HUMANIZED EDUCATION

A MASTERY-BASED FRAMEWORK TO PROMOTE STUDENT GROWTH AND STRENGTH

MIKE RUYLE
AWACHÍIKAATE (JASON D. CUMMINS)
LIBBY CHILD
DONYALL D. DICKEY

with Hawar Khalandi and Nancy Weinstein
Foreword by Mario I. Acosta

MARZANO Resources

555 North Morton Street
Bloomington, IN 47404
888.849.0851
FAX: 866.801.1447

email: info@MarzanoResources.com
MarzanoResources.com

Visit **MarzanoResources.com/reproducibles** to download the free reproducibles in this book.

Printed in the United States of America

FSC
www.fsc.org
MIX
Paper | Supporting responsible forestry
FSC® C008955

Library of Congress Cataloging-in-Publication Data
Names: Ruyle, Mike, author. | Awachíikaate, author. | Child, Libby, author. | Dickey, Donyall D., author.
Title: Humanized education : a mastery-based framework to promote student growth and strength / Mike Ruyle, Awachíikaate (Jason D. Cummins), Libby Child, Donyall D. Dickey.
Description: Bloomington, IN : Marzano Resources, [2024] | Includes bibliographical references and index.
Identifiers: LCCN 2024016196 (print) | LCCN 2024016197 (ebook) | ISBN 9781943360864 (paperback) | ISBN 9781943360871 (ebook)
Subjects: LCSH: Children with mental disabilities--Education--United States. | Academic achievement--United States. | Psychic trauma in children--United States. | Affective education--United States. | Competency-based education--United States. | Mastery learning--United States.
Classification: LCC LC4631 .R886 2024 (print) | LCC LC4631 (ebook) | DDC 371.920973--dc23/eng/20240627
LC record available at https://lccn.loc.gov/2024016196
LC ebook record available at https://lccn.loc.gov/2024016197

Production Team
President and Publisher: Douglas M. Rife
Associate Publishers: Todd Brakke and Kendra Slayton
Editorial Director: Laurel Hecker
Art Director: Rian Anderson
Copy Chief: Jessi Finn
Senior Production Editor: Tonya Maddox Cupp
Copy Editor: Mark Hain
Acquisitions Editors: Carol Collins and Hilary Goff
Content Development Specialist: Amy Rubenstein
Associate Editors: Sarah Ludwig and Elijah Oates
Editorial Assistant: Anne Marie Watkins

Acknowledgments

Many Tribal Nations in the Great Plains region of the United States and Canada have histories and relationships with what is commonly translated into English as *medicine wheels* or *sacred hoops*. Many known medicine wheels in Montana, South Dakota, Wyoming, Alberta, and Saskatchewan have inspired an array of practitioners in the realms of education and wellness.

One example is the largest and best-preserved medicine wheel, located in the Bighorn Mountains of Wyoming and Montana, which are among the traditional homelands of the Apsáalooke Nation. The Annáshisee (Large Camp), or Bighorn Medicine Wheel, is high up on Wyoming's Medicine Mountain, close to 10,000 feet in elevation and only accessible in the summer months. In this tradition and story, an individual known as Burnt-Face or Scar-Face received from the Creator the knowledge of how to fashion and practice necessary actions in the medicine wheel for the express intention of the community's survival and well-being (E. Bull Chief, personal communication, 2016). Burnt-Face built four medicine wheels in the Apsáalooke community, and other tribal members built additional medicine wheels after learning the protocols for this practice. The medicine wheels that align with the summer solstice are uniquely Apsáalooke (E. Bull Chief, personal communication, December 6, 2023). Annáshisee remains a place of great significance where people of all nations visit annually.

The school wellness wheel and school fitness flywheel were both inspired by and pay homage to this medicine wheel concept. We consciously strove to approach this work honorably and sought to practice bicultural accountability and respect community-protected knowledge (Windchief & Cummins, 2022). We communicated with members of the Apsáalooke community to ensure our reference to the medicine wheel as an inspiration for this work remained held in high esteem. So, without misappropriating or presuming to use Native practices, we respectfully acknowledge that in ancient times, as well as modern times, there are places where one can learn, heal, receive instruction, wisdom, guidance, and empowerment. We believe schools should also be fitness-focused, empowering institutions that enhance human potential, safety, growth, and inspiration.

Marzano Resources would like to thank the following reviewers:

Brad Neuendorf
Principal
Lander Valley High School
Lander, Wyoming

Janet Nuzzie
District Intervention Specialist, K–12 Mathematics
Pasadena ISD
Pasadena, Texas

David Pillar
Assistant Director
Hoosier Hills Career Center
Bloomington, Indiana

Melisha Plummer
Assistant Principal
Atlanta Public Schools
Atlanta, Georgia

Bo Ryan
Principal/Solution Tree and Marzano Associate/Author
Ana Grace Academy of the Arts Middle School
Bloomfield, Connecticut

Ringnolda Jofee' Tremain
Director of Professional Learning
Texas Leadership Public Schools
Arlington, Texas

Visit **MarzanoResources.com/reproducibles** to download the free reproducibles in this book.

Table of Contents

Reproducibles are in italics.

About the Authors

Mike Ruyle, EdD, has served as a classroom teacher, athletic coach, school principal, alternative program director, university professor, and school consultant for over thirty years. He led the creation and implementation of personalized, competency-based schools in Montana and California, has authored an array of books, and is a recognized authority in the areas of educational leadership, healing- and resilience-centered schooling, instruction, and assessment. Mike's leadership experience and dynamic presentation style have made him a sought-after national and international speaker for numerous schools, districts, state agencies, and conferences.

Mike earned bachelor of arts degrees in history and English from the University of San Francisco, as well as master's and doctoral degrees in educational leadership from Montana State University.

Awachíikaate (Jason D. Cummins, EdD), is an enrolled member of the Apsáalooke Nation and has served over twenty years in education in many different leadership roles, implementing initiatives from traditional school improvement efforts to culturally sustaining, trauma-informed, and restorative approaches. He is a contributing author of the School Wellness Wheel and a professor of Educational Leadership at Montana State University. He recently served as deputy director of the White House Initiative EO 14049 and is a recognized leader in shifting how schools innovate by providing relevant and purposeful educational experiences.

Jason and his wife, Velvett, have been married for thirty years and in their spare time enjoy all things outdoors. He is a Clark Scholar, Little Big Horn Tribal College alumnus, and earned his master's and doctorate degrees from Montana State University.

Libby Child has spent over twenty-seven years in education as a high school special education teacher, a special education program coordinator, and an educational consultant for the Montana Office of Public Instruction in the areas of inclusive education, secondary transition practices for students with special needs, paraeducator development, and co-teaching. Her career has been deeply rooted in the belief that every student deserves an education with dignity and the best possible opportunity to learn and achieve at their greatest capacity. She is a coauthor of the book *The School Wellness Wheel: A Framework Addressing Trauma, Culture, and Mastery to Raise Student Achievement.*

Libby holds a bachelor of arts degree in elementary and special education from Carroll College and a master's degree in educational leadership from Montana State University.

Donyall D. Dickey, EdD, is a nationally recognized authority on curriculum, instruction, organizational development, and school administration. Unparalleled levels of student achievement and school improvement distinguish Donyall's twenty-plus-year career as an educational leader. Donyall has led at nearly every level in public education. After a decade of successful site-based leadership, he served as assistant superintendent and chief academic officer of the school district of Philadelphia and later as chief schools officer and chief academic officer of Atlanta Public Schools. In each case, his leadership resulted in record gains in student outcomes and state assessment scores, as well as significant improvements in organizational effectiveness.

Donyall is the chief executive officer and lead consultant for Educational Epiphany, where he and his national consulting team partner with urban, suburban, and rural school districts in over forty U.S. states. Through this work, they serve as a leading provider of standards-informed instructional materials for the core content areas and professional development for teachers, school leaders, central office personnel, state departments of education, and professional associations.

Donyall is a graduate of the University of Texas at Austin, Loyola University—Maryland, and George Washington University—D.C., where he earned a doctorate in educational leadership and policy.

Hawar Khalandi, EdD, brings an abundance of experience and passion to the field of education both as a teacher and as an administrator. Since 2007, she has been dedicated to fostering an equitable and inclusive learning environment for all students. She helped lead the development and implementation of standards-based learning policy and a discipline philosophy centered on restorative practices in the North Kansas City School District and was a driving force in creating an educational experience that empowers all students to reach their full potential. After that, she became director of college and career readiness at Platte County School District in Kansas City, Missouri. Hawar's diverse background, extensive knowledge, and practical experience uniquely position her to provide practical and insightful perspectives that bridge the gap between educational theory and the real-world challenges faced in classrooms and schools.

Hawar earned a bachelor of education degree with an emphasis in biology from the University of Missouri–Kansas City, a master of science from Emporia State University in Emporia, Kansas, and an education specialist and doctoral degree in educational leadership from William Woods University in Fulton, Missouri.

Nancy Weinstein is the founder and CEO of MindPrint Learning, an education technology company that identifies student learning strengths to support differentiated instruction and improve learning outcomes. Prior to founding MindPrint, Nancy worked at Bristol-Myers Squibb, the Walt Disney Company, and Goldman Sachs. She is coauthor of *The Empowered Student* and is a national speaker on using the science of learning best practices to improve student outcomes. She is the principal investigator on four National Science Foundation grants.

Nancy earned a bachelor of science in bioengineering from the University of Pennsylvania and a master of business administration from Harvard University.

Foreword

By Mario I. Acosta

As educators, we stand at a crossroads in an educational era marked by challenge and change yet brimming with the potential for transformation. *Humanized Education: A Mastery-Based Framework to Promote Student Growth and Strength* by Mike Ruyle, Awachíikaate, Libby Child, and Donyall Dickey, gives direction to all who seek not only to navigate these waters but also to chart a new course for the future of education. This book integrates research spanning neuroscience, psychology, biology, genetics, and education, converging into a framework that is not just theoretical, but also pragmatically designed for schools. It speaks directly to the heart of the challenges schools face as they emerge from a period of unprecedented disruption.

The authors present a three-principle framework intended to provide educators with powerful and practical action steps: (1) mastery-based learning, (2) growth-based schooling, and (2) strength-based teaching.

Growth-based schooling, the book's first guiding principle, recognizes the need for a compassionate and nurturing educational environment. It serves as an antidote to turmoil, fostering resilience and a deep-seated love of learning that can help students recover and grow in the aftermath of societal upheaval.

Strength-based teaching, the second principle, resonates profoundly in a world where diversity of experience and adversity have been more pronounced than ever. This approach encourages educators to shift the focus from a deficit-based model to one that acknowledges and harnesses the unique strengths and talents that each student brings to the classroom, fostering an inclusive culture that supports healing and empowerment.

Mastery-based learning, the third principle, challenges traditional metrics of education, emphasizing the importance of applying knowledge rather than the mere completion of tasks. It insists on a demonstration of mastery over specific knowledge and competencies, ensuring that when students step out into the world, they do so not with a repository of information, but with a tool kit of capabilities.

This book is an imperative tool in the cache of anyone committed to the real essence of education. It is a guide to not only improve schools but also to elevate them as communities where students do not just learn but thrive. The strategies and insights within these pages offer a path to not just mend the fractures in our system but also to rebuild it stronger and more attuned to the needs of the future. *Humanized Education* is an essential read for those ready to lead the charge in this era, ensuring that our schools become vessels of growth, strength, and mastery for every student.

Mario I. Acosta is an accomplished author and associate with Marzano Resources. He is a twenty-year veteran teacher, instructional coach, assistant principal, academic director, and principal.

INTRODUCTION

Knowledge without transformation is not wisdom.

—PAULO COELHO

Human beings are complex creatures with three core dimensions—(1) mind, (2) body, and (3) soul or spirit—that are interconnected, equally important, and constantly interacting. This holistic perspective crosses cultures and has been an integral part of humanity from the beginning of recorded history (Campbell, 1991; Pang et al., 2023).

Modern medicine recognizes that weakness or imbalance in one of these components can negatively effect the others. For example, emotional stress can impact a usually healthy body by increasing blood pressure, inflammation, and susceptibility to other illnesses (van der Kolk, 2015). Likewise, physical injury or illness can impact an otherwise healthy mind and can lead to depression or anxiety (Kellezi et al., 2017). Psychological elements such as loneliness or lack of belonging can result in an array of both physical and mental ailments (Godman & Howley, 2023). The balance between and among these three pillars of humanity forms the bedrock of our well-being and can have a significant, positive impact on us across a lifespan.

Humans have a remarkable capacity to learn, evolve, grow, and adapt. Learning is fundamentally an act of the brain, and our brains are all fundamentally different. Thus, learning does not look the same for every person. This concept of *cognitive variability* is well understood by researchers and explains why one young student may exhibit highly advanced verbal skills but have weaker gross and fine motor control and, therefore, not be able to write clearly to share their thoughts. A different student may present as physically advanced but have trouble mastering their social skills, while yet another learner may be cognitively advanced but exhibit emotional immaturity. Scientists know that our brains begin to grow before birth and continue to develop and change throughout the lifespan. But brains do not mature at the same rate for everyone. In addition, environmental factors like chronic stress and trauma can impede that development and can result in negative long-term effects. The good news is that the brain is extraordinarily resilient and can heal and grow with the right interventions and a sustained positive environment (Noam & Triggs, 2015; Weinstein & Algeri, 2018).

Thanks to advancements in a host of scientific fields, we know more about the human brain today than we ever have. We also have a better grasp of some of the internal and external factors that can profoundly impact students' readiness, learning, and academic performance. For example, it is clear that vital structural brain development occurs during a child's early years as well as during adolescence. This development can be profoundly impacted by traumatic experiences such as abuse, neglect, and violence, as well as other issues such as poverty and inequity. As a result, if such students are unable to efficiently engage in learning as they struggle with factors outside of school, consequences such as cognitive loss, learning problems, and physical, emotional, and social delays will most likely become apparent (Weinstein & Algeri, 2018). Efficient cognition relies on a healthy, well-regulated brain. As such, the responsibility for teachers to understand and facilitate high-level learning for every student is now more important—yet also more challenging—than ever before.

While teachers certainly need not be experts on all aspects of the brain, it is important that they have a general understanding of how brains mature, the natural differences that may be present in those brains, and how environment and interventions can impact that development. Since the brain is key to learning readiness for all students, it is critical for educators to consider an array of factors when designing lessons, providing instruction, and using assessments.

Teachers and administrators have expressed widespread frustration because of relentless student behavior issues and decreased engagement since the spring of 2020 (Evans, Farah, & Hackman, 2021; Nawaz & Norris, 2023; Tsai, Jaeggi, Eccles, Atherton, & Robbins, 2020). Roughly 70 percent of educators state that the rise in student behavior concerns continues to worsen (EAB, 2023; Prothero, 2023). Low stakeholder engagement is further evidenced by the fact that in 2022, two million fewer students were enrolled in U.S. schools than had been just two years prior (Houston, Peterson, & West, 2023), and there were also 300,000 fewer teachers in 2022 (Preston, 2022). The struggle is profound, and people are just beginning to come to grips with the fact that schools will not ever return to "normal." A new normal is upon us. Yet, from our experience and observations, far too often we continue to see 1990s-era educational applications in a 2020s reality. Thus, we urgently need an evolved model of schooling that is both more humanized than standardized and that effectively addresses the vast complexity of the learning process.

As such, this book makes four critical assertions.

1. **Educators have the moral responsibility to evolve schools into a contemporary, humanized model based on updated research and knowledge.** Until we create schools that actively focus on the overall health of the brains, bodies, and psyches of the humans in the building, the quality of the curriculum, instruction, and assessments is irrelevant. Thus, teachers and school leaders must be able to adjust their professional orientation away from simply delivering curriculum, providing instruction, and maintaining traditional grading systems to adopting and evolving practices within a humanized educational model that recognizes students' individuality and helps them grow to their greatest capacity possible.
2. **The three evidence-based constructs of mastery-based learning, growth-based schooling, and strength-based teaching have the immense power—when combined—to transform the entire school model.** Simply focusing on only one pivot point does not lead to any substantive change or improvement. When a school or district offers professional learning sessions in areas such as social-emotional learning (SEL) or culturally responsive instruction, but doesn't revise or evolve the overarching academic structure, it only adds more to teachers' already full plates. Thus, there is a deep, purposeful overlap between elements in the three pivot points. It's imperative that teachers don't see the pivot points in isolation, but rather see them integrating to create a better, healthier school.
3. **Healing and resilience go deeper than wellness, and teachers must embrace these foundational concepts together to help every learner reach their fullest capacity.** Ultimately, the job of schools is to prepare every student with the mindset and skills to be successful in life beyond the school building. In this sense, teachers and school professionals have an incredible opportunity to impact the lives of their students and families by helping increase protective factors that can foster mental, psychological, and academic fitness.

4. **True equity, cultural affirmation, inclusion, healing, and fitness can be fully realized best in schools where mastery-based learning principles are embraced and implemented.** In such a framework, *equity* means having high expectations for every learner along with blueprints to success while also embracing diversity, respecting individual identities, and valuing cultural heritage. This is what author Ken Williams (2022) refers to as *ruthless equity*. When teachers have the means and expertise to ensure every student is proficient in identified knowledge and skills and able to meet high expectations regardless of their socioeconomic status, race, ethnicity, or cultural background, mastery-based principles can empower all students to reach their full potential while promoting a more equitable, inclusive society.

This book presents a humanized framework—the school fitness flywheel—that includes these elements and considerations. The school fitness flywheel helps schools become healing- and resilience-centered institutions where fostering mental, psychological, and academic fitness is foundational. Before we get to that evolved model, we discuss the mental health issue facing educators and what schools can and should be. Finally, we explain what to expect in this book.

The Mental Health Issue

Mental health has become one of the most pressing human issues worldwide. According to a large-scale study in twenty-nine countries, co-led by researchers from Harvard Medical School and the University of Queensland, one out of every two people in the world will develop a mental health disorder in their lifetime (McGrath et al., 2023). The World Health Organization (WHO, 2020) has declared that the global economy suffers a loss of over $1 trillion annually due to decreased productivity resulting from untreated mental health conditions. Thus, the gravity of the mental health crisis cannot be overstated as it significantly contributes to the global burden of disease; this staggering financial toll alone clearly speaks to the urgency of prioritizing mental health and implementing effective interventions.

The impact of mental health challenges on children and adolescents has been especially profound. Research published in *Pediatrics* identified a dramatic increase in depression and anxiety to such an extent that suicidal ideation and attempts among young people in the U.S. doubled between 2008 and 2015. By 2018, suicide was the second leading cause of death for all youth aged 10–24 (American Academy of Pediatrics, n.d.; Plemmons et al., 2018). The COVID-19 pandemic accelerated this sobering trend (Center on Reinventing Public Education, 2022). As a result, in October 2021, the American Academy of Pediatrics, the Children's Hospital Association, and the American Academy of Child and Adolescent Psychiatry issued a joint statement that declared children's mental health a national emergency. Similar assertions have been made internationally (McGrath et al., 2023)

Furthermore, the link between mental health and societal inequity is compelling. Although all people can experience mental health problems, there is an emerging yet robust body of research suggesting that risks to mental health and well-being have a disproportionately negative impact on people of color, women, the LGBTQA+ community, immigrants, those with low income, and other marginalized groups (Patel et al., 2020; Shim, 2021; WHO, 2020; WHO & & Calouste Gulbenkian Foundation, 2014). Research by Columbia University suggested that this phenomenon is strongly associated with both gender inequality and social disadvantage, with people in minority communities more likely to experience an array of stressors that affects their psychological safety (Vance, 2019). For example, a "Black adult is 20 percent more likely to experience a serious mental health concern than a White adult" (Vance, 2019, p. 1). Yet these challenges spread far beyond race, gender, or economic inequality in that people with disabilities also confront social exclusion due to the lack of accessibility. Simply stated, research (Patel et al., 2020; Shim, 2021; WHO, 2020; WHO & Calouste Gulbenkian Foundation, 2014) has repeatedly linked an array of inequity and discrimination with negative mental health outcomes.

These worrisome trends are not limited to certain socioeconomic or cultural subgroups. Rather, mental health and equity challenges impact many of our highest functioning learners and are becoming increasingly prevalent among college students. For example, between 2013 and 2021, more than 350,000 students from over three hundred college campuses participated in a study that analyzed data from annual surveys on mental health and the rates at which racial and ethnic groups sought professional assistance. The findings were stunning. All groups experienced worsened mental health over the course of the study, and by its last two years, more than 60 percent of students had one or more mental health problem per the criteria. College students reported the following as well (Eisenberg, Ketchen Lipson, & Heinze, 2021; Federal Student Aid, n.d.).

- Eighty-one percent said their academic performance was impacted negatively by emotional or mental challenges.
- Sixty-eight percent reported often feeling isolated or lonely.
- Forty-five percent felt hopeless.

Despite how well publicized mental health has become, dramatic racial and ethnic disparities in mental health care and assistance still remain in the United States. The highest rate of mental health treatment for Asian, Black, Arab American, and Latinx students remained below the lowest rate for White students (Center for Collegiate Mental Health, n.d.). Furthermore, American Indian and Alaskan Native students have experienced the largest increases in suicidal ideation, depression, and anxiety since 2014 (Thulin, Lipson, Heinze, & Zhou, 2023). Students from these groups utilized mental health service at the lowest rates, however, primarily due to an array of issues such as the stigmas and different cultural perceptions associated with mental health, lack of transportation or childcare, language barriers, and the general lack of qualified providers in many local communities (Gone, 2021).

Similar disparities exist in Australia and Canada. For example, Aboriginal and Torres Strait Islander peoples experience notable mental health care disparities (Kairuz, Casanelia, Bennet-Brook, Coombes, & Yadav, 2021), and "racial discrimination predicts barriers to health care in general, as well as accessing mental health services" (Bastos, Harnois, & Paradies, 2018, p. 216). Black Caribbeans in Canada report "wait times for mental health care averaged 16 months, more than twice those for Whites" (Mental Health Commission of Canada, 2021, p. 1). First Nations adolescents are between five to seven times more likely to commit suicide than non-Indigenous youth, and Inuit adolescents are eleven times more likely (Kumar & Tjepkema, 2019). Clearly, this is a worldwide issue.

The impact of this reality on the education field is profound. Mental health issues such as anxiety, depression, eating disorders, and substance use are associated with lower college GPA. Over 30 percent of students who dropped out of college reported mental health concerns as one of their top reasons for leaving school. Counseling service demands at schools have grown five times faster than student enrollment (Lipson et al., 2022). Clearly, it is no longer acceptable to assert that "caring for students' mental and emotional needs is primarily the responsibility of those outside" of our schools and academic programs (Rim, 2022). The disruption to existing paradigms is apparent, and it is time to confront modern issues with a more updated knowledge base and perspective. In this way, schools have the potential to make a tremendous difference.

What Schools Can and Should Be

Schools have considered the idea of educating the *whole child* and attending to social and emotional development for well over a century. In fact, education groundbreaker John Dewey specifically addressed the movement as early as 1916. Despite educators typically agreeing with the whole-child movement conceptually, there has been very little clarity around how to integrate such an approach into existing school programs, including what to teach and how to define concepts. As an example, a study of 136 SEL frameworks revealed that different terminology is commonly used for concepts that have similar definitions; in addition, similar terms are often used for concepts that have different definitions (Berg et al., 2017). As a result, implementing SEL or culturally affirming principles in a traditional classroom setting is often confusing and ineffective.

On top of everything else, schools remain faced with the challenge of ensuring student mastery of high-level standards while also attempting to differentiate the educational experience for students. Thus, many SEL frameworks narrow the focus of complex human constructs to lists of social-emotional skills that educators should address. This approach reflects a deep lack of understanding regarding the human developmental process. It also pressures educators to add content on top of their subject-specific academic priorities without providing the resources they need to effectively teach complex topics like respect, empathy, emotional regulation, and perseverance.

Schools typically address these challenges by simply providing teachers and school personnel with professional development sessions on concepts such as standards-based school practices, trauma-informed care, and culturally responsive pedagogy—while also asking them to continue operating in a traditional school mindset. That approach is clearly ineffective in bringing sustainable growth and lasting change (Thompson & Wiliam, 2007). Placing more on the plates of teachers and administrators without evolving the entire existing educational construct is, ultimately, futile.

Yet by understanding cognitive and developmental variability among groups of learners, teachers can be more strategic about which developmental competencies to prioritize and how to approach them for successful outcomes. We assert that schools have the moral responsibility as well as the means to address mental health and brain development. School systems are, indeed, the best organizations to do this critical work.

This systemic evolution in education is vital and significant because childhood trauma and stress in the critical early years when the brain is continually evolving can have devastating effects on a person's subsequent overall mental and physical health (Bloom, 2020; De Bellis & Zisk, 2014). Trauma, toxic stress, and some mental health conditions can hinder brain development, especially in the areas of executive functioning, memory, attention, language, and self-regulation, which are critical regions for learning (Weinstein

& Algeri, 2018). Trauma can also delay personal development and impede social integration, which serves to perpetuate a vicious cycle of underachievement and diminished well-being. Conversely, if people can acquire skills such as engagement, self-regulation, flexible thinking, and communication, and develop agency and trusting relationships during childhood and adolescence, they will be better able as adults to enhance their brain health, leading to better overall cognitive, emotional, and physical outcomes (Cantor, Osher, Berg, Steyer, & Rose, 2019; Harris, 2021).

The good news is that mounting evidence from neuroscience and neuropsychology suggests that relatively simple classroom routines and strategies can improve executive function, memory, and self-regulation—all key to learning. For example, regular mindfulness practices as well as supportive, responsive, and developmentally appropriate relationships with a caring, trustworthy adult can prevent or even reverse the damage done by chronic stress (Center on the Developing Child, 2007; Weinstein & Algeri, 2018). Schools and educators can play a direct and fundamental role in fostering students' emotional development, mental health, and academic growth. As stable, caring adults in many children's lives, we are part of the protective factor and can continue providing that support throughout their time as our students.

The claim that educators could play an important role in facilitating their students' emotional development is not without controversy. Social-emotional learning has become a flashpoint in the political debate, as some critics allege SEL intrudes into parental authority and aims to instill into children ideological, religious, and political values that parents or families may not share (Abrams, 2023). In addition, some stakeholders and parents claim schools should not be involved in mental and emotional health in any way because a focus on well-being removes attention from academics.

Yet schools are, indeed, the most appropriate place to address mental and emotional health since learning and thinking are fundamentally acts of the brain. The Collaborative for Academic, Social, and Emotional Learning (CASEL; n.d.) identifies social-emotional learning as follows:

> SEL is the process through which all young people and adults acquire and apply the knowledge, skills, and attitudes to develop healthy identities, manage emotions and achieve personal and collective goals, feel and show empathy for others, establish and maintain supportive relationships, and make responsible and caring decisions.

These social and psychological factors are critical in an educational domain because when students face emotional or mental health challenges, those can also impact their motivation and attitudes toward school and learning.

Most public schools offer students some level of mental health services. In fact, 96 percent of schools provided some iteration of those services in the 2021–2022 school year alone. This, along with the fact that learning isn't possible without a degree of self-regulation and executive function and that educators are a constant in children's lives throughout their formative years, makes our education system a critical source of mental health delivery for children and adolescents (National Center for Education Statistics, 2022; Singer & Ludlow-Broback, 2022). Effective SEL practices can advance academic excellence and educational equity; despite infrequent backlash against its presence in schools, many families and stakeholders across the political spectrum broadly support teaching self-regulation and related skills in schools (Tyner, 2021).

The School Fitness Flywheel

Just as federal, state, and provincial free- and reduced-lunch programs have been adopted based on the understanding that a hungry child can't learn, it is also clear that a stressed, tired, cluttered, or troubled mind cannot focus on learning. If educators approach the aforementioned critical issues from a different perspective, it can open a new world of possibilities.

The most effective way to evolve schools is to adopt an updated, evidence-based educational model that addresses all three human components that make high-level learning possible. The school fitness flywheel we present in this book provides that clear vision and comprehensive framework.

Terminology is important to grasping the power of the model. Thus, an explanation of the central concepts is vital. First, we employ the term *fitness* because it is synonymous with health. Just as exercise can help to improve physical fitness, consciously focusing on healing and overall human wellness can enhance academic, cognitive, and psychological fitness.

Second, although inspired by the Native American medicine wheel, we also adapted author Jim Collins's (2001) metaphor of the *flywheel* as presented in his book *Good to Great: Why Some Companies Make the Leap and Others Don't* to describe the effect that can happen when small wins build on each other over time and eventually gain so much momentum that growth almost seems to happen by itself:

> No matter how dramatic the end result, good-to-great transformations never happen in one fell swoop. In building a great company or social sector enterprise, there is no single defining action, no grand program, no one killer innovation, no solitary lucky break, no miracle moment. Rather, the process

resembles relentlessly pushing a giant, heavy flywheel, turn upon turn, building momentum until a point of breakthrough, and beyond. (p. 14)

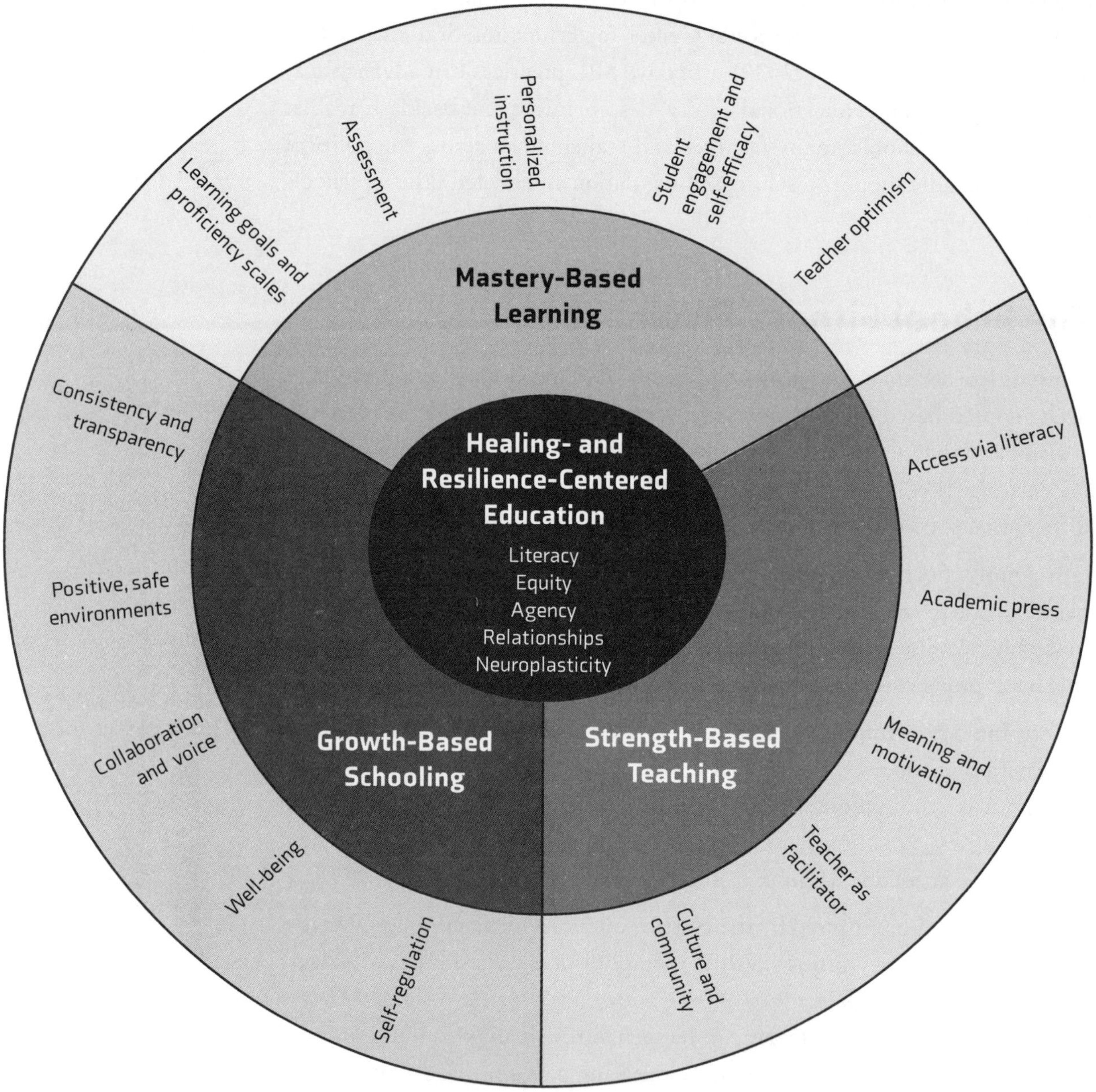

FIGURE I.1: The school fitness flywheel with its fifteen indicators of humanized education.

Visit ***MarzanoResources.com/reproducibles*** *for a free reproducible version of this figure.*

We assert that, in a school setting, critical organizational shifts implemented with vision, purpose, and commitment can create an evolved system that increases momentum and, ultimately, powers itself. The school fitness flywheel is presented in figure I.1.

The school fitness flywheel is a framework that does two things.

1. It aligns and synthesizes research and knowledge from an array of fields such as education, neuroscience, biology, and psychology and other social sciences into a dynamic, holistic, and contextualized structure that empowers all educational organizations to meet the needs of every learner and community.
2. It addresses the capacity of people to grow, improve, heal, and build their mental, psychological, and academic capacity.

But schools can only continue to evolve into the future if they adopt an integrated school model focused on healing and resilience that works for their specific situation. Although we present a comprehensive framework here, it is critical that schools customize the model to fit their specific needs and circumstances; they do so in part by using accepted language and creating a visual representation that is compelling to their communities. Strategies and examples of how to customize the school fitness flywheel appear in chapter 5 (page 119).

Schools that effectively implement all three segments of mastery-based learning, growth-based schooling, and strength-based teaching will witness a corresponding increase in the wellness, learning, academic growth, and college and career readiness of the students they serve. While an earlier iteration of the healing- and resilience-centered model, *The School Wellness Wheel: A Framework Addressing Trauma, Culture, and Mastery to Raise Student Achievement* (Ruyle, Child, & Dome, 2022), provided a solid research-based framework for evolving the larger educational paradigm, *Humanized Education* takes a deep dive into concrete strategies that teachers, school leaders, and communities can embrace to bring the new system to fruition. It also uses updated terms and language that can more powerfully, positively communicate a vision of the educational mission. This is the right work and can better help address modern issues with a relevant and advanced school model.

About This Book

We maintain that the primary purpose of contemporary schooling is to help every student reach their fullest potential—as students, certainly, but also as human beings. If we know that trauma, toxic stress, and mental health issues can negatively impact and even damage the brain and make it impossible to learn, we also now know that there are actions educators and adults can take to reverse those effects, heal the brain, and build resilience even in nontraumatized brains. The research is clear: if people engage in these actions, they get better and stronger (Bloom & Farragher, 2013b; R. Macy, personal communication, March 2020). Thus, this book does the following.

- It provides a framework in which all resources, practices, strategies, and interventions make sense in a larger organizational context.
- It focuses on the big picture of an updated, evidence-based education structure that attends to the academic, mental, and psychological fitness of people to provide the best opportunity for authentic learning and mastery of critical skills and knowledge.
- It delves into timely topics such as trauma-informed classrooms and culturally responsive teaching, presents them from strength-based and growth-based perspectives, and provides teaching strategies for them.
- It helps teachers consider how to make change happen every day around literacy, equity, agency, mental health, and academic mastery.
- It includes implementation strategies from the micro to the macro perspective by including planning on current concepts such as Portraits of a Graduate, school vision statement, and learner profiles for individual students.

Students' brains are malleable and educators can support and help heal them through a three-pronged approach of (1) mastery-based learning principles, (2) growth-based school protocols, and (3) strength-based teaching practices that can specifically address mental, psychological, and academic fitness. Thus, the purpose of this book is to help schools become institutions in which brain growth and human empowerment become the foundational elements. We've written this book for all K–12 educators, as well as school boards and state- and province-level agencies. It is vital that everyone involved in educating young people believe that healing and resilience serve as precursors to academics so that achievement can follow.

A massive paradigm shift like adopting a more humanized model focused on healing and resilience does not happen without strong leadership, along with the entire staff's commitment and combined energy. The transformation only happens because of changes in the educators' hearts, minds, and practices. Indeed, all the work in healing and resilience to enhance mental, psychological, and academic fitness must start with the adults. Our young people will not be well if the adults are wounded. Thus, we assert that this book is for everyone in an educational organization to delve into and digest over time.

Since the main function of schools is to foster healthy and resilient people who have the skills, strengths, and capacity to be successful in life beyond the school building, we have designed the chapters of the book in alignment with the three segments of the school fitness flywheel: mastery-based learning, growth-based schooling, and strength-based teaching. Each chapter delves into the critical components that *must* happen for healing- and resilience-centered education to take root. Each chapter provides specific strategies and actions that teachers and school stakeholders can take to enhance mental, psychological, and academic fitness.

Chapter 1 provides the deep theoretical and philosophical underpinnings that form the foundation of a humanized education system centered on the school fitness flywheel. Teachers must recognize these constructs to better address academic content and student need. The foundational elements of a healing- and resilience-centered school speak specifically to strategies that can strengthen neurophysiology, build connection and relationships, improve literacy, address equity, and empower learner agency.

Chapter 2 focuses on the educational construct of mastery-based learning and revolves around the elements of learner voice and autonomy. It also explores teachers' academic optimism that can result from the shift to mastery-based learning, as well as how to best personalize the educational experience for every learner, how to utilize clear learning goals and learning progressions, and how to improve the assessment literacy of every teacher to improve student learning. The central element of developing learner agency is deeply embedded in the mastery-based learning segment of the school fitness flywheel.

Chapter 3 addresses growth-based schooling and includes the power of cultivating a positive, safe environment; student ownership of their own learning; wellness for all stakeholders; and self-regulation in students and co-regulation in educators. The central elements of strengthening neurophysiology and developmentally appropriate relationships are fundamental to the growth-based schooling segment of the school fitness flywheel.

Chapter 4 discusses the critical elements of a strength-based teaching model and revolves around the necessary role that culture and community play in learning. It also looks at how being aware and responsive to the specific perspectives of learners leads to an increased sense of hope so that they can meet higher-level academic expectations. We further examine how literacy practices can increase access to curriculum and standards for every learner, resulting in higher motivation. Building powerful student-teacher partnerships supports this motivation, creates a deeper sense of purpose, and prepares young brains for optimal learning. The central elements of improving literacy and striving for equity and educational justice are vital to the strength-based teaching segment of the school fitness flywheel.

Chapter 5 discusses implementation strategies, important tools, and the critical leadership qualities to bring the vision to fruition.

Chapters 2–5 all contain vignettes, quotes, examples, and advice from educators and learners who have actively engaged in transforming their schools into academic, mental, and psychology-focused places of learning. Also, since the shift to the school fitness flywheel educational model is difficult to achieve without focused, strong leadership, each chapter ends with leadership qualities critical to realizing the transformation. These chapters also present reproducible proficiency scales for assessing a school's mastery level in each segment of the wheel.

Before beginning, we point out that all three segments—mastery-based learning, growth-based schooling, and strength-based teaching—are equally important to cultivating a healing- and resilience-centered school model. They do not exist in a hierarchy or in isolation. Elements from the three segments continually interact. Thus, the metaphor of a flywheel is important to demonstrate how the three segments ultimately work in concert to shift the educational paradigm to a holistic model of academic, mental, and psychological fitness to grow healthy people who can learn and operate at their highest levels. We recommend starting at the center.

1

Healing- and Resilience-Centered Education

Ever since I was a child, I have had this instinctive urge for expansion and growth. To me, the function and duty of a quality human being is the sincere and honest development of one's potential.

—BRUCE LEE

We live in societies, countries, regions, and a world in great need of wellness, health, and growth. As such, it is long past time to cultivate an innovative, modern school experience for students based on updated knowledge and research. This chapter addresses the healing and resilience in schools that result from nurturing student literacy, equity, agency, relationships, and neuroplasticity.

Learning is personal. One's cultural heritage is personal. Trauma is personal. Yet, most traditional educational systems remain highly standardized. We strongly make the point that schools must undertake the journey to become more personalized and humanized as there are no more personal and human endeavors than teaching and learning. When educators purposefully focus on the following elements with their students, they can create a powerful school environment that better supports high-level learning.

- **Literacy:** Literacy skills are vital to learning because students who can't read or communicate effectively fail to grasp important concepts, score poorly on tests, and ultimately fail to meet educational standards (Dickey, 2022; Marzano, 2020).
- **Equity:** Focusing on systemwide equity can provide disadvantaged students—indeed, all students—the opportunity to overcome barriers, grow, and improve an array of life skills that facilitate greater ultimate success (Williams, 2022).
- **Agency:** High levels of agency empower learners to act on their own behalf and play an active role in their learning, which

increases motivation and engagement (Organisation for Economic Co-operation and Development [OECD], 2019).

- **Relationships:** Authentic relationships improve academic performance by increasing engagement and providing learners a sense of belonging (Marzano et al., 2017).
- **Neuroplasticity:** Education informed by neuroscience can help promote learning, motivation, high-level information processing, deepening memory skills, and executive functioning in all learners (Cantor et al., 2019; Goldberg, 2022).

Read on to learn more about these elements.

Healing- and Resilience-Centered Education Defined

At its center, the school fitness flywheel revolves around the dual concepts of healing and resilience. *Wellness* is a common buzzword, yet we assert that healing and cultivating resilience are something much deeper. Inspired by the Native American medicine wheel, the school fitness flywheel is a strength-based framework that addresses the capacity of people to grow, improve, heal, connect, and build their mental and emotional capacity. At the core of this belief is empowering students with the personalized strategies they need to succeed in the face of whatever adversity they encounter. Every student is unique, and every situation is different. A healing- and resilience-centered school shows students how to adapt to succeed given their personal circumstances.

Fundamental components of healing- and resilience-centered schools include cultivating academic, mental, and psychological fitness to help improve overall wellness and enhance learning.

- **Academic fitness** relates to academic goals and a learner's ability to demonstrate mastery of identified standards, critical skills, and knowledge. It also refers to a learner's cognitive faculties and entails the act of learning, having a vast knowledge base, reasoning, understanding, problem solving, analytical thinking, and adapting to new information or situations. It requires challenging and empowering every student to meet high expectations, to work hard to achieve mastery of critical skills and knowledge, and to develop disciplined learning habits. Schools can foster academic fitness by effectively implementing mastery-based learning principles.
- **Mental fitness** is a positive state of well-being. It requires enhancing the ability to keep one's brain and emotional health in good shape. It entails mental toughness (persevering, making good

decisions, and ignoring negative self-talk), resilience (recovering from setbacks), and focus (making decisions effectively and efficiently). Mental fitness requires building crucial skills that allow one to navigate and adapt to challenges and to bounce back from adversity. This fitness concept revolves around the idea that the brain needs regular exercise, just like the body does, to stay healthy. Educators can nurture mental fitness when they consistently employ growth-based schooling principles.

- **Psychological fitness** relates to how the mind functions and the factors that influence mental processes, including meaning, determination, and motivation. Psychological fitness includes cognitive, emotional, and behavioral components in that it requires self-regulation, a positive mindset, and effective behavioral processing. It also entails coping skills that enhance social interactions, community involvement, and making and connecting with something outside of oneself. Fostering healthy relationships, increasing academic access, understanding one's own emotions and triggers, and cultivating a sense of belonging are important elements of strength-based teaching, which can bolster psychological fitness. *Mental health* and *psychological health* might be incorrectly used interchangeably. Although interconnected, they represent distinct aspects of a person's overall well-being. Ultimately, mental fitness is about the quality of one's life, while psychological fitness is more about the coping mechanisms one can access to deepen quality of life.

In these ways, a healing- and resilience-centered school can help students learn how to adapt to succeed given *their* personal circumstances. The three main segments of the flywheel allow this personalization. Table 1.1 lists the critical indicators at the heart of the school fitness flywheel's three segments, which we describe in chapters 2–4.

Table 1.1: Embedded Critical Elements of the School Fitness Flywheel

Mastery-Based Learning Academic Fitness	Growth-Based Schooling Mental Fitness	Strength-Based Teaching Psychological Fitness
Learning goals and proficiency scales	Positive, safe environments	Access via literacy
Assessment	Collaboration and voice	Academic press
Personalized instruction	Well-being	Meaning and motivation
Student engagement and self-efficacy	Self-regulation	Teacher as facilitator
Teacher optimism	Consistency and transparency	Culture and community

Visit ***MarzanoResources.com/reproducibles*** *for a free reproducible version of this table.*

Humans have the profound ability to heal themselves and each other. In fact, negative experiences can spur positive change that can result in post-traumatic growth, which could include the following.

- Personal realization of strength and resilience
- A deeper ability to learn
- Improved interpersonal relationships
- Increased openness to the exploration of new possibilities
- A greater appreciation for life and well-being (Tedeschi et al., 2018)

This growth and increased resilience can often happen naturally, without formal interventions such as psychotherapy or medical treatment. Thus, educators have the potential to serve as expert companions for students and each other through personal connection, learning partnerships, and by offering community and hope. Simply stated, teachers and school leaders can help the students in their daily care nurture their academic, mental, and psychological fitness.

We in no way are suggesting that teachers serve as mental health counselors or personally respond to the highest needs of the learners they work with. However, educators cannot ignore the big picture since learning is inextricably linked with mental and psychological fitness. Yet, as schools rush to keep up with the increasing demand for resources, it has become clear that many educators in traditional school systems lack the expertise to effectively deal with student mental health challenges. This is simply not an area for which most teaching staffs are adequately prepared.

Adding complexity to this situation, the National Association of School Psychologists (n.d.) recommends one school psychologist for every five hundred students. The organization estimates that, on average in the United States, there is one school psychologist for more than twice that number of students. There tends to be great variability between states, with some approaching a ratio of one counselor for every five thousand students. Canadian schools have seen a dramatic decrease in the number of candidates entering the education field (Kang & Shaw, 2024) and Australia reports a critical and immediate need to grow the candidate pool in school psychologists (Australian Psychological Society, 2022) .

We strongly suggest, however, that all educators can join efforts to address the issue. Helping students learn how to manage emotions and stress and purposefully engaging in healing and resilience—what we refer to as *mental fitness*—will benefit them in the classroom and throughout life. Thus, school must be about more than simply imparting reading, writing, and arithmetic. The most powerful knowledge we have at our disposal is that despite trauma and stress negatively altering brain structure, healing can positively impact brain structure.

The critical elements of a healing- and resilience-centered framework focus on elements that improve students' literacy, equity, agency, relationships, and neurophysiology (LEARN). We examine each of these elements in the following section.

Literacy

The most vital and focused efforts in education must always revolve around the concept of providing every learner with access to a quality education by ensuring literacy and language knowledge. To imbue students with the ability to read, write, speak, and listen so that they can communicate effectively and engage with the world around them is one of school's foundational purposes.

We assert that much of the world, including the United States, is in a literacy crisis. If students do not have high-level literacy skills, they cannot access the curriculum. Academic, mental, and psychological fitness are all directly impacted by literacy. Research points to a significant association between literacy and mental health outcomes across multiple countries; people with lower literacy in a global systematic review had greater mental health difficulties such as anxiety and depression (Hunn, Teague, & Fisher, 2023). Scientists "can't say for sure that poor literacy causes poor mental health, but there is a strong association" according to clinical psychologist Lucy Hunn (cited in University of East Anglia, 2023).

That association is made through what several researchers have proven: that literacy is "linked to a variety of positive outcomes, such as higher education, income, health and civil engagement" (Rothwell, 2020, p. 3). Yet, despite countless reforms in public education and billions of dollars in investments in literacy, the following statistics still apply (Rothwell, 2020).

- Nearly 70 percent of all U.S. school-aged children are not reading proficiently (Irwin et al., 2023).
- The majority of Native American, African American, Latinx, and Asian American-Pacific Islander students are not reading proficiently (National Assessment of Educational Progress, 2022).
- None of the U.S. students living with a disability were reading proficiently in grade 4 (National Assessment of Educational Progress, 2022).
- Forty percent of Canadian and Australian students do not read proficiently (OECD, 2023).

Furthermore, the U.S. Department of Education reported that over half of adults in the United States—roughly 130 million people—have difficulty reading, thinking critically about what they have read, and speaking or writing in response to a given text (Rothwell, 2020).

We implore readers to refrain from viewing this persistent issue as having a causal relationship with race or ethnicity, socioeconomics, or English proficiency. Instead, we ask you to think of chronic underperformance as a direct result of the lack of student access to daily instruction planned, delivered, and supported by teachers and leaders who possess the training and capacity necessary to successfully transfer literacy skills to students (Dickey, 2022). Literacy correlates with Benjamin S. Bloom's (1956) taxonomy, bridging the space between those skills and abilities and Abraham Maslow's (1943) proposed hierarchy of needs. The higher levels of Maslow's hierarchy are much more accessible when one has been empowered to master literacy. Figure 1.1 illustrates this relationship.

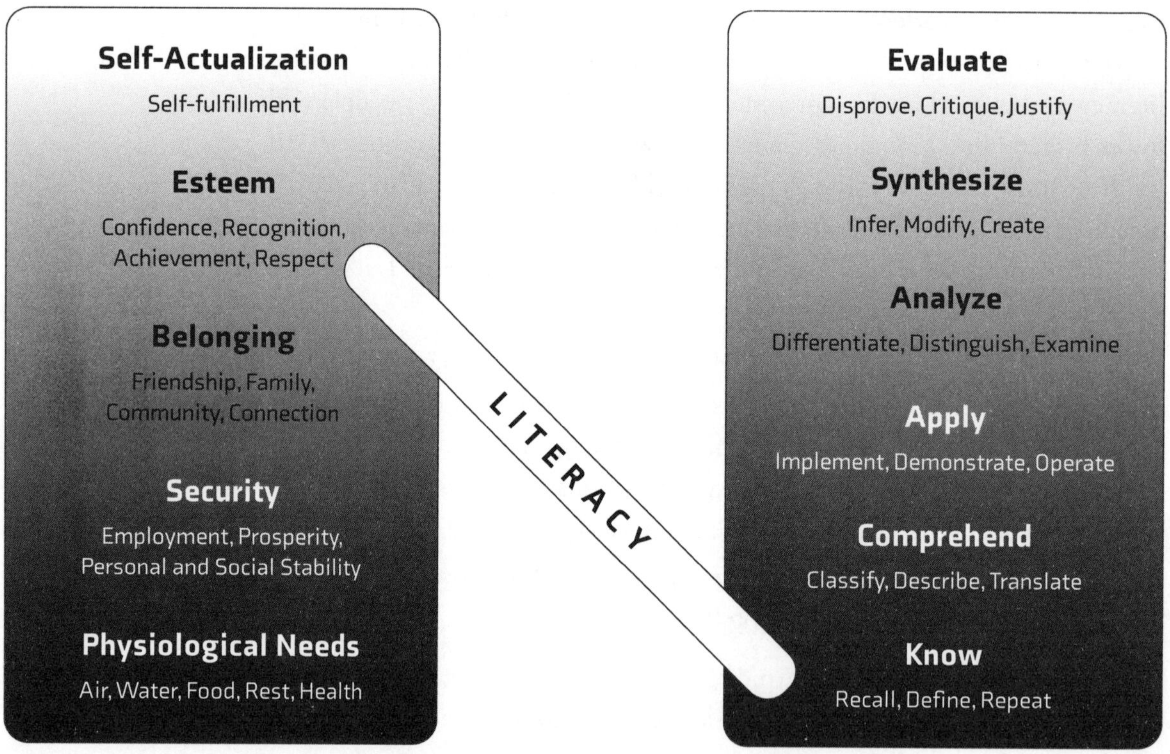

Sources: Adapted from Bloom, 1956; Maslow, 1943.

FIGURE 1.1: Literacy impacts skills and abilities, which impacts need satisfaction.

To address the crisis and to ensure equitable access, drastically improving literacy instruction is urgently needed and therefore must be established, solidified, communicated, taught, modeled, and clinically monitored in all preK–12 classrooms. The literacy focus includes an understanding of what it takes to both prevent and mitigate gaps in foundational skills and knowledge-based competencies, both of which comprise what is known as *the science of reading*. To that end, the gold standard for literacy instruction must include, but not be limited to, the following learning strands: print concepts, phonemic awareness, phonological awareness, phonics, fluency, decoding, vocabulary, oral language skills, background knowledge, and comprehension (National Reading Panel, 2000).

Literacy plays a significant role in reducing educational inequity and empowers students to be thoughtful contributors to their school, community, and society. In short, literacy is key for interacting in the world, which is why it is fundamental to strength-based teaching. But how can we ensure improvements in literacy outcomes when so many children do not have equitable access to high-quality foundational instruction? We explore this question in the following section.

Equity

In a healing- and resilience-centered school model, a core belief is that every student—regardless of financial constraints, geographic location, primary language, cognitive or physical challenges, and existing practices—deserves equitable access to quality education. According to the National Equity Project (n.d.), educational equity means that each student "receives what they need to develop to their full academic and social potential." While the term *equality* focuses on providing the same resources to all students, *equity* emphasizes supporting students according to their individual needs.

Such an education entails an array of pedagogical components, including the following.

- Holding students to mastery of high-level standards
- Increasing the assessment fluency of every teacher to ensure equitable grading practices and quality feedback about learner growth
- Expecting all teachers to enhance literacy skills in the school
- Personalizing the educational experience based on student needs
- Implementing mastery-based learning (Joseph, 2021)

However, educational equity goes beyond providing equal resources and opportunities. It must also address the systemic barriers that disproportionately affect marginalized students. For example, *equal* resources could include things such as internet access or highly skilled teachers, but equity requires understanding students' needs and meeting them where they are. This could include examining whether the same curriculum that works for students whose parents have high socioeconomic status might not be culturally responsive or have the multiformat approach that engages and benefits students whose parents have low socioeconomic status. It could also entail removing prerequisites for honors and Advanced Placement classes (Joseph, 2021). Examining current practices and assumptions with an eye for equity will be an ongoing process for educators to consider.

Creating an inclusive, welcoming environment is also a fundamental aspect of promoting equity. By nurturing a sense of belonging for all students, regardless of their background, race, ethnicity, socioeconomic status, or ability, culturally responsive schools counteract the marginalization and exclusion that perpetuate inequities. Culturally responsive teaching practices, social-emotional learning, and celebrating diverse identities and perspectives contribute to a school culture where students feel they belong and are valued, seen, and heard.

School culture refers to the collective beliefs, values, attitudes, traditions, and behaviors that shape the climate and interactions within a school (Deal & Peterson, 2009). It encompasses the relationships among students, teachers, administrators, parents, and the broader community, as well as the unwritten rules and shared understandings that govern daily life within the school. Thus, schools are not simply institutions for academic learning. Rather, they are microcosms of society where students from diverse backgrounds come together to learn and grow.

When embracing cultural responsiveness, a school implementing the school fitness flywheel promotes educational equity when valuing and leveraging the assets that each student brings to the learning environment. It does that work by affirming their identities and lived experiences, thereby increasing their engagement and facilitating a deeper connection to the curriculum. Celebrating diverse identities and perspectives (including cultural backgrounds and experiences other than those of the majority of students) integrates these students into the educational process. Adapting instructional strategies and materials to reflect the backgrounds and interests of all students accomplishes this for a start. This speaks to modern iterations of culturally responsive teaching, which is rooted in the work of, among others, Gloria Ladson-Billings (1995, 2009, 2014, 2021a, 2021b) and Geneva Gay (2002, 2018), and asserts that a person's cognition and learning are influenced by the environment in which they live, including the family, community, and other social relationships.

Specifically, culturally responsive teaching taps into a students' prior knowledge, which may aid in academic comprehension (Brod, 2021). Prior knowledge draws from students' cultural background and experiences to make connections between what they know and what they need to learn. As an example, a teacher could project a historical landmark during a related history unit and ask learners to brainstorm everything they know about it. The teacher could then connect that knowledge to the new content or skills they will be learning. Another example could entail a teacher employing an affinity chart that shows a word or concept written in big letters and asking students to use sticky notes to write as many other words connected to it as they can come up with in a short time. The teacher could then keep the chart posted, group the sticky notes into common themes, and refer to the chart as the lesson continues, providing opportunities to add to the word list over time.

In addition, this healing- and resilience-centered school model recognizes the importance of addressing systemic injustices and empowering students to advocate for change. By incorporating humanized education, critical consciousness, and activism into the curriculum, students begin understanding complex human, political, and economic dynamics. In this model, students engage in discussions and projects that address social issues, fostering citizenship through empathy, compassion, and a commitment to social advancement. This focus on healing and resilience equips students with the knowledge, skills, and motivation to challenge inequities in and beyond the educational setting, contributing to a more just and equitable society. An educator from Montana spoke to this specifically:

> When I was a student from the reservation, we had multiple situations when we were discriminated against on athletic trips and field trips. Many Native American students have a similar story. I remember our teachers and coaches always told us to ignore it, let it go, and be the bigger person, while there was no accountability for the perpetrators. I felt powerless and frustrated when this happened. I am very happy that my staff and I refused to accept this as normal and realized we needed to protect our students in all situations and if a similar situation arose, we decided to identity this mistreatment in a peaceful and productive manner as well as prepare our students to assert and protect their dignity, rather than teaching kids to accept this type of mistreatment. (J. C., personal communication, May, 2019)

Chapter 3 (page 59) presents a detailed array of strategies on equity.

Agency

Healing- and resilience-centered schooling seeks to create a supportive educational environment that values and fosters student *agency*—the capacity to make choices, take ownership of one's learning, and effect positive change.

Creating a supportive educational environment that values and fosters student agency offers numerous benefits to academic, mental, and psychological fitness, including the following.

- Higher motivation, increased satisfaction with one's education, and a greater likelihood of academic success (Williams, as cited in O'Rourke & Addison, 2017)
- Increased responsibility for students' own education, leading to increased motivation, engagement, and a greater sense of purpose (Zima, 2021)
- Deeper learning and novel problem solving (Fullan, Hill, & Rincón-Gallardo, 2017; Victorian Department of Education and Training, 2017)
- Increased metacognitive skills and self-regulation leading to greater growth (Siddall, 2016)

Even though teachers generally intuitively recognize that students are unique individuals with diverse strengths, interests, and cognitive variability, they often teach all students the same way. By providing opportunities for student voice and choice in their education, schools foster autonomy and ownership—agency—by encouraging learners to actively participate in decision-making processes. Those decisions could be selecting project types or topics of study, setting goals, and determining how they demonstrate their learning. Student voice opportunities such as these are vital elements of mastery-based learning.

Student agency begins with shared vision and standard classroom operating procedures such as guidelines for student collaborative work or behavioral expectations. This vision and these procedures lay the groundwork for student agency by providing clear expectations for students regarding their roles and responsibilities, processes for goal setting and decision making, and establishing mechanisms for individual accountability in a group. Student voice is critical when teachers create classroom standard operating procedures.

Student-led conferences are another way to help students own their learning experience in that they can clearly articulate what a unit's proficiency scales mean in their own words. A ninth-grade student in North Dakota explained his experience in mastery-based learning to his parents in this way:

> Level 1, I am beginning to learn. It means, I'm just starting to kinda get it, but I need more help.
>
> Level 2 means I can show evidence and can remember details. It's where I probably already know it or can do it . . . . I just need to remember a few things still.

> Level 3 is when I totally know it, and I'm really good at it. This is where I need to be.
>
> Level 4 is advanced. I can show my knowledge in lots of ways or I can could teach it to someone else. (Cale V., personal communication, April, 2019)

Self-efficacy—the belief in one's ability to achieve goals—is fostered when teachers offer constructive feedback, support, strategies, and create a space where students feel comfortable taking risks and making mistakes. Self-efficacy is strongly correlated with higher levels of physical and emotional healing and recovery (Harris, 2021). This is an indicator of mental fitness. To provide this, teachers know students' strengths and where they need specific support. The relationships that teachers have with students and the informal and formal assessment data they receive provide that necessary information. They are able to provide the following, which leads to agency.

- Content in a student's zone of proximal development (Vygotsky, 1978), so they're challenged with something at which they can succeed after productive struggle
- Personalized feedback so students receive individualized support and guidance based on where they sit on a learning progression and can act on that
- A place safe for risk taking so they are willing to make mistakes

Through these practices, students obtain the attitudes and skills to actively participate in learning and enact positive change in their communities and beyond. We present an array of strategies around agency more fully in the rest of this book.

Relationships

The fourth core principle that underpins healing- and resilience-centered schooling is strong, positive, developmentally appropriate relationships. Such relationships with a trusting adult as well as with peers are one antidote to childhood trauma (Buchanan, Walker, Boden, Mansoor, & Newton-Howes, 2023; Sieving et al., 2017). Our successful evolution as a species is due to our ability to empathize and connect (B. Farragher, personal communication, January, 2018). Although connection and empathy are deeply part of the human condition, it is not uncommon for systems to push it aside to make way for academics.

Empathy is an action word that describes vicariously experiencing someone else's reality. As a reminder, empathy, as often defined by emotion researchers, can be the "ability to sense other people's emotions, coupled with the ability to imagine what someone else might be thinking or feeling" (Greater Good Magazine, n.d.). Empathy is a quality that helps facilitate connection and is a skill that most people must learn and have nurtured. Humans are creatures of connection and, thus, relationships are crucial to our survival. Finding ways to connect with students builds the protective factor students need (Centers for Disease Control and Prevention [CDC], 2022). From acknowledging students by name—and correctly pronouncing that name—to knowing some of their interests or asking about their activities, there are many ways teachers can connect and build such relationships.

Displaying curiosity (instead of making a judgment) is a good step toward building trusting relationships as well. The following are examples of such open-ended questions:

- How are things going in [*a particular setting*]?
- What happened? Tell me in your own words.
- Can you tell me why . . . ?
- Can you tell me what you mean by . . . ?
- Can you tell me more about how that makes you feel?
- Can you give me an example?
- Why do you think that is? (Turnaround for Children, 2020, p. 7)

Relational poverty, which is a profound lack of connectedness with others (and can be more destructive and debilitating than economic poverty), negatively impacts all groups of people regardless of race, gender, or socioeconomic status (Perry, 2022; Szalavitz & Perry, 2010). We assert that the mental health challenges and increased behavioral issues partly point to many students showing up to school more dysregulated and suffering from relational poverty than in previous generations. Informal and formal surveys point to the same conclusion (Dubinski, 2023).

One reason for this increase in relational poverty revolves around the fact that many modern societies are more focused on economics and financial status than relationships, often with broken social structures that prove challenging for young people's ability to relate to each other (Lawson & Elwood, 2018). This phenomenon has manifested in the creeping realization that empathy, the ability to sense other people's emotions and understand their feelings, has begun to decline (Konrath, 2019). This lack of empathy can be the root cause of racism, crime, violence, war, abuse, and social inequity (Williams, 2022). Thus, there is an urgent need to develop a deeper emotional vocabulary to develop empathy.

In addition, innovative technology means young people spend more time in front of phones, computers, game systems, or television sets rather than interacting with significant adults (Lee et al., 2022). Screen time is a major factor in relational poverty (Perry & Winfrey, 2021). Finally, schools provide environments in which students experience hundreds of daily interactions with peers and teachers—yet these interactions are often profoundly lacking in relational connections such as touch, rich conversation, or intergenerational mentoring. Relational poverty contributes to our alienation.

Empathy is a cure for relational poverty. The psychological benefits of empathy can be profound. It can lead to trust, deeper personal connection, generosity of spirit, and love (Perry, 2022). Personal connection can reduce stress hormones and result in many of the same neurological benefits mindfulness offers, including calming the amygdala and increasing brain *neuroplasticity*, or pliability (Caballero et al., 2019; Hammond, 2015).

Psychologist Daniel Goleman (2017) identified three types of empathy that teachers can directly address in classrooms. Table 1.2 connects those empathy types to the three school fitness flywheel components.

Table 1.2: Connecting Empathy to the School Fitness Flywheel Components

Goleman's (2017) Empathy Type and When It Occurs	Where the Flywheel Helps
Emotional (or affective) empathy occurs when we share in another's feelings and emotions.	The strength-based teaching segment speaks directly to emotional empathy because understanding and respecting the culture, background, and community that helped shaped a learner can enhance a sense of meaning and motivation between teacher and student.
Compassionate empathy occurs when our empathic feelings inspire us to act on another's behalf with compassion. In turn, compassion is the "feeling that arises when witnessing another's suffering and that motivates a desire to help" (Goetz, Keltner, & Simon-Thomas, 2010, p. 351).	The growth-based schooling segment can help an educator embrace compassionate empathy with students by deepening connections and co-regulating.
Cognitive empathy occurs when we comprehend another's perspective. In education, cognitive empathy can mean stepping into a student's shoes and understanding variability in performance.	The mastery-based learning segment can help a teacher personalize learning using proficiency scales and learner profiles and, thereby, more deeply understanding where students are on their learning journey.

Teaching students active listening skills can help them develop empathy. This can be accomplished in a number of ways such as team building activities, restorative circles, advisory periods, and flexible grouping strategies (Hammond, 2015; Marzano, 2017). We present an array of other strategies on deepening and enhancing relationships more fully in chapters 2 (page 31), 3 (page 59), and 4 (page 93).

Neuroplasticity

One of the most powerful points we make in this book is that schools have the capacity to help repair and strengthen the brain. Educators from healing- and resilience-centered schools recognize that a healthy brain is essential for optimal cognitive functioning, efficient learning, and educational success.

Neuroplasticity is a brain's capacity to reorganize and form new neural connections throughout one's lifespan based on new learning, experiences, and thoughts (Dost, 2023). It means the brain can heal, change, and grow. Neuroplasticity is an important element in helping heal students who are struggling with any number of issues, from depression and anxiety to memory and executive function issues (Weinstein & Algeri, 2018). Schools can create an environment conducive to enhancing neuroplasticity by incorporating practices that support brain development. These practices may include mindfulness and physical activities (both discussed in chapter 3, page 59) and rich learning experiences, especially via mastery-based learning protocols (Jowkar, Kojuri, Kohoulat, & Hayat, 2014). By engaging in activities that stimulate different regions of the brain, students can strengthen neural pathways and enhance their capacity for learning, memory, and cognitive flexibility (Harris, 2021; Ruyle et al., 2022; Weinstein & Algeri, 2018).

Chronic stress can specifically impair our ability to learn and remember, and it can negatively impact overall brain health as well (Posner & Barbey, 2020). Conversely, reduced stress levels empower students to optimize their cognitive resources including memory, attention, and reasoning, thus enabling them to engage in learning more effectively (Posner & Barbey, 2020). By fostering positive relationships and implementing stress-reduction techniques such as mindfulness, deep-breathing exercises, gratitude, and movement, the school fitness flywheel model can help teachers and students regulate stress responses and support healthy neuroplasticity changes. School systems that work in ways that ameliorate toxic stress and trauma require educators who can teach skills and strategies that could potentially boost synaptic plasticity in the brain—which could, ultimately, facilitate academic, mental, and psychological fitness (Cantor et al., 2019; Perry, 2022; Yehuda, Daskalakis, et al., 2016; Yehuda, Spiegel, et al., 2016).

Furthermore, resilience is closely linked to neuroplasticity in that it speaks to a person's ability to bounce back and effectively adapt to challenging situations. Resilient students sustain high levels of achievement motivation and performance despite the presence of trauma or stressful events (Jowkar et al., 2014; Zima, 2021). Resilience can enhance mental fitness by helping people look beyond problems and challenges and discover multiple ways to enjoy life and better handle stress (Mayo Clinic Staff, n.d.b). Cultivating students' ability to show resilience means recognizing that a resilient brain is better equipped to handle challenges and setbacks.

Doing the following strengthens the neural circuits involved in emotional regulation and impulse control.

- Encouraging a sense of agency and self-efficacy (chapter 2)
- Practicing emotional regulation strategies (chapter 3)
- Enhancing learning strengths (chapter 4)

Specific strategies centered on relationships are also explained in chapters 3 (page 59) and 4 (page 93). We also present a number of strategies centered on brain development more fully in chapters 2–4 and introduce specific tools in chapter 5 (page 119).

Summary

We have a once-in-a-century opportunity to evolve our schools into the future. Thus, it is critical that stakeholders seize this moment to shift from a standardized approach to education to one that is humanized, recognizing the fact that teaching and learning are fundamentally among the greatest of human endeavors. As stated earlier, schools must serve as dynamic centers for human development in which students can connect their personal backgrounds and aspirations with their teachers, peers, educational culture, and daily environment to learn and grow emotionally and cognitively. The following chapters provide ways to connect the dots so that classroom teaching does not only consist of a variety of discrete actions and strategies for content delivery, but instead does that and leads to higher levels of student learning and human development. Visit **MarzanoResources.com/reproducibles** for a free reproducible version of this book's next steps.

We advise these three next steps as most important from this chapter for school leaders.

1. Personally embrace the urgent need to evolve schools to a healing- and resilience-centered educational framework.
2. Facilitate the shift in hearts and minds of staff and community, which are vital to moving to a mastery-based school model.
3. Engage the larger community to help them understand the power of culture to enhance a strength-based teaching mindset.

We advise these three next steps as most important from this chapter for teachers and other classroom staff.

1. Use professional collaborative learning to engage in the roles that schools and teachers can play in strengthening neuroplasticity.
2. Consider the need to address healing and resilience in our own lives by understanding how mental health impacts our own capacity to learn and grow.
3. Engage in professional development to enhance literacy practices across the curriculum.

2

Mastery-Based Learning

A mind once stretched by a new idea never regains its original dimensions.

—OLIVER WENDELL HOLMES

As educators strive to meet the diverse needs of their students and cultivate deeper learning experiences, there has been a growing recognition of the limitations of traditional models of instruction that focus on seat time, deadlines, and completion of assignments. Thus, mastery-based learning represents a transformative shift in education by actively fostering a student-centered and competency-driven approach. By focusing attention on proficiency rather than seat time, mastery-based learning protocols empower students to take control of their learning while providing educators with valuable insights to inform and personalize instruction.

Mastery-based learning has three foundational components: (1) learning goals, (2) proficiency scales, and (3) aligned assessments. Using these three components in daily classroom practice improves students' academic fitness by providing them with clearly articulated standards along with pathways to mastery. Doing so also encourages agency and enhances the ability for learners to own their education and learning.

This paradigm shift to helping ensure every learner is held accountable for demonstrating proficiency is a massive change in structure and practice, the significance of which cannot be overstated. The following three shifts can increase student engagement as well as teacher optimism.

- Embracing academic mastery by identifying the skills and content to practice
- Providing learning progressions to show students the blueprint to success

- Creating assessment philosophies that provide valuable feedback rather than simply grades

Altogether, these actions completely evolve the traditional educational model to a more relevant system that better meets learners' unique needs (Bloom, 1971; Guskey, 2015; Hattie, 2015b; Levine & Patrick, 2019; Norford & Marzano, 2016).

Mastery-Based Learning Defined

Mastery-based learning is an educational approach that focuses on the demonstrated mastery of specific knowledge, skills, and competencies. At its core, mastery-based learning operates on the belief that all students can achieve proficiency in essential learning objectives if provided with appropriate instructional guidance, support, resources, and time. Mastery-based learning has three foundational components.

1. Learning goals
2. Proficiency scales
3. Aligned assessments

Using these three components in daily classroom practice improves students' academic fitness by providing them with goals and pathways to mastery. Doing so also encourages agency and enhances the ability for learners to own their education and learning. Altogether, these actions completely evolve the traditional educational model to a more relevant system that better meets learners' unique needs (Bloom, 1971; Guskey, 2015; Hattie, 2015b; Levine & Patrick, 2019; Norford & Marzano, 2016).

This paradigm shift to helping ensure every learner is held accountable for demonstrating proficiency is a massive change from traditional school structure and practice, the significance of which cannot be overstated. The mastery-based approach accomplishes several things.

- It encourages students to actively engage in their learning process, taking ownership of their academic journey (Zima, 2021).
- It promotes personalized learning experiences by tailoring instruction to individual needs and providing flexibility in pacing. This allows students to progress at a rate that suits their abilities, enabling them to delve into topics of interest, revisit challenging areas, or accelerate their learning when ready (Levine & Patrick, 2019; Zima, 2021).
- It acknowledges that students may require additional support or opportunities for enrichment. When students struggle to grasp

certain concepts, they receive targeted interventions or remediation strategies based on proficiency scales to address their specific needs. Similarly, students who quickly master content are offered opportunities for deeper exploration, extensions, or more complex challenges to further enhance their learning (Marzano et al., 2017).

Simply stated, mastery-based learning prioritizes students' ability to apply knowledge rather than merely demanding teachers deliver curriculum and students complete assignments. Although a school's structure in this model is different from the traditional model, the fundamental elements of using proficiency scales, aligning assessments to scales, and personalizing instruction based on assessment data are actions that any teacher can do. As a powerful support to this argument, a meta-analysis of the mastery-based learning approach related to academic achievement by David Arhin and Winifred Bonsu Opoku (2020) finds that mastery-based learning "has positive effects on learners' academic achievements," leading them to conclude "that the empirical evidence from this study warrants a generalization without hesitation" (p. 102).

The following sections explore the practical implementation of personalized, mastery-based learning using the critical elements of learning goals and learning progressions, assessment, personalized instruction, self-efficacy from voice and choice, and teacher optimism. In addition, we highlight successful strategies and real-world examples that illustrate the potential for mastery-based learning to transform educational outcomes.

Learning Goals and Proficiency Scales

The fundamental, nonnegotiable component of a mastery-based approach entails the effective regular use of learning goals and proficiency scales by teachers and students to provide a pathway for students to follow on their journey to mastery and a way to monitor their progress. In the context of a healing- and resilience-centered school, the focus extends beyond academics to encompass students' overall well-being and growth with learning goals and proficiency scales.

Learning Goals

A *guaranteed and viable curriculum* articulates knowledge and skills learners are expected to learn in the allotted time frame of a school term. The key to determining a guaranteed and viable curriculum lies in prioritizing and unpacking standards, which, ultimately, results in the expression of curriculum through *learning goals* (Marzano, 2017). We have heard learning goals referred to by a host of terms such as *prioritized standards*, *core competencies*, *essential understandings*, *educational outcomes*, *measurement topics*, or other nomenclature. It boils down to academic knowledge and skills, thinking skills, life (social and personal) skills, work habits, dispositions, and other domains that the school and community believe are important for students to master.

Learning goals must do the following.

- Align with state, provincial, or national standards
- Be clearly defined and articulated at the expressed level of the standard

Unpacking and prioritizing standards—or establishing learning goals—is necessary because most standards documents (whether Common Core State Standards or other individual state or provincial standards documents) simply contain too much content to teach and assess in a typical school term (Marzano, 2017). Teachers are placed in the position where they are forced to plow through content, as opposed to helping students understand and master critical skills and knowledge.

Teacher teams who are content experts usually are responsible for prioritizing identified standards or establishing learning goals. In our experience, the vast majority of schools have gone through some sort of prioritizing process since the mid-1990s or 2010s. It is important, therefore, that content teams no longer get bogged down in the prioritization process.

Educators avoid some issues if they communicate those learning goals to students and families in a way that ensures three things.

1. Educators present goals in a way that is student and family friendly, and not simply an iteration of a document with typical standards language.
2. Students have a clear understanding of what the goal entails and what mastery of the goal looks, sounds, and feels like.
3. The pathways to master that goal are in students' hands (hard copy, digital copy, or both), recognizing that students start with different strengths and needs and might require different supports.

Until they grasp these critical steps, schools and educational teams commonly revert to old habits of simply plowing through curriculum. It's easy for teachers to state that their standards documents have been streamlined and priorities established, but until students are able to clearly understand and explain how daily activities lead them to proficiency on the overarching goal, and until teachers are able to alter their practice to help every learner master the identified goal, schooling tends to look the same as it always has (Ruyle, O'Neill, Iberlin, Evans, & Midles, 2019).

As an example, the Critical Concepts (Marzano Resources, n.d.) are a powerful tool for providing high-level learning goals along with solid, clear steps or learning progressions like those in table 2.1 (page 36). These concepts help guide both teachers and students toward mastery and are presented in a way that makes great sense to teachers, students, and families. Rather than simply focusing student effort on submitting work and completing tasks, asking students to demonstrate mastery on a finite number of skills and identified content knowledge is much easier for students to embrace, for families to understand, and for educators to teach.

In this instance, learning goals are presented as measurement topics—overarching themes that students will be held to master—and specific proficiency scales have been created that correspond to each topic. Thus, the overwhelming weight of a full group of standards are presented in a much more learner-friendly version that students have a much easier time understanding. An array of states have already adopted similar versions of their measurement topics for distribution among their schools. In classrooms, students are able to monitor their progress and see how learning immediate, daily targets will lead them to mastery.

Proficiency Scales

After establishing learning goals, proficiency scales articulate via clear steps or learning progressions the knowledge and skills students must master. Proficiency scales are the critical element—they are game changers in mastery-based learning that provide teachers, students, and parents with a clear picture of what knowledge and skills students must demonstrate while establishing the steps toward mastery (Marzano, 2017; Ruyle et al., 2019). They also identify a focus for instruction and assessment. Simply stated, students use the scales to learn their way through basic content and skills until they can demonstrate mastery of the standard; level 3 of the scale expresses what mastery looks like. Teachers plan and then provide direct instruction, appropriate groupings, projects, activities, and tasks, helping students apply their knowledge and skills so that they can provide evidence of mastery.

Proficiency scales can also do the following for students.

- Nurture individual learning strengths, enhance student agency, and foster stronger student-teacher connections, making them also a critical element of growth-based schooling.
- Cultivate a positive learning environment that values progress over perfection, encouraging students to embrace challenges, persist in the face of obstacles, and celebrate their achievements along the journey.

Table 2.1: Example Mathematics Learning Progressions by Grade

Grade 5	Grade 6
Multiplication and Division	Signed Numbers and Absolute Value
Fraction Addition and Subtraction	Factors and Multiples
Fraction Multiplication	Long Division
Fraction Division	Fraction Division
Decimal Place Values	Evaluating Algebraic Expressions
Decimal Addition and Subtraction	Ratios, Rates, and Percentages
Decimal Multiplication and Division	Algebraic Equations
Exponents	Inequalities
Numerical Expressions	Independent and Dependent Variables
Numerical Patterns	Measurement Conversions
Measurement Conversions	Area and Volume
Volume	Coordinate Plane
Two-Dimensional Figures	Measures of Central Tendency
Coordinate Plane	Measures of Variability
	Displaying Distributions
	Analyzing Distributions
Grade 7	**Grade 8**
Signed Numbers and Absolute Value	Exponents
Converting Fractions, Decimals, and Percentages	Cube and Square Roots
Linear Equations	Scientific Notation
Proportional Relationships	Rational and Irrational Numbers
Inequalities	Linear Equations
Area and Volume	Systems of Linear Equations
Analyzing Geometric Figures	Quadratic Equations
Transformations of Geometric Figures	Concept of Functions
Angle Relationships	Linear Functions
Constructing Triangles	Volume
Circles	Transformations, Similarity, and Congruence
Comparing Distributions	Angles of Two-Dimensional Figures
Representative Samples	Line and Angle Constructions
Simple Probability Models	Pythagorean Theorem
Probability of Compound Events	Bivariate Categorical Data
	Bivariate Measurement Data

Source: Simms, 2016.

- Encourage seeing setbacks as opportunities for learning and development by emphasizing academic growth as well as individualized academic, mental, and psychological fitness. (Students can recognize that this wellness does not occur in a specific progression and that their efforts and resilience contribute to their overall well-being.)
- Empower taking control over their learning by fostering self-awareness and a deeper understanding of their own growth.

Figure 2.1 (page 38) depicts an example proficiency scale.

Proficiency scales in this model enable educators to assess students' progress in a holistic manner. Effective use can provide a comprehensive picture of a student's well-being beyond just academic performance and can thus enhance academic, mental, and psychological fitness. This allows educators to identify areas of strength and areas that require additional support, ensuring a more personalized and student-centered approach to education.

As a teacher from California said:

> Kids understand better what the concept behind their grade is. Rather than having a 90 or a 70 percent, a B or a C, the proficiency scale specifically states what things they need to master and what they need to practice more. The parents really see that their kids have ownership and knowledge over what they are learning. What's best of all is that the expectation is that learners not only can but will revisit material to be able to demonstrate proficiency. Using proficiency scales, at the beginning and middle of the year, most kids are still going to be getting 1s and 2s because they're still learning. But by the end of the year, they are getting 3s, if not 4s. (N. Bethany, personal communication, November, 2019)

Again, consistently, effectively using proficiency scales in classroom practice is the foundation of mastery-based learning. It also happens to be a vital component of growth-based schooling and strength-based teaching.

Pathways to Mastery

One of the fundamental tenets of mastery-based learning is the acknowledgment of *cognitive variability*—the recognition that students learn at different rates and various pathways. This understanding empowers teachers to take a more deliberate, strength-based approach to delivering instruction, which, in turn, encourages students to express their own voice and exercise greater autonomy over their learning. By empowering students to have a voice in their

4.0	**The student will:** • Investigate the outcome of a collision between two satellites (for example, diagram the forces acting on two satellites orbiting Earth heading toward one another and determine whether they will continue to orbit after they collide using known equations)
3.5	In addition to score 3.0 performance, partial success at score 4.0 content
3.0	**The student will:** **G1—Use Newton's law of gravitation to describe the gravitational forces between objects** (for example, using known equations and Newton's law of gravitation, find the values for force, acceleration, velocity, mass, or the distance between two objects based on given information) **G2—Predict the motion of orbiting objects in the solar system** (for example, use equations to find the velocity, period, frequency, and distance of objects in both circular and elliptical orbits)
2.5	No major errors or omissions regarding score 2.0 content, and partial success at score 3.0 content
2.0	**G1—The student will** recognize or recall specific vocabulary (for example, *acceleration, attraction, constant, distance, exert, force, gravity, mass, Newton* [unit], *Newton's law of gravitation, Newton's third law, opposite, proportional, radius, range, relationship, substitute, universal, universal gravitation constant, variable*) and perform basic processes such the following. • State Newton's law of gravitation. • Use Newton's law of gravitation $F = G \frac{m_1 m_2}{r_2}$ to explain the proportional relationships between the force of gravity, mass, and the distance between two objects. • Use Newton's third law to explain the equal and opposite gravitational force a person standing on the surface of the Earth experiences (the force of gravity and the force exerted by the Earth back toward them). • Explain the phrase "gravity is universal." • Substitute values for variables, constants (for example, the universal gravitation constant or the acceleration of gravity), and applicable equations as necessary. **G2—The student will** recognize or recall specific vocabulary (for example, *acceleration, apogee, astronomical unit, axis, circle, circumference, distance, eccentricity, ellipse, focus, force, frequency, gravity, Kepler's constant, Kepler's laws of planetary motion, law of ellipses, law of equal areas, law of harmonies, mass, motion, Newton's second law of motion, Newton's law of gravitation, orbit, perigee, period, radius, satellite, semi-major axis, semi-minor axis, solar system, sun, velocity*) and perform basic processes such the following. • Use Newton's second law of motion $F_{net} = ma$ and law of gravitation $F_g = G \frac{m_1 m_2}{r_2}$ as well as the equation for acceleration $a = \frac{v^2}{r}$ to find an object's velocity in a circular orbit. • Determine the period and frequency of an object in a circular orbit using $2\pi r$ and an object's velocity. • Explain each of Kepler's laws of planetary motion (the law of ellipses, the law of equal areas, and the law of harmonies) in relation to knowledge of orbiting objects. • Diagram an object in space's elliptical orbit. • Use Kepler's third law ($P^2 \propto a^3$, where P = period and a = semi-major axis) and a knowledge of astronomical units (AU) to determine the distance of an object from the sun.
1.5	Partial success at score 2.0 content and major errors or omissions regarding score 3.0 content
1.0	With help, partial success at score 2.0 content and score 3.0 content
0.5	With help, partial success at score 2.0 content but not at score 3.0 content
0.0	Even with help, no success

Source: © 2016 by Julia A. Simms. Adapted with permission.

FIGURE 2.1: Example high school science proficiency scale.

education and exercise autonomy over their own learning, they become more engaged and, ultimately, grow and learn at higher levels.

When students can embrace their own learning and demonstrate their knowledge in ways that are meaningful to them as opposed to simply completing assignments as directed by a teacher, their voice becomes magnified and motivation increases (Zima, 2021). For example, students in a 9–12 program in California access their proficiency scales through hard copies provided in a student notebook. The students in this program also have full access to their scales online. By having this information clearly articulated and in their possession, all their work and assignments make sense, and their learning efforts become more meaningful and their engagement increases.

The students in the program speak to the power of using scales as the foundational element of competency-based learning:

> "I like how the work today gets me to level 3."
> —Middle school student
>
> "I like how I have options at level 3."
> —Middle school student
>
> "I want to get credit when I show my knowledge and not just turn in the work."
> —High school student

A high school in Kansas City, Missouri, empowers students to take ownership of their learning by assessing their level of mastery. This takes the form of an exit ticket. In self-reflecting on their progress, students share evidence of their learning.

In both examples, students can be specific about where they are in their learning progression, how their daily work fits into the proficiency scale, and they can monitor their progress toward mastery of the goal. This results in higher levels of motivation and engagement and empowers students to take control of their own learning. It also enhances the student-teacher connection, in that teachers can provide targeted instruction and help students grow from where they currently sit on the scale (Ruyle et al., 2019). Thus, the effective use of learning goals and proficiency scales is a critical component of growth-based schooling and strength-based teaching in addition to being the foundational piece of mastery-based learning. This is also an example of how the school fitness flywheel can continually bring all the segments of an academic, mental, and psychological fitness-based framework to life.

Assessment

Schools and teachers often struggle to update their assessment practice. Teachers are familiar with their own school experience as students, and it is challenging to evolve protocols that have been so common in schools for decades. In traditional school models, assessments are usually seen as more closely aligned with grading as opposed to learning. This concept is deeply engrained in the collective school psyche, and it can be daunting to challenge. Unfortunately, many traditional grading systems often rank students and assign labels and grades that can hinder academic motivation and stifle growth (Chamberlin, Yasué, & Chiang, 2018).

But in terms of a mastery-based learning framework, high-quality assessment practices are about providing regular feedback that drives subsequent teaching and learning. By aligning assessment practices with growth-oriented goals, educators inspire students to view feedback as a valuable tool for improvement. Grades remain an accepted, nonnegotiable element of schools and play an important role in reporting student status and progress toward mastery. But assessment in a healing- and resilience-centered school model serves primarily as a feedback tool in which generating grades based on the points from assessments becomes an endeavor of secondary importance.

For our purposes here, we refer to this mindset shift and the corresponding improvement in teacher expertise as *assessment literacy*, in that all teachers should be adept in using sound assessment practices at a professional level just as clearly and effectively as they speak in their native language. This is some of the most important work for teachers to engage in and for schools to expend professional development efforts on. Teachers can deepen their assessment literacy by ensuring their assessment practices are valid, reliable, and equitable, and serve as a continuous feedback tool. Cultivating such deeper levels of teacher assessment skill can help healing- and resilience-centered schools to enhance both academic and psychological fitness.

For a more in-depth examination of assessment and grading, we suggest teachers focus on high-quality assessment design through professional development and collaborative teams. *The New Art and Science of Classroom Assessment* (Marzano, Norford, & Ruyle, 2019) is a particularly valuable book in this area. In the following sections, we discuss the critical elements of high-quality assessment practices that can empower teachers to provide regular evidence of learning and feedback regarding a student's progression of learning toward mastery.

Valid

Assessment *validity* refers to the extent to which an assessment measures what it is designed to measure. Teachers can address validity through such foundational questions as, How valid is this test for the decisions that I need to make? or How valid is the interpretation I propose for the test? In other words, teachers should continually examine the purpose of the assessment, the type or form of an assessment they're using, and the population for whom it is intended. A common analogy to explain validity is the bathroom scale. If a person uses the bathroom scale to measure their weight, it is a valid use of the instrument. If they use the scale to measure their vision, it is an invalid use of the instrument. To illustrate this point in a classroom setting, consider a learning goal at level 3, which states that students will *predict the motion of orbiting objects in the solar system.* If a unit test provides evidence that a learner can apply Newton's law by correctly predicting motion in a test setting, then the criteria for validity have been met.

Teachers and teacher teams can speak directly to improving validity in their assessment practices by doing the following.

- Describe degrees of cognition required for an assessment.
- Make proficiency scales readily available to students and publicly accessible.
- Ensure that assessments can clearly measure goals and objectives by directly aligning to a proficiency scale.
- Ensure that assessments reflect appropriate levels of thinking to accurately monitor growth and achievement.
- Obtain feedback from others by having colleagues or collaborative teams review assessments.
- Involve students and solicit their feedback in terms of clarity, troublesome wording, or other difficulties.
- Compare the assessment with other measures or available data, when possible.

Reliability is the next concern.

Reliable

Reliability speaks to an assessment's accuracy, precision, and consistency. It is the degree to which an assessment tool produces stable, consistent results. Using the bathroom scale example from the validity discussion, if a person uses a scale to measure their weight, the tool is valid. If, however, a person gets on the scale ten times in a row and the scale indicates a different weight each time, the scale is not reliably reporting weight. In a classroom, reliability is more of a theoretical construct explained by the analogy that if a student were to take an assessment ten times, their score should be the same or very similar each time. Reliability is an important element of high-quality assessment design.

To address reliability in classroom settings, use multiple, parallel assessments. Simply stated, reliability is strengthened by providing students with multiple opportunities to demonstrate mastery by employing an array of assessments that are of similar depth of knowledge. As an example, when teachers place a greater weight on certain assessments than on others—such as with a final exam—the resulting score is no more of a valuable indicator of knowledge than any other task or assignment created at similar levels of thinking. But if a student provides an array of evidence—a collection of multiple assessments in the form of tests, quizzes, conversations, assignments, and tasks—both the teacher and student have a much more reliable idea of the student's true level of knowledge. This provides a robust score that teachers can update in real time and provide learners with clear indicators of their current learning status. For example, consider the learning goal at level 3 that states students will *predict the motion of orbiting objects in the solar system.* If a unit test provides evidence that a learner can apply Newton's law by correctly predicting motion in a test setting, and if the student has also effectively predicted motion in an experiment, as well as communicated their prediction skill using Newton's law in a conversation with peers or a teacher, then that student has provided three pieces of evidence that they can meet the identified standard. This is a much more reliable indicator of knowledge than a benchmark assessment score.

Mastery-based academic programs that provide students with multiple opportunities to demonstrate mastery of learning objectives do not penalize learners for mistakes or low performance. If a student does not initially meet the criteria for mastery, they receive additional instruction, support, and opportunities to reassess their understanding. By allowing students to revise and improve their work, the focus shifts from grades to true mastery and the development of a growth mindset.

The Marzano Calculator (http://marzanocalc.empowerlearning.net) is a free tool that can help teachers understand the importance and power of multiple parallel assessments using technology. One can enter an array of scores from assessments aligned to proficiency scales into the calculator, which then interprets the scores to determine the most reliable indicator of student learning. For example, if a teacher were to record a number of scores on many similar assessments, that collection of evidence of learning, taken all together, would provide a much more reliable score than taking scores and calculating an average.

Equitable

Transforming assessment paradigms so the focus is on providing feedback that can drive learning and instruction rather than using points to determine a grade can transform the entire educational system.

A critical point is that using valid and reliable assessment practices can enhance academic fitness by providing clear learning feedback for students and driving instruction for teachers. Sound assessment practices can also strengthen psychological fitness by helping learners operate from a position of strength by being able to show what they know as opposed to what they miss. This builds motivation, meaning, and engagement.

We have seen many schools and districts attempt to quickly embrace equitable grading philosophies. But, implementing new policies and procedures without engaging teachers in meaningful, effective professional education to enhance their assessment literacy is insufficient despite teachers' best efforts. Presenting assessment theory along with updated assessment research for educators as well as the larger community and providing regular opportunities for teachers to collaborate and receive coaching to evolve their practice are vital.

Equitable assessment practices ensure that students are held to high expectations by demonstrating mastery on clearly defined standards. By communicating honest and accurate reports about where they are in their learning journey, equitable assessment practice can also serve to inspire, motivate, and drive teacher actions that truly improve their learning. This includes providing additional supports, relevant and engaging curriculum and instruction, and multiple pathways to access and demonstrate learning.

Educational thought leader Joe Feldman (2023) made the case that equitable grading has three pillars: (1) accuracy, (2) bias resistance, and (3) intrinsic motivation. Our assessment practices should directly address these constructs to acknowledge how tests and assignments can provide feedback rather simply garner points to calculate a grade.

Accuracy

Equitable assessments should accurately indicate a student's level of content knowledge or skill acquisition. Ensuring that assessments clearly describe the degrees of cognition allows for a more accurate assessment of knowledge and skill. When assessments are aligned to a high level of expectation as articulated at the level of the standard, teachers can ensure that all students are held to mastery of the same standards. This is the essence of equity.

Assessments should also exclude nonacademic information. When teachers combine both academic and nonacademic information or tasks, the assessment can include too much disparate information. By ensuring that assessments directly align with proficiency scales, teachers increase assessment validity and can clearly identify academic levels of performance, which will deepen meaning in terms of mastering content goals (Marzano et al., 2019).

Bias Resistance

It is critical that reporting a student's progress isn't compromised by a teacher's opinion or emotions about a student. Teachers can be tempted to reduce expectations for some students out of compassion for those with traumatic, stressful, or challenging backgrounds. Unfortunately, this empathic move does not serve students. When assessments are not valid or rigorous, students are held to lower expectations. Likewise, grades generated by these practices can mislead students and caregivers into believing that their true course content understanding is higher than it is (Hammond, 2015). Simply stated, bias in assessments threatens the reliability and validity of assessment scores and outcomes, limiting their usefulness and instilling a lack of trust and confidence among students.

When an assessment is fair or free of bias, however, students have equal opportunity to demonstrate knowledge, skills, and abilities regardless of identity and personal characteristics. To reduce or eliminate bias and create fair assessments, avoid stereotyping, unfamiliar cultural phenomena, or unfair representations of culture, race, or gender. Also make sure questions and directions are written well enough to be completely clear to all students.

Intrinsic Motivation

A vital component of assessment in a mastery-based learning system is student involvement, choice, and reflection. Thus, assessment strategies should include self-assessments, reflections like that in figure 2.2, portfolios, observations, and group activities that gauge students' ability to demonstrate mastery of an identified standard.

By providing all students with a learning progression such as the following articulated in a proficiency scale, teachers can show them that no matter where they start, growth and success are always possible.

- **Level 4:** Exceeding the standard
- **Level 3:** Meeting the standard
- **Level 2:** Approaching the standard
- **Level 1:** Beginning the journey to mastery
- **Level 0:** Insufficient evidence

Students can see the lowest level as simply no evidence rather than failing. In this way, teachers provide hope for every learner, which increases motivation.

Tracking My Own Learning

Student Name: *Henry C.*

Learning Goal: *Mathematics: Understand and use decoding and spacers*

My score at beginning: *2*

My goal: *3* by *Nov. 3*

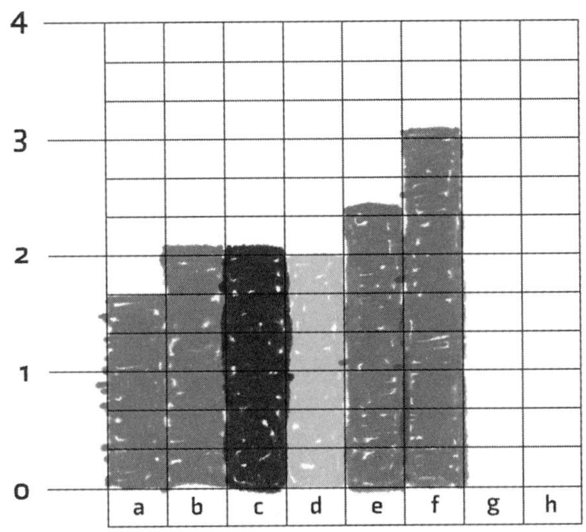

(a) *Oct. 5 (2)*

(b) *Oct. 12 (2)*

(c) *Oct. 19 (2)*

(d) *Oct. 20 (2)*

(e) *Oct. 22 (2)*

(f) *Oct. 27 (3!)*

4	*I made no mistakes. I understand completely.*
3	*I made no major mistakes. Maybe I need a little more time to understand what is important.*
2	*I made some major mistakes. My errors show I don't understand some important parts.*
1	*I made many major mistakes. I just don't understand yet.*

FIGURE 2.2: Example of student tracking their own learning.

Instead of limiting students to one learning path, encouraging choice in mastery demonstration provides students the opportunity to lead their learning and increases agency, which are important in motivating students to engage (Ackerman, 2018; Ryan & Deci, 2000).

As high school learners from North Dakota said:

> "Goals and scales are huge—I get school now. I like that I can follow my own progress, and that I can do lots of things like quizzes, posters, worksheets, essays, and power points. I like

> essays and power points the best because then I get to show what I know better."
>
> "I love seeing myself progress on my measurement topics. I couldn't go to school without goals and scales anymore!!!"

Valid, reliable, and equitable classroom assessments should be the most effective and frequently used tools in our instructional tool kit because they provide evidence of growth and progress toward specific learning goals in a way that can empower and motivate learners (Marzano et al., 2019). Teachers should be able to really *see* the student and *see* the evidence, and that knowledge of the student from the evidence gathered should be reflected in the gradebook.

Our teachers and leaders should be provided with the knowledge and guidance to improve and become fluent with contemporary research regarding classroom assessments. They need time to study, discuss, practice, and evolve their learning. They need continued support to make this critical piece of educational evolution a norm in all schools.

Personalized Instruction

Personalized instruction empowers students to take ownership of their learning by giving them a voice in setting goals, encouraging them to make choices about their learning paths, and helping them reflect on their progress. This student ownership enhances motivation and engagement as students develop a sense of purpose and responsibility for their educational journey. When students develop the metacognitive awareness of what they need to succeed, they are on the path to becoming independent learners capable of succeeding in any environment (Ruyle et al., 2019; Ruyle et al., 2022; Zima, 2021).

Personalizing the learning experience aligns with mastery-based learning because teachers aim and differentiate specifically for every learner, in appropriately challenging and personally relevant ways within individualized time frames. Teachers fluidly identify where students sit on a proficiency scale and provide targeted instructional strategies that they have cultivated through their own learning and practice.

This is where the adoption of an instructional model such as the one Robert J. Marzano (2017) presented in *The New Art and Science of Teaching* becomes vital. A framework that aligns instructional strategies more closely with individual students' needs allows for personalized, targeted interventions. Consider the following examples (Marzano, 2017).

- A teacher identifies a group of learners as operating at level 1 or the lower segments of level 2 on a proficiency scale, making direct instruction of specific content vital. When content is new, students need to understand which parts of a topic are important and how those parts fit together. In this case, the elements of chunking content, processing content, and representing content are important components to effective direct instruction.
- A group of students are operating near or at level 3. They need time to deepen their skills, so it is important to provide structured practice sessions where students can examine similarities and differences as well as errors in their own reasoning.
- Students who have already mastered the standard as articulated at level 4 should receive instructional guidance and strategies that can help them apply their knowledge in new and novel ways by engaging in cognitively complex tasks and generating and defending claims.

Tailoring instruction to individuals or groups of student interests can be a powerful teaching tool that helps students recognize their own cultural background knowledge. Doing so can also enhance their psychological fitness as well as empower their voice and collaboration skills, thereby facilitating their mental fitness. Personalizing instruction this way demands more of teachers than has been expected in the past. It requires that teachers spend the time and cognitive energy to know their students on a deeper level and understand where their skills fit on a learning progression. This can be extremely challenging; many teachers already feel overwhelmed. But in the long run, helping students learn can help teachers grow healthy, thoughtful learners.

As a high school student in Montana said:

> This way of doing school is so much more motivating because kids can follow their own interests and learn in the way that's best for them. I know where I am on the proficiency scale and all our assignments match up to the scale so it's not always just busy work—but the work today helps get me to mastery level 3. And I have options at level 3. The teachers don't just throw work at us. I understand what I need to do and how it all fits together. It's really all about mastery, and I know I can do things at a high level with the scale showing me the way. (P. Bethany, personal communication, June, 2022)

By embracing personalized instruction in the context of mastery-based learning, educators can use specific strategies and create learning experiences that maximize student engagement, motivation, and achievement, ultimately unlocking the full potential of every learner (Ruyle et al., 2019; Ruyle et al., 2022; Zima, 2021).

Student Engagement and Self-Efficacy

Highly engaged students are a highly sought-after goal. Unfortunately, the traditional industrialized educational system often fosters a passive learning environment. The good news is that expanding research indicates that implementing mastery-based learning principles in schools tends to lead to higher student engagement, motivation, and agency (Hammond, 2015; Lombardi et al., 2019; Priest, Rudenstine, Weisstein, & Gerwin, 2012; Ruyle et al., 2019). Based on our collective experience and research, students in such schools continually report that they are more engaged in their academic progress, take a more active role in their learning, and find the work they complete more meaningful to them than when they are subjected to more traditional methods.

In addition, student self-efficacy is also positively impacted when mastery-based learning principles are effectively implemented, which directly correlates with subsequent learner success (Bai & Wang, 2023; Zima, 2021). *Self-efficacy* is a person's belief in their ability to successfully do specific things (Bandura, 1977, 1986, 1997). This concept reveals how much impact a person believes they have over their motivation and behavior, as well as over their social sphere. High self-efficacy is likely to lead to intrinsically motivated students who challenge themselves (American Psychological Association, n.d.). High self-efficacy also leads to students trying hard to succeed and meet commitments, recovering quickly from setbacks, and taking responsibility for failures rather than blaming someone or something else. Learners in mastery-based learning models consistently demonstrate higher levels of agency, confidence, self-efficacy, and engagement (Guskey, 2008, 2015; Ruyle et al., 2019; Zima, 2021).

For example, individuals who have low self-efficacy often do not believe they can succeed, which makes them less likely to try hard, and they may avoid challenges altogether (Bandura, 1997; Margolis & McCabe, 2006). Their goals tend to be easily attainable. This low self-concept can result in a negative cycle, since humans have a "tendency to search for information that supports their beliefs and ignore or distort data contradicting them" (Peters, 2020, p. 1351). Fixing problems or helping these students complete tasks does not increase their self-efficacy. Thus, educators must avoid hovering or rescuing students when they face challenges or fail (Martínez-Martí & Ruch, 2017).

Conversely, high self-efficacy is likely to lead to intrinsically motivated students who challenge themselves (American Psychological Association, n.d.). High self-efficacy also leads to students trying hard to succeed and meet commitments, recovering quickly from setbacks, and taking responsibility for failures rather than blaming someone or something else. Powerfully, learners in mastery-based learning models consistently demonstrate higher levels of agency, confidence, self-efficacy, and engagement (Guskey, 2008, 2015; Ruyle et al., 2019; Zima, 2021).

Albert Bandura (1997) identified four sources from which students can increase their self-efficacy.

1. **Mastery experience:** This most powerful source of self-efficacy happens when students experience and demonstrate success. In a mastery-based learning classroom, there are many opportunities for experiences where students can provide an array of evidence that demonstrates mastery (through tests, exit tickets aligned to a proficiency scale, extended discussions with peers and teacher, and a class presentation).
2. **Vicarious experience:** When a student witnesses a peer experience success, it can improve confidence in their own abilities and increase motivation. In a mastery-based learning classroom, students see peers demonstrate mastery of a skill or unit, often through a demonstration of expertise. The other students' success can provide an example for a learner that speaks more to their personal experience and provides vicarious experience of self-efficacy as well.
3. **Verbal persuasion:** When teachers provide clear communication and focused feedback to help guide students on their path toward mastery, that is verbal persuasion. When a teacher provides a student with a proficiency scale that clearly defines what mastery entails, along with the path to success and an explanation of how all the tasks or assignments fit in the big picture, the teacher is better able to guide and inspire a student toward mastery of the standard and self-efficacy.
4. **Emotional state:** When students are in a positive emotional state, their belief in their own abilities and their motivation can increase. Teachers can help by reducing stressful situations, enhancing mindful practices, and lowering anxiety surrounding events like exams or presentations.

As such, teachers can use the following elements of mastery-based learning to build self-efficacy in various ways.

- Use proficiency scales to establish specific, short-term learning targets to help learners see the acquisition of knowledge as challenging yet attainable. Student-friendly steps let learners feel a sense of confidence and empowerment (Ruyle et al., 2022).
- Help students plan a detailed learning strategy and have them verbalize or record their plan. Teaching them to take notes or use other tools to document their learning as they move up the proficiency scale increases motivation (Zima, 2021).
- Capitalize on student engagement by linking the course content to student interests (hobbies, sports, movies, music, and other topics). By having a greater understanding of student culture, strengths, and background knowledge, teachers can better connect with their students and create a positive emotional state (Marzano, 2017).
- Provide opportunities for self-reflection and encourage students to reflect on their strengths. Understanding how these abilities can contribute to their personal growth is a powerful way for learners to monitor their own growth. Students can identify their strengths in learner profiles (chapter 5, page 119). Self-reflection activities, such as journaling or group discussions, can deepen students' self-awareness and help them connect their strengths and feel efficacious (Margolis & McCabe, 2006).

Furthermore, increasing student voice and choice are fundamental components of mastery-based learning and are important considerations to improve student engagement and self-efficacy (Guskey, 2008, 2015; Ruyle et al., 2019; Zima, 2021). Although teachers may think of voice and autonomy as more appropriate for older students, students of all ages can benefit from making their own decisions and advocating for themselves (Bandura, 1986; Center on the Developing Child, 2007; Delpit, 1993). For example, preschool-age students notice when their teachers listen to them for the purpose of assessing their knowledge and understanding of a topic as the students write, record, and seriously document their interests, preferences, observations, hypotheses, questions, and emotions. Feeling that their voice is heard is a fundamental part of their cognitive and social-emotional development (Treacy & Leavey, 2023).

These engagement and self-efficacy efforts in mastery-based learning link directly to the efforts of growth-based schooling (page 59) to create a positive learning environment. Students who have voice and choice in the classroom about their well-being show benefits, especially in engagement and self-efficacy—so much so that the act of checking in with students about their well-being is something researchers reported is an "accessible, evidence-based, and developmentally beneficial approach to the implementation of positive education" (Halliday, Kern, Garrett, & Turnbull, 2018).

Teacher Optimism

The school fitness flywheel presents an educational model that nurtures a culture of independence and empowers students to delve deeper into subjects that resonate with them, fostering a sense of intrinsic motivation and engagement. As such, we see students who are more invested in their education. This phenomenon tends to have a direct, corresponding impact on teachers who are more engaged personally with their students and, thus, are happier, empowered, and more optimistic in their jobs when they engage in mastery-based learning principles (Ruyle et al., 2019).

A powerful way to measure and monitor that increased engagement in the teaching ranks is through the educational and psychological construct of *academic optimism*, which is defined by three elements: (1) collective efficacy, (2) academic emphasis, and (3) faculty trust (Hoy et al., 2006b). Measuring academic optimism can help monitor teacher buy-in and shed light on the most vital things to begin addressing.

Assessing academic optimism is easily completed using the School Academic Optimism Survey (SAOS; https://waynekhoy.com/pdfs/saos.pdf), a free tool that teachers can complete in minimal time. In schools that have implemented mastery-based learning, we see significantly higher levels of academic optimism based on the SAOS than in those schools that are *not* using these principles. Also, as a school faculty progresses through the process of implementing mastery-based learning by using learning goals and proficiency scales, personalizing instruction based on the scales, and aligning assessments to the various levels of the scale, academic optimism tends to rise over time (Ruyle et al., 2019).

By surveying teachers periodically during the implementation phase, leaders can gather data that indicate how teachers feel about their growth in a simple yet very effective way. As a teacher in Montana said:

> We took the SAOS as a staff. It was so empowering to see that the teachers who have bought into the system the most have the highest academic optimism scores, and their students are performing better and attending school at a higher rate! How about that? That data gave us just the boost we needed and inspired us to keep moving and go deeper. (R. Kaela, personal communication, May, 2022)

In addition to measuring academic optimism, it is critical to manage expectations for change when implementing a new model of schooling. Immediate academic improvement is not common in terms of test scores or other common metrics. Learning is not linear, and it takes time to make up for years of insufficient support. In contrast, academic optimism can change quickly and is highly correlated with increased student achievement over time (Feldman & Kubota, 2015; Hoy, Tarter, & Hoy, 2006a, 2006b). In short, when academic optimism increases, student achievement will typically follow.

The link between mastery-based learning in schools and teacher optimism is significant. With its instructional and curricular designs, the mastery-based learning model often dramatically increases levels of teacher academic optimism in our professional experience. This, in turn, fuels their commitment to fostering positive learning environments, empowering students, and continuously improving their instructional practices. Collective efficacy, academic emphasis, and faculty trust are integral parts of a mastery-based learning experience.

Collective Efficacy

Collective efficacy is the collective belief of a school faculty in its abilities to achieve a desired outcome. In the case of mastery-based learning schools, it is the perception of a teaching staff that they possess the skills and expertise to help every student master identified content at the level of the standard. Educator Wayne K. Hoy and his colleagues (2006a, 2006b) asserted that collective efficacy represents the cognitive aspect of academic optimism. As such, collective efficacy is a critical element of mastery-based learning and, thus, also related to enhanced academic fitness for students in that it helps empower learners to achieve high skill levels by providing a clear vision of the learning goals as well as a road map and a dedicated teaching staff to help every student achieve mastery.

Collaboration and shared responsibility are part of the culture when teachers work collectively to design mastery-based learning experiences, develop common assessments, and analyze student performance data. This collaborative approach fosters a sense of collective efficacy, whereby a group of people believe their collective efforts can positively influence outcomes (Bandura, 1997). By encouraging teachers to engage in a repeated practice of sharing everyday examples with peers while also sharing their feelings of doubt, confusion, struggle, as well as moments of clarity and excitement, staff's ability to build collective efficacy and grow together is amplified (Ruyle et al., 2022; Sugarman, 2021). Building trust within a team to inspire respect and collaboration by setting goals together, sharing knowledge through instructional rounds protocols, recognizing when milestones are achieved, and celebrating successes together can help get everyone on the same page. In these ways, educators' trust and collective efficacy relate to their mastery-based learning efforts. In addition, teachers collaborative efforts around implementing mastery-based learning principles in their daily practice can help them understand how these strategies can also enhance student voice, increase student access to the curriculum and content, and provide feedback in a way that is motivational to students. In this way, increasing academic fitness through mastery-based learning strategies can also strengthen students' psychological and mental fitness.

Shifting a school program this way is a heavy lift. Moving to mastery-based learning takes the combined efforts of an array of stakeholders to bring to fruition. As such, collaborative teams take on an even greater importance as teacher teams must work together to deepen their understanding of an innovative system and refine their expertise to make it happen in the classroom. The four fundamental components of the model focus all collaboration. In this way, teachers we work with do report higher professional satisfaction because they know and understand that their colleagues are working for the same purpose and that the collaboration it will take to change classroom dynamics is critical. Using something like the reproducible "Proficiency Scale for Educator Collaboration Growth and Effectiveness" (page 56) to monitor collaboration growth and effectiveness is a way to ensure all participants have the same vision.

In addition to keeping efforts trained on implementing effective instruction and assessment, as well as understanding where each student is and what they need to master a skill or standard, teachers can improve collective efficacy by sharing stories and celebrating growth. Continually examining data and celebrating growth can lead to collective efficacy among faculty (Sugarman, 2021). A California teacher powerfully addressed this concept when she said:

> The biggest change is that we were able to have a voice in the process. We were motivated to be a part of something that made things better for staff and students. The support provided by the principal during this time was amazing. (S. Jones, May 2022)

The next topic is academic emphasis.

Academic Emphasis

Academic emphasis is the push for high but achievable learning goals in a school. Academic emphasis and academic optimism speak to faculty perceptions and actions regarding high expectations for student and teacher achievement and excellence (Hoy et al., 2006a, 2006b). Academic emphasis is a critical element of strength-based teaching, related to enhanced psychological fitness for students in that it can help create a school climate that encourages "both teachers and students to plan more, persist longer, accept responsibility for achievement, and overcome temporary setbacks" (Goddard, Sweetland, & Hoy, 2000, p. 698). Increased levels of academic emphasis can also strengthen teachers' sense of purpose, motivation, and confidence (Ruyle et al., 2019).

In mastery-based learning, level 3 of any given proficiency scale addresses increased academic emphasis. Level 3 language should clearly articulate high levels of academic expectation by presenting content or skills at the level of the standard. Unfortunately, the vast majority of high schools we've worked with rarely strive to ensure that every learner is held to demonstrating mastery of the standards at that high level.

When teachers witness students progressing and demonstrating mastery of targeted skills, it reinforces their trust in collective efficacy and confidence in students' potential and affirms their high expectations. As a result, teacher academic optimism is bolstered, creating a positive cycle of belief in students' capabilities and a commitment to providing meaningful and rigorous instruction.

Faculty Trust

Faculty trust speaks to the level of a trusting relationship among teachers and students along with their parents. This is an emotional aspect of academic optimism that involves people being vulnerable to others, with the corresponding hope that the others will display understanding and connection and act in the original person's best interest (Hoy et al., 2006a).

Faculty trust is a critical element of growth-based schooling and thus related to enhanced mental fitness for students. That is the case because it can enhance a deeper sense of student connection and relationship with peers as well as with trusting adults. Researchers on a thirty-five-year meta-analysis claimed that "to improve student learning, school leaders need to enlist all effective practices in order to build trust in schools and pay equal attention to improving teachers' trust as they do other efforts to improve instructional programs and teaching practices" (Sun, Zhang, & Forsyth, 2023). In schools that have implemented mastery-based learning, we see correspondingly high levels of faculty trust between teachers and the students and families they serve.

Summary

As one of the centerpieces of the school fitness flywheel, mastery-based learning offers a transformative approach to education. The change in focus from exposing students to content and delivering curriculum to one where every learner is held to mastery of high-level standards is a massive paradigm shift. However, mastery-based learning is aligned with research and evidence-based practices. It epitomizes the science of learning and can result in deeper well-being and growth for students. The "Professional Development in Mastery-Based Learning: Proficiency Scale" (page 57) is one way a school can monitor its progress toward mastery as defined in level 3.

We advise these three next steps as most important from this chapter for school leaders.

1. Deepen their own knowledge through professional learning and collaboration to understand the critical leadership elements of implementing a mastery-based learning educational model.
2. Use proficiency scales with teachers to help monitor their own growth in the shift toward mastery-based learning.
3. Identify vital professional development for teachers and administrators to shift the mindset of assessment toward providing feedback about learning.

We advise these three next steps as most important from this chapter for teachers and other classroom staff.

1. Begin the process of identifying learning goals and implementing proficiency scales in classrooms (academic fitness).
2. Work in collaborative teams to increase assessment literacy by using valid and reliable assessment practices in the classroom.
3. Use proficiency scales to identify student placement on a learning progression and effectively use strategies to personalize learning experiences in the classroom.

Proficiency Scale for Educator Collaboration Growth and Effectiveness

Teachers			
Score 4.0		**In addition to Score 3.0, in-depth inferences and applications that go beyond what was taught.** **The teacher:** • Creates and utilizes an array of proficiency scales on schoolwide initiatives and can capture evidence of mastery from all learners	**Sample Activities**
	3.5	In addition to score 3.0 performance, in-depth inferences and applications with partial success.	
Score 3.0		**The teacher:** • Demonstrates regular collaboration in teams with established norms and goals • Exhibits deliberate reflection on the six questions of the collaborative cycle: (1) "What is it we want our students to know?", (2) "How will we know if our students are learning?", (3) "How will we respond when students do not learn?", (4) "How will we enrich and extend the learning for students who are proficient?", (5) "How will we increase our instructional competence?", and (6) "How will we coordinate our efforts as a school?" (Marzano et al., 2016, p. 4). • Demonstrates improved assessment literacy by using valid and reliable assessment practices in their classrooms • Produces, posts, edits, and updates artifacts that demonstrate and inform their work **The leader exhibits no major errors or omissions.**	• *The New Art and Science of Teaching* (Marzano, 2017) proficiency scales • District proficiency scales
	2.5	No major errors or omissions regarding score 2.0 content, and partial knowledge of score 3.0 content	
Score 2.0		The teacher will recognize or recall specific vocabulary (for example, *norms, priority standard, proficiency scale, learning progression, scaffolding, aligned assessment, teacher development and evaluation*) and perform basic processes such as the following. • Explain the six questions of the collaborative cycle. • Describe how PLCs can function to operationalize master-based learning in every classroom. • Discuss artifacts that could be used to demonstrate and inform their work. • Describe why a proficiency scale is an accurate picture of student performance. • Monitor trust in collaborative teams. • Monitor quality and depth of interaction between team members • Produce and post a norms document describing standard operating procedures. • Explain how to create assessment other than tests from a proficiency scale. • Create student-friendly scales and provide students and families copies of them.	• *The School Wellness Wheel* (Ruyle, Child, & Dome, 2021) • *The New Art and Science of Teaching* (Marzano, 2017) • *Collaborative Teams That Transform Schools* (Marzano et al., 2016) • Critical Concepts (Simms, 2016) • Proficiency scale template • Identified norms document
	1.5	Partial knowledge of score 2.0 content, but major errors or omissions regarding score 3.0 content.	
Score 1.0		With help, a partial understanding of some of the simpler details and processes and some of the more complex ideas and processes	
	0.5	With help, a partial understanding of score 2.0 content, but not of score 3.0 content.	
Score 0.0		Even with help, no understanding or skill demonstrated	

Sources: Marzano, R. J., Heflebower, T., Hoegh, J. K., Warrick, P., & Grift, G. (2016). Collaborative teams that transform schools: The next steps in PLCs. *Bloomington, IN: Marzano Resources; © 2016 by Julia A. Simms (adapted with permission).*

Professional Development in Mastery-Based Learning: Proficiency Scale

<table>
<tr><th colspan="4">Teachers</th></tr>
<tr><td rowspan="2">Score 4.0</td><td colspan="2" rowspan="2">In addition to score 3.0, in-depth inferences and applications that go beyond what was taught
The teacher:
• Can create and utilize an array of proficiency scales on schoolwide initiatives and can capture evidence of mastery from all learners</td><td>Sample Resources and Activities</td></tr>
<tr><td></td></tr>
<tr><td></td><td>3.5</td><td>In addition to score 3.0 performance, in-depth inferences and applications with partial success</td><td></td></tr>
<tr><td>Score 3.0</td><td colspan="2">The teacher:
• Is skilled at using learning goals and proficiency scales in their daily classroom practice
• Demonstrates fluency in their assessment literacy by using valid and reliable assessment practices in their classrooms
• Uses an array of strategies to personalize learning experiences in their classrooms
• Clearly communicates and presents the foundational educational construct of mastery-based learning to a wide variety of stakeholders
The teacher exhibits no major errors or omissions.</td><td>• District- or school-created proficiency scales
• The New Art and Science of Teaching (Marzano, 2017)
• The New Art and Science of Classroom Assessment (Marzano, Norford, & Ruyle, 2019)
• School Academic Optimism Survey data reports (https://waynekhoy.com/pdfs/saos.pdf)</td></tr>
<tr><td></td><td>2.5</td><td>No major errors or omissions regarding 2.0 content and partial knowledge of the 3.0 content</td><td></td></tr>
</table>

Score		Description	Resources
Score 2.0		**The teacher will** recognize or recall specific vocabulary (for example, *aligned assessments, collaborative teams, learning goal, learning progression, priority standard, proficiency scale, reliability, scaffolding, teacher development and evaluation, validity,* and *zone of proximal development*) and perform basic processes such as the following. • Explain that standards are not designed to provide a clear pathway to learning in our classrooms and describe the impact of clarity and transparency on leaners. • Describe how a proficiency scale provides an accurate picture of student learning performance. • Describe the structure of a proficiency scale. • Identify the difference between an activity and a learning outcome. • Provide the learning goal and proficiency scale for students. • Demonstrate how to create assessments other than tests from a proficiency scale. • Describe how collaborative teams can function to operationalize mastery-based learning in every classroom. • Compare scales and rubrics. • Explain how mastery-based learning is becoming normalized and mandated at the legislative level. • Create student-friendly scales and get them into the hands of learners and families.	• *The School Wellness Wheel* (Ruyle, Child, & Dome, 2021) • *Mindsets and Skill Sets for Learning: A Framework for Building Student Agency* (Zima, 2021) • *Leading the Evolution: How to Make Personalized Competency-Based Education a Reality* (Ruyle, O'Neill, Iberlin, Evans, & Midles, 2019)
	1.5	Partial knowledge of the 2.0 content, but major errors or omissions regarding the 3.0 content	
Score 1.0		With help, a partial understanding of some of the simpler details and processes and some of the more complex ideas and processes	
	0.5	With help, a partial understanding of the 2.0 content but not the 3.0 content	
Score 0.0		Even with help, no understanding or skill demonstrated	

3

Growth-Based Schooling

The purpose of learning is growth, and our minds, unlike our bodies, can continue growing as we continue to live.

—MORTIMER ADLER

Growth-based schooling has the capacity to enhance and deepen mental fitness. Educators can accomplish this by promoting emotional well-being and building social support systems that nurture healing and growth. By creating safe, positive learning environments, being consistent and transparent, empowering students to collaborate in learning and giving them voice, encouraging their well-being, and teaching and modeling self-regulation, teachers can help students develop a strong foundation of emotional resilience. Students learn to identify and regulate their emotions and develop coping strategies to manage stress and adversity effectively with a school that, in part, focuses on growth. Cultivating emotional well-being enhances students' capacity to navigate challenges, build healthy relationships, and maintain a positive outlook, contributing to their overall resilience (Harris, 2018; Perry, 2015; Ruyle et al., 2022).

As such, a major focus of this book is acknowledging the profound impact that mental health, trauma, and toxic stress can have on students' and adults' educational experiences and overall well-being, as well as the growth that can happen despite these challenges. This is why growth-based schooling encompasses mental fitness. Many people of all ages face various traumas or toxic stress that can significantly hinder their ability to learn, form healthy relationships, and thrive. Growth-based schooling provides a way for adults and students alike to overcome these obstacles.

Growth-Based Schooling Defined

Understanding the impact of trauma, toxic stress, and mental health challenges can be immeasurably valuable. We strongly assert, however, that focusing on the trauma and stress alone without providing a way forward is not helpful or fruitful. Doing such is like a doctor recognizing a diagnosis but failing to follow up with a treatment plan. Rather, put the emphasis on providing the paths to growth and the empowerment that can result. A school leader in Arkansas explains the nuances of being *trauma informed* versus *trauma sensitive* in our educational practices:

> I truly understand trauma and its effects on my students, community, and even in my own personal life . . . but where do we go from here? We don't want to make trauma and a tough home life an excuse to fail or a reason not to take responsibility for our lives. (Don P., personal communication, June, 2021)

Thus, *growth-based schooling* presents a forward-thinking, positive approach to education that focuses on nurturing students' individual potential, fosters a love of learning, and equips them with the habits to thrive. Growth-based schooling is an updated, strength-based version of *trauma-responsive* or *trauma-informed teaching* terminology commonly used.

Thus, while not all students may have experienced trauma (or do not believe they have), we believe that all students can benefit from a growth-based schooling model just as all people can benefit from healthier daily habits. By equipping educators with the knowledge and skills necessary to create growth-based classrooms, schools can transform educational outcomes. They can do this by fostering post-traumatic growth and creating a comprehensive system of support that extends beyond individual interventions.

The following sections serve as a guide for educators, administrators, and policymakers seeking to embrace growth-based principles and practices of consistency and transparency, a positive and safe environment, as well as collaboration and voice empowerment, resilience strengthened through emotional regulation, and the fundamental mission of enhancing human well-being for all stakeholders (Fallot & Harris, 2008, 2011; Harris, 2021).

Consistency and Transparency

Consistent, transparent expectations and information to all stakeholders are important for creating a feeling of safety and positivity. Consistent routines and transparent expectations are particularly helpful for students who experience poverty or trauma, because predictable routines and reliable environments can help balance the lack of safety and predictability they often encounter in their lives outside school (Bloom, 2020). The Calgary Board of Education addressed this specifically in 2014: "Build safety through routines. Create predictable environments and responses. Use routines to assist students to know what will happen next. Predictability around key trouble spots such as transitions and leave-takings help students with getting to calm" (p. 1).

Consistency

The predictability of routines and procedures "gives a child the sense that the world is a safe place for exploring, learning, and growing. This is important to the developing brain because it lowers stress and reinforces a sense of well-being" (Child Welfare Information Gateway, 2017, p. 4). Making sure that you have established routines and procedures for your classroom and moments in it (such as transitions) helps reduce the odds that students will become nervous and show dysregulated behavior (TREP Project, n.d.).

Schedules that teachers and schools follow help students anticipate the move from one activity to the next. The following items help create consistency and predictability:

- Daily or class-specific schedules and agendas posted in the same place in every classroom
- Clearly defined and posted behavior expectations
- Clearly defined sequence of actions for transitions
- Calls to attention and nonverbal signals for behavioral expectations
- Preparation warnings and countdowns to transitions (Trickey, 2022)

In addition, administrators and teachers should be mindful of consistency in terms of addressing student behavioral expectations. There is a vast research base indicating that educator bias is instrumental in disparate discipline outcomes (Carter, Skiba, Arredondo, & Pollock, 2017; Cole-Lewis, Hope, Mustafaa, & Jagers, 2021; Whitford, Katsiyannis, & Counts, 2016). To consciously address issues such as educator bias and to ensure consistency, it is important that administrators collaborate with colleagues and bring others into discipline decisions. Also, we suggest creating data systems that monitor incidents of student discipline disaggregated by subgroup categories; this allows you to determine who is excluded from the classroom and where behavioral infractions commonly occur. Employ and then regularly monitor systems such as Multi-tiered Systems of Support (MTSS) to examine whether staff are prepared to recognize and respond to signs of trauma and whether there are sufficient resources to support students who are experiencing trauma. Finally, ensuring that collaborative teams have the time and focus to examine effective instructional and disciplinary approaches and determine what is working are important elements of consistency and transparency.

Simply stated, the brain loves routine and strives to identify patterns to make sense of the world and learn new material (Marzano, 2017). As such, consistency in practice through routines, procedures, and rituals not only helps students trust the classroom teacher and administrators, but also provides an environment in which the brain can learn most efficiently.

Transparency

In addition, nurturing a transparent and connective culture is a fundamental component in schools as it allows educators to create "welcoming, engaging and positive learning environments where everyone in the school building can thrive" (Marzano & Marzano, 2015, p. 14). Transparency promotes connectivity by fostering a culture of empathy and collaboration. Removing the mystery can help everyone see administrators make decisions and schools move in certain directions. That transparency can include being clear with students about what the school goals are.

Transparency can also be an effective tool in building trust and can help build higher levels of engagement, collaboration, and satisfaction, which can result in direct academic gains (Gallup, n.d.; Ruyle et al., 2019). In terms of parents and guardians, working to help teachers engage in regular, clear, open, and collaborative conversations with students and their families is a way of building trust and promoting transparency.

Clearly communicated classroom rules and expectations are foundational and deserve regular revisitation. Seemingly small gestures such as framing classroom rules in a positive manner are an important strategy. As an example, rather than posting comments such as *Don't be disrespectful*, a teacher should clearly communicate that *We all will respect all people in class at all times*, which makes the strategy active and places the onus on students to behave in a more proactive manner. This can increase student agency and be effective via student involvement in creating class standard operating procedures, as mentioned in the previous chapter.

A group of educators, students, and administrators at the previously mentioned Kansas City high school collaboratively created the building expectations shown in figure 3.1. These expectations were converted into posters, which then were laminated and posted in every classroom and hallway throughout the building.

Creating proficiency scales around critical behavior expectations and including examples for what mastery of those behaviors looks like is a powerful way to communicate expectations. The scales can help teachers remember that many behaviors need to be directly taught rather an expectation. Just as with academic proficiency scales, behavior scales clearly express the expected

Expectations

TAKE CARE OF YOURSELF.

- ✔ Be on time.
- ✔ Be an active participant.
- ✔ Ask for help.

TAKE CARE OF EACH OTHER.

- ✔ Participate in group discussions.
- ✔ Treat each other with respect.
- ✔ Help each other and show empathy.

TAKE CARE OF THIS PLACE.

- ✔ Clean up after yourself or others.
- ✔ Manage hallways.
- ✔ Manage common areas.

You belong here!

Source: © 2022 by North Kansas City School. Adapted with permission.

FIGURE 3.1: Example classroom poster with expectations.

behavior, provide clear definitions of what the behavior looks like, and provide a learning progression so that students can monitor their own progress. Adding student voice in the creation of such scales can be a way to increase student investment and agency as well. To accomplish this, groups of teachers should determine a limited number of important behaviors that they will teach and reinforce over the course of the year. They provide clear indicators of what mastery of the behavior looks like at level 3 and articulate lower-level skills at level 2. Teachers should also demonstrate a scaffold of higher-level behavior expectations as students progress through their educational experience. For example, teachers might expect more from a twelfth grader than a ninth grader.

Figure 3.2 (page 64) presents an example of such a scale.

Another powerful way to provide transparency (and include voice and choice for students at the same time) is using social contracts. With such contracts, students collectively discuss and decide how specific aspects of their class will look. One of the most effective ways teachers can empower student voice is by encouraging them to directly participate in developing classroom

4.0	**The student will:** • Evaluate how well the class in general has done at behaving appropriately and offer useful suggestions for whole-class improvement
3.5	In addition to score 3.0 performance, partial success at score 4.0 content
3.0	**B1—The student will:** • **Follow behavioral directions** (for example, following a routine or spontaneous direction given by the teacher). • **Help others follow complex directions** (for example, providing assistance to other students who might find a given set of directions confusing or too complex to follow) • **Not disrespect, tease, or bully others** (for example, treating other students in a courteous and respectful manner and following the school's student code of conduct regarding bullying behaviors that have been established as inappropriate behavior in school)
2.5	No major errors or omissions regarding score 2.0 content, and partial success at score 3.0 content
2.0	**B1—The student will:** • Understand the critical features of following directions (for example, describing important features of following directions, such as listening to or reading every step carefully and following every step). • Understand the characteristics of helping others follow directions (for example, describing what it looks like to help others follow directions) • Understand the characteristics of respecting others and refraining from teasing and bullying others (for example, describing what it looks like to refrain from teasing and bullying others).
1.5	Partial success at score 2.0 content and major errors or omissions regarding score 3.0 content
1.0	With help, partial success at score 2.0 content and score 3.0 content
0.5	With help, partial success at score 2.0 content but not at score 3.0 content
0.0	Even with help, no success

Source: © 2016 by Julia A. Simms. Adapted with permission.

FIGURE 3.2: Behavior—Grades 6–8 life skills.

rules or behavior expectations. Just as teachers value school leaders who seek out their opinions and ideas when establishing professional norms or when implementing a new initiative, they can bring that same value to the learners in their classrooms.

After beginning with a classroom discussion about creating classroom norms, teachers can lead students in creating a web chart or mind map.

1. A teacher organizes teams of learners into small groups with chart paper and writing implements. The center of the paper should be labeled with wording like *class expectations*.
2. Students then draw lines going from the center to new circles encompassing important ideas or norms for the class to follow.
3. After a short time, students share their ideas with the larger class.
4. The class then designs a web chart, like that in figure 3.3, incorporating the most-used norms.

Social Contract

Fair
Appreciated
Encouraging
Calm
RESPECTFUL
Nice
Like family
Listen
Helpful
Responsible
FUN
Understanding
Honest
No put downs
Like a fifth grader
Effort

This class agrees to . . .

Being attentive & judgment free during open discussions, lessons, & small group time. We will be a supportive, motivational, & respectful democracy in this class.

Source: © 2024 by North Kansas City High School. Adapted with permission.

FIGURE 3.3: Agreed-on class norms.

For older students, creating an affinity chart to establish class norms can be equally engaging and powerful.

1. A teacher places students into small groups with an array of sticky notes.
2. Learners work individually to generate as many ideas as they can—one idea per sticky note.
3. After a short time, the group comes together and places all the sticky notes on chart paper, organized by general theme.
4. After an appropriate amount of time, all the groups can come together to share their chart.
5. The teacher or student writes the classroom affinity chart and hangs it in the room.

Along academic lines of transparency, university researcher Mary-Ann Winkelmes and her colleagues (2016) conducted two studies with college students. They demonstrated that transparent instructional and assessment practices had significant, equitable benefits for undergraduate students, and that those benefits were long term. The researchers suggested that merely *two* instances of transparent instruction during a grading period significantly helped improve students' academic success; first-generation, low-income, and underrepresented college student gains were even more profound (Winkelmes et al., 2016). They also asserted that by making assignments more transparent, they ensured that the content was more accessible and relevant for the students, thereby enhancing their confidence, belonging, and ability to monitor their progression of knowledge toward mastery, all of which are critical elements of equity (Winkelmes et al., 2016). We strongly suggest that these findings also apply in the preK–12 educational realm through the effective implementation of strength-based and mastery-based school principles (Dickey, 2022; Guskey, 2007, 2015; Ruyle et al., 2019). Mastery-based learning's use of proficiency scales makes expectations and teaching methods transparent.

Proficiency scales are vital learning tools that clearly articulate important academic standards or learning goals for students to master. Proficiency scales are often seen as equivalent to a rubric, but the purpose of the two instruments is different. A rubric can help identify levels of completion and is commonly used as a grading tool. A proficiency scale, on the other hand, is a learning tool and must be provided for the learner since it identifies a standard to be mastered along with a learning progression or the important steps to achieve mastery. When teachers use proficiency scales to communicate *why* and *how* students are learning academic content in certain ways, they are being transparent about teaching and learning.

In schools that have successfully implemented mastery-based learning practices, we see a bidirectional increase in trust between students and families and teachers based on providing clear learning goals and pathways to success via the successful implementation of proficiency scales and equitable assessment practices (Ruyle et al., 2019). Part of this positive shift is developing proficiency scales involving a collaborative effort among educators, mental health professionals, and community members. Engaging all stakeholders ensures that diverse perspectives are considered, resulting in a more comprehensive and culturally responsive framework. This collaboration promotes a shared vision and fosters a sense of ownership among all involved parties. We delve deeper into the use of proficiency scales and equitable assessment practices in chapter 4 (page 93).

Positive, Safe Environments

Another core principle that underpins growth-based schooling is cultivating a positive, safe environment. This environment is not a luxury but a necessity for educational excellence. Begin first by knowing that if a person does not feel safe, they cannot learn (Dean, 2023; Lacoe, 2020). Safety is the bedrock on which a thriving educational community is built. This certainly entails physical safety, but emotional, mental, and psychological safety are equally vital in every school environment.

In a school with a positive culture, there is a palpable sense of trust and belonging.

- Trust is fostered when all members of the school community genuinely listen to each other, demonstrate respect for each other's ideas and opinions, and show personal care regarding each other's well-being.
- Belonging is enhanced when teachers know, see, and hear their students, promote interaction and collaboration in classrooms, and recognize and celebrate diversity. These are all skills that stakeholders can teach, model, reinforce, and authentically learn (Marzano & Marzano, 2015; Ruyle et al., 2022).

In these healing-focused schools, students feel valued, motivated, and empowered to learn. Teachers are enthusiastic, innovative, and supportive of each other. Administrators are approachable, transparent, and committed to continuous improvement. Such an environment fosters not only academic growth but also personal and social development (Altman, 2016; Berkowitz, Moore, Astor, & Benbenishty, 2017; Darling-Hammond & Cook-Harvey, 2018; Frazier, Cross, Cross, & Kim, 2021).

A major issue with many school initiatives is that they often fail to address the systemic nature of the mental health crisis, focusing on crisis *response* rather than crisis *prevention*. A positive, safe environment, on the other hand, cultivates a strength-based perspective focused on what learners *can* do as opposed to issuing consequences for what they fail to do. Research revealed, in fact, that "the adverse effects of trauma can be mitigated by the presence of even just one empowering and empathetic presence in a student's life" (Todd, 2022). To illustrate this point, a school principal from Montana shared the following story:

> In the summer of 2023, when sharing about the school wellness wheel with a large group of educators and education leaders—emphasizing the research behind a healthy and positive school environment in relation to poverty and low socioeconomic

> status—a teacher attending the session approached and shared that she had scored a nine out of ten on the [adverse childhood experience] evaluation—she had experienced everything except the death of parent. She stated that it was her teachers at school who provided a safe, empowering place for her. She gave permission to share her story with the hopes that other educators would realize their tremendous opportunity they have in the lives of their students, as her teachers had given her a path forward and a rich and healthy life through the power of education. (M. J., personal communication, May, 2022)

The critical components for facilitating a positive, safe environment include relationships, nurtured learning strengths, and prioritized celebration and recognition. Also, understanding and managing emotions, making good decisions, and interacting positively and appropriately with others are learned behaviors that can be taught and reinforced in schools. These elements, among others, can be vital in addressing one of the most pressing current social issues: school violence and shootings. The organization Rachel's Challenge (https://rachelschallenge.org) helps schools focus on culture and create student wellness programs that facilitate connection, hope, and resilience. The organization also help schools recognize and address many of the root causes of school violence including bullying, prejudice, harassment, and lack of connection. Schools that place a conscious, daily emphasis on their culture as well as build and sustain programs such as the one developed by Rachel's Challenge report fewer reported incidents of bullying, decreased disciplinary referrals, and less student isolation (Rachel's Challenge, n.d.).

Connection and Relationships

The first critical component of a safe environment is purposefully allocating time for enhancing connection and relationships. Some methods require little effort. For example, a low-effort method is greeting students as they enter the classroom. This simple element also allows teachers to gauge learner well-being, read body language, and demonstrate care.

Higher-effort examples includes check-ins, advisories, mindfulness activities, or movement and involve as many adults as possible (including administrators, custodians, aides, and volunteers) to keep student-adult ratios small. Some schools adopt long-term advisory programs where an adult remains with the students for multiple years, while others use a cross-section approach to have an adult build connections between older and younger students. Meeting times for such initiatives vary, with some groups meeting daily for shorter periods and others meeting weekly for longer periods. In our experience, it is the consistency of practice that matters more than the time structure in nurturing positive teacher-student and student-student relationships.

A practice in some larger elementary schools is creating a cohort model so that students can stay together multiple years, when possible, to create relationships with each other to strengthen the sense of school community. Some middle and high schools use a model they call *houses* so students build a community within a very large school setting. A middle school teacher in an eastern U.S. rural community spoke to this concept:

> In our school, we were surprised that many students did not seem to know each other and seemed disconnected from a sense of school community. We instituted a cohort model, so students could form relationships that many smaller schools have among their student bodies and found it to be tremendously helpful in creating a strong sense of community. (J. C., personal communication, November, 2023)

Also, since conflict is a normal part of the human experience, helping students master conflict resolution skills by promoting peer mediation or regular circle activities can empower students to resolve disputes peacefully, which can reduce emotional stress and create a more harmonious learning environment. Once these elements become commonplace in schools, school counselors and psychologists can provide valuable assistance and individualized support for more high-needs learners and staff members.

To cultivate a learning environment that prioritizes building relationships, a high school in Kansas City, Missouri, changed its traditional bell schedule system (H. K., personal communication, May, 2024). The revamped bell schedule dedicates fifty minutes every school day for connecting with students. During the designated time, students have the opportunity for academic, social, and emotional support. Every Monday, advisory teachers confer with their students, reflect on their goals, and identify necessary support. On Fridays, advisory teachers facilitate a community-building activity, establishing and nurturing positive relationship with students. During multitiered systems of support, teachers provide targeted intervention based on student needs.

Another option schools have is weekly relationship building. Advisory teachers at the same high school facilitate weekly circles this often, for example. Circles serve as a valuable tool for managing conflicts and tensions, allowing for the repair of harm and restoration of relationships. Prioritizing strong, trusting relationships with all students, community circles are an ideal way for teachers to connect with students and for students to connect with each other. Figure 3.4 (page 70) shows the circle planning template provided to all teachers at the Kansas City high school to use during advisory time.

Circle topic:

Type of circle (check-in, relationship building, problem solving):

Goal of circle:

Group Circle Norms

Invite everyone to sit in a circle, so they can see each other's faces. If using a talking piece, introduce it and describe its meaning.

- Listen intently.
- Speak from the heart.
- Share the room (one voice at a time).
- Keep technology put away.
- Be open and honest.
- You can pass, but stay engaged.

Circle Questions

Round one:

Round two:

Round three:

Example Circle Questions:

What's a helpful thing you've heard someone say?

What are you excited about in life?

What do you wish you could do more often?

What is it like for you to apologize to someone?

What would you do differently if you knew you wouldn't be judged?

How do you express gratitude?

If you could teach anything, what would it be?

What are you clinging to that you need to let go of?

What brings a smile to your face?

Source: © 2022 by North Kansas City High School. Adapted with permission.

FIGURE 3.4: Circle planning template.

Visit ***MarzanoResources.com/reproducibles*** *for a free reproducible version of this figure.*

The kinds of relationships built by these practices are pivotal in all communities. Thus, expanding a school's reach to enhance connection and relationships with caregivers, families, and the larger community is of critical importance. Building a strong relationship with families requires educators to communicate with them about the good and the bad that happen in classrooms. Keeping families updated on classroom and school occurrences is just one facet of that communication. Social media or a classroom website is where teachers can share the positive things happening every day. Additionally, educators may offer support services and interventions like the following to address the specific needs of marginalized students, bridging the opportunity gap and promoting equity in education wraparound services.

- Authentic parent empowerment by connecting families to physical and mental health, transportation, financial, employment, and legal services and resources
- Specified training for staff that is uniquely relevant to the community they are serving rather than generalized training
- Specified and tailored training built around specific school and community needs vital for staff success

One building leader from Montana shared the following:

> We were able to create a parent resource guide for our school community that had all the county services available and the contact information. These were things from law enforcement contact information to programs that would help cover heating and electricity bills in the cold winter. About eight years ago we were able to work with a homeless family and help them get into their first house. Did we have to print off the applications needed, help them schedule meetings and such? No, we didn't... but seeing the joy in our students' lives was priceless and it didn't take much time out of our daily lives. Some might say that is the social worker's job, but as teachers we are often at the frontlines of our students' lived experiences and can make a real difference. Many families who need assistance the most often do not know what resources are available to them. (J. Cummins, personal communication, May, 2024)

Sharing photos and other visuals to help families see what is happening in classrooms is a powerful way to nurture connection between schools and home (though it is important to know the school or district's policies about posting photos of students before doing so). Sending a quick note home—or better yet, calling home—about a student's success can pay off handsomely down the road in ensuring teachers and families are on the same page and working together for the benefit of the student. The relationship needs to be sincere, with educators delivering information and tasks to families, but with all sides doing their best together for the student. To build authentic trust, educators must not attempt to control the parent and school relationship if they desire a real connection with the community they serve (Awachíikaate & Chang, 2020).

Nurtured Strengths

Emphasizing learning strengths and the belief that a person can develop their intelligence and abilities means students "succeed at a higher level, but they will also cultivate an identity that strengthens their sense of belonging and perceived potential of success" (Branova, 2023). So too does viewing students as active learners who have unique strengths, interests, and background knowledge, as well as articulating that aloud to them and crafting experiences that reinforce the fact. Focusing on strengths means educators help students develop the belief that they can improve their abilities with dedication, practice, and learning from failures. By acknowledging and validating their abilities, educators create a foundation for positive learning experiences. With this mindset, students approach challenges with resilience, adaptability, and a belief in their capacity to overcome difficulties (Dweck & Yeager, 2019; Hammond, 2015). All of this psychological flexibility contributes to mental fitness (Tindle & Moustafa, 2021).

Furthermore, mastery-based learning shifts focus from grades and performance to growth and progress. Instead of comparing students against each other or external standards, instruction and assessments celebrate individual growth and progress. Teachers provide feedback that acknowledges and encourages students' effort, resilience, and improvement over time. This approach promotes a growth mindset, fosters intrinsic motivation, and builds students' confidence and self-esteem (Marzano et al., 2017; Ruyle et al., 2022).

Positive reinforcement can be a powerful motivator and can help promote positive work habits; recognizing and praising effort and growth is critical (University of Kansas, n.d.). Affirming students' effort to persevere, risk failure, and engage in productive struggle is vital to helping them learn to be persistent and positive so as to be able to problem solve through challenges in their futures (Kansas University, n.d.).

Celebration and Recognition

Celebration and recognition are the final components of this desired environment. Although classroom parties to recognize certain milestones or events are common, the importance of celebration is an often-overlooked element of a positive culture. Celebrating student learning is vital in that it shows students that their work is meaningful and something to be proud of. Celebration isn't just a party, but rather can serve to help students feel that they matter and that their efforts have meaning. In addition, reinforcing students' effort is associated with a gain in student achievement because helping students see a direct relationship between how hard they work and how much they learn is an important part of reinforcing effort (Marzano, 2017). Celebration and recognition speak directly to the esteem needs in Maslow's (1943) hierarchy of needs in that an individual's esteem in a community is highly dependent on their own self-concept.

As an additional consideration, negative talk is often common in high-poverty communities, and the link between negativity and toxic cultures can be profoundly strong (Fell & Hewstone, 2015). In addition, people who have untreated post-traumatic stress disorder tend to use negative self-talk (Hollowood, 2017). Negative talk can entail any speech directed toward self or others that has the purpose of mocking or disparaging an individual, their efforts, or their worth. Thus, celebration, recognition, and positive talk are fundamental for those young people suffering most. Establishing protocols around celebration such as cheering for others' success and recognizing effort is a great strategy that cultivate a deeper sense of positivity, which facilitates growth and the three types of fitness. Providing verbal feedback specifically explaining what a student has done well or on evidence of learning—one to one or shared in a larger class setting—can have a deep impact on feelings of competence and significance, which help students grow a sense of esteem (Marzano et al., 2017). For example, weekly celebrations in which teachers recognize students' advancement on proficiency scales can be quite effective at the elementary level, as can making classroom announcements when students master a standard or proficiency scale in the upper grades. Asking students how they would like to celebrate, both individually and as a class, is important and can lead to even greater motivation and agency.

Making a conscious effort to recognize both great achievements and small victories in demonstrating skills such as perseverance, kindness, care, or collaboration goes a long way in nurturing a positive environment. Focusing on genuine, authentic "praise for a job that's well done goes a long way toward building trust, helping students feel seen," and enhancing a sense of belonging (Prieur, 2022). This, in turn, increases the likelihood that students will repeat the desired behaviors (University of Kansas, n.d.).

This can bring joy to a classroom by celebrating the time shared together, recognizing the gifts all students bring to the space, and highlighting the learning that is to come, like an assistant principal shared:

> At North Kansas City High School, student leaders take charge of coordinating quarterly assemblies to recognize and celebrate both staff and students. These assemblies highlight students with high attendance, academic achievement, and the embodiment of the Portrait of a Graduate competencies. Additionally, the high school actively embraces and celebrates its diversity by hosting events such as the Black History assembly, Hispanic Heritage assembly, and the Multicultural assembly and Multicultural Festival. (H. Khalandi, personal communication, March, 2024)

Collaboration and Voice

Collaboration is a cornerstone of effective education and is the second critical component of a growth-based school approach. Students must not only possess content knowledge, but also the ability to work together, communicate, and solve complex problems. In fact, "research shows that educational experiences that are active, social, contextual, engaging, and student-owned lead to deeper learning" (Center for Teaching Innovation, n.d.). Thus, creating a collaborative environment in schools is crucial for preparing students and building confidence for their future success.

Teachers play a pivotal role in fostering collaboration within the school environment. They must model collaborative behavior, craft collaborative experiences in lessons, share ideas, and respect diverse perspectives as part of their job as professional educators. They can assign tasks that require students to collaborate, such as group discussions, debates, or cooperative research projects. In this setting, mutually agreeing on open, respectful communication is essential. That means modeling and facilitating an atmosphere where students feel comfortable expressing their thoughts and opinions without fear of criticism (from the teacher or peers). As such, teaching students how to manage conflicts and disagreements constructively is crucial. At the elementary level, telling or reading stories about how other young people managed conflict can be an effective teaching strategy. In the upper grades, restorative circles have become a popular method for enhancing collaboration and voice due to their effectiveness and relatively simple protocols; fidelity and follow-through are critical, however. Conflict can arise in any collaborative effort, but when students know how to resolve it positively, it can strengthen their teamwork skills and other essential skills for life and workforce success.

Using culturally responsive strategies such as the following honor and celebrate those differences and come from a place of seeing them as assets. In this way, strength-based teaching connects with growth-based schooling.

- Learning information about students' cultural backgrounds
- Customizing word problems, or more broadly, assignments to reflect students' cultural backgrounds
- Incorporating language from students' family language in addition to the predominantly spoken language in class
- Using books and other media that positively depict a range of cultures
- Hosting guest speakers from different backgrounds

Also, purposefully mixing students from different backgrounds and abilities in collaborative groups can encourage diverse perspectives and foster empathy and understanding (León-Jiménez, Villarejo-Carballido, de Aguileta, & Puigvert, 2020). In the same way, ensuring that students with special needs have the necessary support and accommodations to participate fully in collaborative activities is an important component of a growth-based model of schooling. Finally, encouraging the use of collaborative software tools like Google Workspace, Microsoft Teams, or Slack can enable students to work together on documents, spreadsheets, and presentations at any time and from any place.

A powerful byproduct of collaboration and partnerships is empowering students to find their voice and encourage them to explore choices. See page 23 for more about student voice.

Teachers can incorporate collaboration and voice into their classrooms a variety of ways regardless of grade level (Marzano, 2017; Zima, 2021).

- Encouraging students to choose topics or themes for projects or assignments within a given scope or subject area can heighten student investment (Zima, 2021).
- Offering a variety of options for assignment formats such as written essays, multimedia presentations, or probing discussions allows students to choose the format that aligns with their strengths and interests (Marzano, 2017).
- Providing students with a multitude of resources and activities such as reading text, watching a video, or engaging in hands-on experiments can help teachers cater to different learning strengths and then allows students to choose the pathway that best suits their learning needs (Zima, 2021).
- Offering alternative assessment methods that might include presentations, portfolios, or self-assessments provides students with a choice for demonstrating their understanding of concepts (Marzano et al., 2019).

- Creating flexible seating arrangements or collaborative spaces within the classroom allows students to fit their specific learning strengths to the task at hand (Marzano, 2017).
- Allocating time for students to pursue self-directed projects or inquiry-based assignments aligned with their interests and goals, along with providing opportunities for students to reflect on their learning experiences and provide input on instructional methods, are powerful methods to enhance student voice as well as peer collaboration (Ruyle et al., 2022).
- Encouraging students to align an assignment or a project to their specific community, family, culture, or area of specific interest is a way to access their own background knowledge and is a culturally responsive way to engender higher levels of meaning and motivations (Ruyle et al., 2022).

Being able to work with others and to express ourselves are two actions that impact our well-being and are skills that are useful over our entire lifespans.

Well-Being

The third core principle that underpins growth-based schooling is cultivating a sense of well-being among all stakeholders in a school. *Well-being* is a broad concept that can entail such concepts as physical, mental, emotional, relational, financial, and social health. Well-being that can be nurtured and enhanced in schools and classrooms is vital. However, in a powerful corollary, we also assert that schools can broaden their influence and have a stronger impact on the community supporting the school by engaging in a true bidirectional partnership of connection, support, healing, and resilience building.

The importance of an explicit focus on well-being for all stakeholders cannot be overemphasized. Consider that "for individuals with trauma, ordinary emotional and social skills often are superseded by trauma-responsive survival skills . . . such as defiance, shutting down, struggling with relational boundaries, becoming overly self-reliant, or becoming too dependent on others" (Lorenzo, Eichert, Pawlo, & Elias, 2019).

Specifically addressing well-being and mental health is a critical factor in learning across the lifespan, and schools can serve as centers of well-being by making efforts to enhance well-being across entire communities, as well as helping all stakeholders embrace the power of mindfulness practices, sleep, and exercise.

Mindfulness Practices

Mindfulness has gained popularity as an in-school activity. Research has found that mindfulness activities lead to the following outcomes.

- Better educational outcomes in adolescents (Caballero et al., 2019)
- Decreased stress and negative affect (Schonert-Reichl & Lawlor, 2010)
- Improved cognitive function (Cásedas, Pirruccio, Vadillo, & Lupiáñez, 2020; Riggs, Black, & Ritt-Olson, 2015)
- Improved brain health (Caballero et al., 2019; Lazar et al., 2005)
- Enhanced self-regulation and a sense of belonging, which can positively impact relationships (Iberlin & Ruyle, 2017)

Thus, mindfulness is a good example of how components of the school fitness flywheel constantly interact, blending together rather than operating as separate constructs.

Educators can use a vast array of mindfulness practices and strategies including, but not limited to, the following.

- **Breathing exercises:** It sounds simple but breathing is a way to effectively address mental fitness. Research has shown that breathing exercises decrease "the mean scores for depression, anxiety, and stress" in an intervention group (Komariah, Ibrahim, Pahria, Rahayuwait, & Somantri, 2022, p. 1). A plethora of options exist, and box breathing is one example, where you inhale for a count of four, hold for a count of four, exhale for a count of four, hold for a count of four, and repeat. They are easily searchable online and appear in books such as *Positive Behaviors Start With Positive Mindsets: Twenty-Eight Actions to Motivate Students and Boost Achievement* (Hierck & Weber, 2024).
- **Five senses exercise:** Ask the whole class (or one-to-one with a student who is having trouble regulating) to name five things they can see, four things they can feel, three things they can hear, two things they can smell, and one thing they can taste.
- **Reading:** Integrate mindfulness practices into literacy activities, such as silent sustained reading or journaling prompts related to the texts.

Incorporating mindfulness and relaxation techniques into daily routines can help students calm their brains and bodies to better manage stress and anxiety. Exercises such as those listed can be taught explicitly and students can practice daily, before tests, big events, or whenever they notice escalating emotions or behaviors.

Sleep Hygiene

Healthy adolescent brain development and the connection to adequate sleep is an area of intense research interest. Sleep issues dramatically impact a person's lifespan. Insufficient sleep is directly associated with negative physical and mental health outcomes, decreased learning, poor decision making, behavioral problems, increased suicidal ideation, and challenges in personal relationships (Galloway, Conner, & Pope, 2013). Good sleep habits, commonly referred to as sleep hygiene, are important for both physical and mental fitness, brain health, learning, and overall quality of life (Irish, Kline, Gunn, Buysse, & Hall, 2015).

Despite being so impactful, sleep is a challenge a huge percentage of people struggle with. Although there are some specific ways in which educators can help to encourage sleep—such as reducing the homework load—mostly they can explicitly explain the value of getting more sleep. Educating students and families on the importance of sleep and the associated data may lead to behavior changes at home.

A school in Utah asked learners to create posters they could take home and share with their families about the importance of good sleep hygiene for healthier brains and bodies focused on such concepts as the following (M. Hickman, personal communication, January, 2023).

- Establish a daily sleep routine to get a good night's sleep, which will help you remember better and feel better.
- Stick to a regular, consistent sleep routine that gives a minimum of nine hours for all days of the week, not just school days. Your body loves routine.
- Always use the blue light filter on your devices in the evenings.
- Turn off all screens at least one hour before you want to sleep. The screen lights keep you stimulated well after you turn them off.
- Unwind before bed. Put away your phone and listen to calming music or read a book. If you are feeling anxious, write down or talk about your concerns to help clear your mind.
- Review key things you need to remember right before you go to sleep. Memories strengthen while you sleep, which is why sleep is so important!
- Monitor the temperature. Try to avoid being too hot or too cold.

We find these campaigns to be particularly effective when they are student led.

A more drastic idea is to start the school day later. California has the first U.S. statewide legislation explicitly designed to address adolescent sleep health by mandating high schools start no earlier than 8:30 a.m. and middle schools no earlier than 8:00 a.m. (Acevedo-Vigo, 2022). This is something that several districts are discussing. Consider this, from a principal in Montana:

> When we moved the school day to 9–4, it was of great relief to students, families, and teachers for many different reasons. For many the tacit assumption is that school day schedules were always unquestioned—like sacred cows. So when we proposed the changing of the school day and the school calendar, it was surprising and even a little shocking—that the idea had never crossed anyone's mind. The previous assumption was that the community should conform to the school, rather that the school should serve the community. (B. Cummins, personal communication, March, 2021)

Sleep hygiene can impact one's physical activities as well.

Exercise

The research linking exercise and brain health is robust and strongly suggests that many kinds of intentional movement practiced regularly have demonstrated some promise in enhancing executive functions in children. Although some schools have explored the idea of reducing or eliminating physical education classes to increase academic time, especially in an effort to make up for lost learning, we assert that those actions will most likely have the opposite effect. In short, letting children and adolescents play and otherwise move is critical for facilitating resilience (Weinstein & Tsai, 2023).

Exercise is connected to academic performance as well, as the following research indicates.

- Cardiorespiratory exercise directly correlates with better middle school grades (Srikanth, Petrie, Greenleaf, & Martin, 2012).
- Focus and memory improve with physical activity (Michael, Merlo, Basch, Wentzel, & Wechsler, 2015).
- A combination of regular brain breaks coupled with high cognitive engagement can lead to a stronger improvement in executive function (Egger, Benzing, Conzelmann, & Schmidt, 2019).

Exercise needn't take long. Five-minute physical brain breaks are enough to help.

Community Issues Such as Intimate Partner Violence

While teachers are often taught to recognize signs of possible abuse and neglect for students and are mandatory reporters in the U.S., it is also helpful to teach students of an appropriate developmental age to see signs of dating violence and abuse as well. School-based prevention programs that focus on educating youth about different types of abuse contain the promise of scalable prevention in a community (Letourneau, Schaeffer, Bradshaw, & Feder, 2017). There is little research concerning the safety of middle- and high school-aged youth who are exposed to or experience mistreatment in romantic relationships—thus the importance of creating effective prevention programming for this overlooked age group (Diaz et al., 2021). There is the following evidence, however.

- One-and-a-half million U.S. students have experienced physical dating violence (Basile et al., 2020).
- 8.2 percent of U.S. students reported sexual dating violence (Basile et al., 2020).
- 9 percent of Canadian youth age 15 years and older reported having experienced "psychological, physical and/or sexual violence within a dating relationship" in the previous five years (Exner-Cortens, Baker, & Craig, 2021).
- The percentage of female students who reported sexual violence increased from 2017 to 2021 (CDC, 2023).

Such violence impacts students' mental and physical health in the short and long term. The CDC (n.d.a) reported that young people who are victims of teen dating violence are more likely to do the following:

- Experience depression and anxiety symptoms
- Engage in unhealthy behaviors like using tobacco, drugs, and alcohol
- Exhibit antisocial behaviors like lying, theft, bullying, or hitting
- Think about suicide

Through education, we can help prevent unhealthy behaviors and assist all students in recognizing early warning signs of abuse and knowing how to get help or deal with those situations. That way students know what relationship abuse is, the different ways it can present, and what is not acceptable or safe. This helps communities at large in myriad ways and results in students not experiencing as much trauma in the longer term.

Resources from organizations such as the National Domestic Violence Hotline (www.thehotline.org) and Love Is Respect (www.loveisrespect.org) can help form curriculum, and are places where students can learn some signs that an abusive person might exhibit:

- Putting you down frequently, especially in front of others
- Checking your phone, email, or social media accounts without your permission
- Preventing or discouraging you from seeing your friends or family
- Isolating you from friends or family, (physically, financially, or emotionally)
- Extreme jealousy or insecurity
- Explosive temper, outbursts, or mood swings
- Pressuring you or forcing you to have sex
- Preventing you from working or going to school
- Threatening to hurt you or themselves to control and manipulate (Love Is Respect, n.d.b)

In short, teachers can communicate in developmentally appropriate ways that all peer relationships happen on a spectrum from healthy to unhealthy to abusive (Love Is Respect, n.d.a).

- **Healthy:** Communicative, respectful, trusting, honest, equal partnering, and time with others as well as with each other
- **Unhealthy:** Not communicative, disrespectful, lacking trust, dishonesty, one person always making decisions, and only spending time together
- **Abusive:** Making threats, being purposefully hurtful, accusations, denying abusive behavior, controlling someone, and isolating someone from others

The resources list many more red flags that middle school- and high school-age students would benefit from knowing. Teachers can teach about these signs and give examples of what this might look like for middle school and high school students and teach them to have healthy boundaries. Students need to be aware of warning signs of an abusive relationship and to have the tools to create healthy emotional, physical, and digital boundaries. They also need to know how to create a safety plan for schools, home, and online as well as seek help from family and educators, if needed.

Some recommended activities to use with middle and high school students from Love Is Respect are sharing examples of unhealthy relational situations with content the students can understand and teaching the relationship spectrum.

By informing students about healthy conflict management and healthy relational interactions, as well as equipping them to recognize signs of people who may not be good at self-regulating, young people can create healthy boundaries and be empowered to grow into socially healthy adults. As educators and educational leaders, we cannot allow these types of harmful behaviors that affect all communities to go unaddressed when we have an opportunity to provide education that strengthens community well-being.

Self-Regulation

Self-regulation is the fourth element of growth-based schooling. This applies because our feelings and emotions are deeply embedded in our neurophysiology as humans, which means emotions and cognition are inextricably linked (Immordino-Yang, 2016b). Self-regulation underpins growth-based schooling because teaching students to regulate their emotions allows high-level learning and improves the odds of successful relationships of all kinds (Cuncic, 2023). *Self-regulation* means managing feelings, thoughts, and behaviors to achieve goals and succeed (Murray, Rosanbalm, Christopoulos, & Hamoudi, 2015). Self-regulation equips students with the tools to cope with adversity and bounce back from failures. In addition, resilient students are more likely to persevere in their academic pursuits, maintain motivation, and continue to learn from their experiences.

Students who can regulate their emotions are better equipped to focus, think critically, and engage in effective problem solving. Emotional regulation facilitates committing information to memory and makes retrieval more efficient (Osher, Cantor, Berg, Steyer, & Rose, 2020; Tyng, Amin, Saad, & Malik, 2017). In fact, the ability to control our attention, emotions, thoughts, desires, and actions is one of our most potent powers and is highly correlated with success (Weinstein & Algeri, 2018). Developing emotional regulation skills in students not only fosters their emotional well-being but also enhances their capacity to learn and thrive academically as well as throughout the lifespan (Darling-Hammond & Cook-Harvey, 2018; Freedman, 2000; Ruyle et al., 2022).

It is important to include emotional education as a core component of the school curriculum (Immordino-Yang, 2016a, 2016b). Understanding the role of emotions, thinking, and behavior is a lifelong skill. Teaching students the language of emotions to enhance their emotional literacy is therefore critical because when students can accurately identify their emotions, they are better equipped to regulate them.

- At the elementary level, a feelings chart showing a wide range of emotions can be a powerful strategy, helping students to recognize and discuss their feelings regularly.

- At the upper grades, teaching students to identify various triggers and healthy ways to express and manage emotions (see mindfulness practices on page 77 as options) is very useful. Incorporating activities such as journaling and role playing also can help students become aware of their emotions, how their emotions drive behaviors, and how to regulate those emotions.

Co-regulation and metacognitive skills are two important pieces of self-regulation.

Co-Regulation

Co-regulation occurs when "caregivers provide external support or scaffolding as children navigate their emotional experiences" (Paley & Hajal, 2022, p. 19). Originally used to describe the way in which adults could soothe or connect with infants, the term is now commonly employed to describe how people can help support and regulate each other across the lifespan (Murray, Rosanbalm, Christopoulos, & Meyer, 2019). Educators can play a vital role in helping a student learn how to self-regulate.

Co-regulation helps teachers regulate a student's brain by regulating their own. For example, assume a student is angry and lashes out. Co-regulating means that, instead of meeting that anger with anger, the teacher controls their emotions and stays in control of themselves. That helps the angry student, who is in the stress-response state, return to a regulated state. If the teacher meets anger with reactivity (anger), the student cannot begin to calm down. Engaging in co-regulation with an upset person usually involves warmth: a soothing tone of voice, communication that acknowledges the person's distress, supportive silence, and an invitation to reflective problem solving (Bath, 2010; Bloom & Farragher, 2013a, 2013b). It can be something simple such as verbalizing our thinking as we experience and manage our emotions in the classroom. As an example, a teacher could model how they may become mindfully aware of a negative emotion, and how they can use mindful breathing to diffuse their anger or anxiety. They could then introduce a similar task for a student by saying, "Think aloud about what you are feeling in your body as you close your eyes and do three rounds of box breathing." Then, as the task winds down, the teacher asks, "Share in your journal something that is going on in your mind."

Many of the students whose behavior we struggle with are dysregulated and need well-regulated adults in their lives to help them manage their emotional world. What happens far too often is that teachers end up being driven by their students' dysregulation rather than the students being influenced by their teachers' solid self-regulation. Teachers cannot help a young student whose heart is racing if their own hearts are racing as well. Mindfulness is a good strategy for teachers and leaders working on their own ability to regulate their feelings. Feelings are contagious.

As a principal from North Dakota said:

> It is amazing how many of us as adults are not aware of our own emotional states and how we operate on scripts and patterns of interactions we had modeled before us when we were children. (S. Thompson, personal communication, November, 2023)

While working with another school, one teacher opened up and mentioned how the school wellness wheel training was helping her as a parent and as a partner, and how her partner commented about the new approaches and behaviors and wanted to know where these changes were coming from (D. Cohn, personal communication, February, 2023). Consistent training, as this examples shows, not only benefited the classrooms and teacher-student interactions, but also benefitted our teachers' home lives. When our private lives are solid, supported, and healthy, our workplace lives become so much easier and more productive.

Schools can address systematic issues prevalent in their area, but they must first be aware of the community's needs. An example comes from Awachíikaate, a school leader in Montana:

> Some areas in North America, the U.S. and Canada included, have a high percentage of MMIP (murdered and missing Indigenous people). Whenever a new incident occurs, a typical question is how the local schools have responded to this problem. To date, very few sustainable school awareness or prevention programs, like "Recognizing Risk" or "Date Rape Prevention," or self-defense classes, have been offered to the community.
>
> In response, we often see visible reactions to horrific incidents needed to bring attention to the issue such as student marches or other visible gatherings. Programmatic changes in our educational systems is a critical need that can address the local and situational issues students currently face. If there are some interventions about this issue, it is usually done individually by committed teachers or staff.

Schools typically remain reactive rather than proactive and are often, sadly, disconnected from their communities' most pressing needs. This can produce negative outcomes, and that causes significant stress. Stress in parents and caregivers results in negative outcomes for the adults and children in a family (Burgdorf, Szabó, & Abbott, 2019).

As mentioned, parents are also co-regulators who can teach their children self-regulation. Thus, we strongly suggest that communities and families could benefit tremendously from the following.

- **Parenting classes:** Providing programs to teach parents, guardians, grandparents, and other adult caregivers about the current dangers facing their children and what types of situations to be aware of can benefit entire communities. Instead of being prescriptive, this offering is a way for families to have more agency, since "agency is connected to adult learning processes" (Koskela, 2021). An array of curricula, such as Parenting Is Sacred (www.nativeamericanfathers.org/fatherhood-and-motherhood-is-sacred) and Positive Parenting Program (www.triplep.net), can teach effective strategies to strengthen family units and provide skills and perspectives to deal with the world our children face. Everyone benefits from instruction in positive conflict management strategies, the importance of boundaries, understanding child and brain development, and healthy communication, as well as the pressures facing students. Parenting classes improve parent and guardian self-efficacy, child behavior, and parent-child interaction and increase feelings of community (Wilder Research, 2016).
- **Mindfulness classes:** We discussed mindfulness practices for the classroom (page 77). Including families in communication about such exercises, and the potential benefits, can improve parents' self-regulation skills. Research indicated that "mindfulness interventions for parents may reduce parenting stress and improve youth psychological functioning" (Burgdorf et al., 2019).

Schools can teach students and the community the social skills and self-regulation that students need to be successful. Through education, we can also prevent unhealthy behaviors and help diminish the chances of traumatized students. Of course, these problems are largely systematic and often complicated, but schools can serve as centers of learning to empower the entire community. Awachíikaate said the following about his school:

> We were able to offer these parenting courses and tailor them to meet our community needs. We advertised through the local family court system and case managers to reach those parents who needed to complete parenting classes to be reunited with their children. It had a massive impact, and the schools began to be held in much higher regard.

And so, co-regulation is a critical strategy that teachers can learn and hone over time, but according to psychologist Howard Bath (2010), it "requires recognition and safe management of one's counter-aggressive impulses" and must be paired with age-appropriate education about emotions. Emotional co-regulation for elementary schoolers includes the following:

- Emotional literacy, including recognizing emotions and using words to express more complex feelings
- Emotion regulation:
  - Ignoring things that are mildly irritating, distracting, or frustrating
  - Calming down using strategies like deep breathing, relaxation, imagery, or positive self-talk
- Social flexibility, such as trying a friend's idea or considering others' perspectives
- Social skills, like being patient and taking turns
- Paying attention and staying focused
- Working independently
- Persistence with difficult tasks
- Problem-solving skills and flexible thinking (Rosanbalm & Murray, 2017, p. 6)

Emotional co-regulation for middle and high schoolers includes the following:

- Awareness of and attention to emotions
- Strategies to tolerate and manage normal levels of stress/distress
- Strategies for seeking help when stress is unmanageable or the context is dangerous
- Effective organization, time management, and task completion skills
- Setting longer-term goals and self-monitoring to achieve them
- Problem-solving complex life situations
  - Effective decision-making "in the moment"
  - Anticipating challenges and problem-solving in advance
- Decision-making with a future perspective
- Compassion for self and others (Rosanbalm & Murray, 2017, p. 7)

This humanizing, holistic perspective is a tremendous expansion of the view of what schools are capable of. But it all starts with the grown-ups. If we want students to be able to self-regulate, teachers must be able to serve as examples first. There are several tools that teachers can use to help them better regulate their emotions (R. Macy, personal communication, September, 2019; Murray et al., 2019). These include getting enough sleep, staying hydrated, engaging in regular exercise, consciously taking breaks, practicing mindfulness strategies, consuming a healthy diet, learning something new, and having strong personal relationships with supportive peers (Hammond, 2015; Iberlin & Ruyle, 2017; Ruyle et al., 2022).

Metacognitive Skills

Schools across the world have recognized the importance of helping learners take ownership of their own learning and have begun stressing an array of social and personal skills that take students beyond simple academic achievement. *Metacognition* is being able to think about what you're thinking about, a skill allows people "to exert executive control over the complex tasks in which we engage" (Marzano, 2017, p. 229). Metacognition is powerfully linked to mental fitness in that being aware of one's thinking helps lead to reflection, resist impulsivity, and make better choices. In addition:

> Mental health problems are also addressed through self-control and self-regulation. A research study indicated that metacognition could affect behavior through individual monitoring and self-regulation of cognitive function, thereby preventing illness and maintaining a healthy state. Metacognition beliefs can predict depression, anxiety, and dysfunctional beliefs related to health. (Li et al., 2023)

This basic level of self-awareness should not be taken for granted. Being aware (and realizing that), as well as reacting to and recognizing your personal perspective in regard to understanding, are invaluable qualities to cultivate.

Several states, provinces, and school districts have adopted updated visions of successful schooling as illustrated by various Portrait of a Graduate frameworks. (We discuss Portrait of a Graduate frameworks in more depth in chapter 5, page 119.) These frameworks help provide all learners with the skills to thrive in their future endeavors, many of which entail high-level metacognitive requirements such as leadership skills, identifying personal strengths and weaknesses, or collaborating with various people to accomplish a variety of tasks.

It is essential that we provide students objective insight into their capacities, strengths, and needs. The young, impressionable mind often does not realize how capable it is and what it might need to unlock its potential. Thus, it is important is that these skills be directly taught and developed over time so that students can actively hone their learning skills and strengthen their cognition. Proficiency scales identifying students' progression toward mastery effectively helps them learn and master these skills and this knowledge. Figure 3.5 is an example of a proficiency scale for the metacognitive strategies of analyzing perspectives and working in groups.

4.0	**The student will:** Describe how they can make the analyzing perspectives process more rigorous or informative.
3.5	In addition to score 3.0 performance, partial success at score 4.0 content
3.0	**The student will:** **AP1—Independently execute an analyzing perspectives process that involves identification and analysis of multiple perspectives, as well as self-analysis**
2.5	No major errors or omissions regarding score 2.0 content, and partial success at score 3.0 content
2.0	**AP1—The student will** perform basic processes such as describe an analyzing perspectives process that involves identification and analysis of multiple perspectives, as well as self-analysis. For example: 1. Identify whether you or others are reacting differently to a specific issue or situation. 2. Describe your own perspective on the issue or situation and the reasons behind your perspective. 3. Describe the other perspective(s) and the reasons behind them. 4. Avoiding judgment or rebuttal, continue to analyze to accurately represent each alternative perspective and the reasons behind them, being aware that the same general perspective might have multiple sets of reasons. 5. Describe what you have learned from the process and determine whether your perspective has become stronger or has changed in any way.
1.5	Partial success at score 2.0 content and major errors or omissions regarding score 3.0 content
1.0	With help, partial success at score 2.0 content and score 3.0 content
0.5	With help, partial success at score 2.0 content but not at score 3.0 content
0.0	Even with help, no success

Source: Adapted from Marzano Resources, n.d.

FIGURE 3.5: Example proficiency scale for analyzing perspectives in grades 6–8.

When using a proficiency scale, level 3 identifies mastery. It is written at the level of the standard and clearly articulates what proficiency—or mastery—of the skill or knowledge looks like. In this case, the goal is that middle school students will *independently execute an analyzing perspectives process that involves identification and analysis of multiple perspectives, as well as self-analysis.* In essence, middle school students must demonstrate the ability to respect and understand the perspectives of different people as well as the ability to reflect on their own perspective. In the case of the proficiency scale in figure 3.6, the goal is that elementary students will be able to take turns in group settings and not interrupt others.

4.0	**The student will:** Provide rudimentary self-evaluations of how well they work in groups
3.5	In addition to score 3.0 performance, partial success at score 4.0 content
3.0	**WG1—The student will:** • Take turns during group activities • Not interrupt others in the group when they are speaking
2.5	No major errors or omissions regarding score 2.0 content, and partial success at score 3.0 content
2.0	**WG1—The student will:** • Understand why it is important to take turns (for example, describing what would happen if group members didn't take turns, such as, "If group members don't take turns, the assignment might take longer to complete than the time allowed") • Understand why it is important to refrain from interrupting others when they are speaking (for example, describing what would happen if group members don't refrain from interrupting, such as, "The rest of the group might get distracted by the interruption and miss an idea that could help the group finish the assignment")
1.5	Partial success at score 2.0 content and major errors or omissions regarding score 3.0 content
1.0	With help, partial success at score 2.0 content and score 3.0 content
0.0	Even with help, no success

Source: © 2016 by Julia A. Simms. Adapted with permission.

FIGURE 3.6: Example proficiency scale for working in groups, K–2.

Both of the skills presented in these two scales will help learners connect better with others, which is fundamental to growth-based schooling. These skills also equip students to listen and consider the opinions of others, which are critical components of strength-based teaching and will also aid them in any endeavor they engage with in life.

The following resources also offer lesson plans and tips for helping students learn vital skills that can facilitate academic, mental, and psychological fitness.

- Collaborative for Academic, Social, and Emotional Learning (https://casel.org)
- Institute for Social and Emotional Learning (www.instituteforsel.net)
- Partnerships in Education and Resilience (www.pearinc.org)

Summary

By nurturing students' mental fitness, empowering a supportive community, teaching personal regulation strategies, and actively integrating mindfulness practices, schools that use growth-based schooling empower students to overcome challenges, persevere in the face of adversity, and thrive. In this way, growth-based schooling equips students with lifelong skills that enable them to navigate the complexities of life with strength, adaptability, and a positive outlook. By creating a culture that celebrates effort, supports individual growth, and empowers students to become lifelong learners, growth-based schooling sets the foundation for personal fulfillment and success in the dynamic landscape.

The reproducible "Professional Development in Growth-Based Schooling: Proficiency Scale" (page 91) is one way a school can monitor its progress toward mastery as defined in level 3.

We advise these three next steps as most important from this chapter for school leaders.

1. Create a professional development plan for staff focused on how mental health and trauma impact cognition and brain health, while also presenting strategies for growth and healing from trauma and stress.
2. Start with the adults by employing mindfulness practices with collaborative teams. Asking different teachers to open a meeting by using a simple four-count breath (inhale four, hold four, exhale four, hold four, repeat) can ensure efficiency and shared leadership in this area.
3. Generate and use proficiency scales in the areas of wellness and student relationships to ensure consistency and transparency, which also provide teachers with personal experience that they can translate to their classrooms.

We advise these three next steps as most important from this chapter for teachers and other classroom staff.

1. Bring mindfulness practices to the daily classroom experience.
2. Create and utilize metacognitive and behavior proficiency scales regularly.
3. Educate students on the impact of trauma and mental health and why directly addressing it can enhance their own brain health, well-being, and academic achievement.

Professional Development in Growth-Based Schooling: Proficiency Scale

<table>
<tr><th colspan="4">Teachers</th></tr>
<tr><td>Score 4.0</td><td colspan="2">In addition to score 3.0, in-depth inferences and applications that go beyond what was taught
The teacher:<ul><li>Can create and utilize an array of proficiency scales on schoolwide initiatives and can capture evidence of healing and growth from all learners</li></ul></td><td>Sample Resources and Activities</td></tr>
<tr><td></td><td>3.5</td><td>In addition to score 3.0 performance, demonstrate in-depth inferences and applications with partial success</td><td></td></tr>
<tr><td>Score 3.0</td><td colspan="2">The teacher:<ul><li>Is skilled at using learning goals and proficiency scales in their daily classroom practice to empower learners to take ownership of their learning</li><li>Demonstrates fluency in their assessment literacy by using valid and reliable assessment practices</li><li>Uses an array of strategies to personalize learning experiences</li><li>Clearly communicates and presents the foundational educational construct of growth-based schooling to a wide variety of stakeholders</li></ul>The teacher exhibits no major errors or omissions.</td><td><ul><li>Humanized Education (Ruyle, Awachíikaate, Child, & Dickey, 2025)</li><li>The Deepest Well: Healing the Long-Term Effects of Childhood Trauma and Adversity (Harris, 2021)</li><li>The New Art and Science of Teaching (Marzano, 2017)</li><li>The Body Keeps the Score: Brain, Mind, and Body in the Healing of Trauma (van der Kolk, 2015)</li><li>The Critical Concepts (Simms, 2016)</li></ul></td></tr>
<tr><td></td><td>2.5</td><td>No major errors or omissions regarding 2.0 content and partial knowledge of the 3.0 content</td><td></td></tr>
<tr><td>Score 2.0</td><td colspan="2">The teacher will recognize or recall specific vocabulary (for example, agency, co-regulation, learning goal, self-regulation, stress, student voice, transparency, and trauma) and perform basic processes such as the following.<ul><li>Explain how the effective use of proficiency scales can provide a clear pathway to mastery in the classroom and describe the impact of clarity and transparency on learners.</li><li>Describe why connection and relationships are the critical components of healing and learning.</li><li>Demonstrate how helping students enhance their learning from a perspective of strength develops students' belief that they can improve their abilities with dedication, practice, and learning from failures.</li><li>Celebrate even small successes for learners who are sometimes reluctant to participate in class.</li><li>Provide evidence of increased collaboration and learner voice in the classroom by being able to show ownership of students' own learning with proficiency scales.</li><li>Collaborate with other teachers to enhance knowledge of healing and cognition.</li></ul></td><td><ul><li>The School Wellness Wheel (Ruyle, Child, & Dome, 2022)</li><li>Growth-based schooling research articles, such as those available at the Flourish Agenda (https://flourishagenda.com)</li></ul></td></tr>
</table>

	1.5	Partial knowledge of the 2.0 content but major errors or omissions regarding the 3.0 content	
Score 1.0	With help, a partial understanding of some of the simpler details and processes and some of the more complex ideas and processes		
	0.5	With help, a partial understanding of the 2.0 content but not the 3.0 content	
Score 0.0	Even with help, no understanding or skill demonstrated		

4

Strength-Based Teaching

Engaged pedagogy does not seek simply to empower students. Any classroom that employs a holistic model of learning will also be a place where teachers grow and are empowered by the process.

—BELL HOOKS

Human learning, behavior, and growth occur within complex ecological systems that entail a variety of interactions, cultures, and societal structures. Neuroscience research shows that culture drives how the brain processes information. A person's cognition and learning are impacted by the environment in which they live, including the family and other social relationships as well as the larger contexts in which their families and communities are situated. Therefore, it is crucial that the teacher understand each student's unique cultural experiences.

Strength-based teaching is a way to nurture psychological fitness. This occurs by focusing on how the mind functions and building mechanisms to enhance personal meaning, determination, and motivation in the educational experience. Ensuring academic access by increasing literacy across all curricula, as well as pressing each student to demonstrate growth bolstered by academic and personal support systems, empowers teachers to serve as experienced guides through the learning process. Cultivating a sense of belonging by embracing students' culture and community can foster psychological strength and deepen the quality of life. Strength-based teaching has a strong impact on all students but can have an especially powerful influence on students from poverty, trauma, historically marginalized communities, and emerging bilingual learners (Gay, 2018; Hammond, 2015; Ladson-Billings, 2014, 2021a, 2021b).

Strength-Based Teaching Defined

Emphasizing student strengths produces increased levels of happiness and engagement in schools (Coleman & Davis, 2020; Seligman, Ernst, Gillham, Reivich, & Linkins, 2009) as well as improved academic achievement (Duckworth & Seligman, 2005; Fortner, Lalas, & Strikwerda, 2021; Park & Peterson, 2008).

The Reinert Center for Transformative Teaching and Learning (n.d.) described *strength-based teaching* as a:

> learner-centered approach to teaching that helps students identify, articulate, and apply their individual skills relevant to their learning needs. Based on research from social work, positive psychology and business, a strengths-based approach can help build student confidence, encourage efficacious behaviors, and support life-long learning pursuits.

Strength-based teaching recognizes and builds on each student's inherent knowledge, strengths, talents, and abilities. It also incorporates and increases an understanding of the diverse range of student experiences and identifying the ways educators can support students' academic, mental, and psychological fitness. Activating students' prior knowledge may help them connect to new learning as well as ensure they can access content through a solid grasp of basic, advanced, and academic vocabulary (Marzano, 2020). In addition, assessment practices that highlight how much a student knows facilitate a more asset-based approach that leads students to feel competent and become more confident and in charge of their own learning (Hammond, 2015). Though grounded in positive psychology research, the strength-based approach boils down to simply focusing on what students do well.

The critical components include full access to literacy instruction, academic press, enhanced meaning and motivation, teachers as a facilitators of learning, and the primacy of culture and community (Hammond, 2015; Kress, Emdin, & Lake, 2021; Ladson-Billings, 2009, 2022). In this chapter, we highlight successful strategies and real-world examples that illustrate the potential for strength-based teaching to transform educational outcomes. By equipping educators with the knowledge and skills necessary to create strength-based classrooms, schools can create a comprehensive system of empowerment that extends beyond classrooms into postschool life success.

Access via Literacy

Educators must conceive of reading as the liberation of the psyche through access to knowledge—freedom that only independent literacy can provide.

To increase equity and enable access to almost all academic content, literacy instruction is key. Improving literacy intertwines with teacher and leader knowledge of the concepts that comprise the standards and the curriculum. Culturally responsive literacy is an additional important piece of that instruction. The research on this topic is robust and clear: "Culturally responsive literacy practices are vital for the academic achievement of socioculturally diverse learners . . . learners with specific learning disabilities (LD) in inclusive settings . . . [and] English Language Learners" (Piazza, Rao, & Protacio, 2015, p. 1). The positive behaviors related to culturally relevant teaching can also lead to higher literacy rates for minority students, who tend to experience more disciplinary actions (Larson, Pas, Bradshaw, Rosenberg, Day-Vines, 2018).

For our purposes in this book, we refer to the science of reading as the best practice for learning reading based on the most current research available (Gentry & Ouellette, 2019). The science of reading consists of two widely accepted major domains: (1) foundational reading skills and (2) knowledge-based competencies. These two domains encompass ten total elements, as shown in table 4.1. Though unique, each of the ten elements should be interconnected and interdependent, together forming the building blocks of reading, critical thinking, and writing proficiency (Castles, Rastle, & Nation, 2018; Petscher et al., 2020; Snowling & Hulme, 2005).

Table 4.1: Science of Reading Elements

Foundational Reading Skills	Knowledge-Based Competencies
Print concepts	Vocabulary development
Phonemic awareness	Background knowledge
Phonological awareness	Oral language skills
Phonics	Reading comprehension
Encoding	
Fluency	

Source: Gough & Tunmer, 1986.

Students who are learning to read need regularly scheduled, in-class learning opportunities and direct-to-student feedback cycles facilitated by a professional educator (teacher assistant, teacher, teacher leader, school leader) trained to recognize gaps in knowledge and ability. K–12 teachers and leaders need diagnostic and prescriptive, short-term and long-term, whole-group and small-group professional learning on foundational literacy skills so they can do the following.

- Understand each element as an independent body of knowledge and how they intertwine with implications for teacher practice.
- Learn to artfully create and draw student attention to the organic interdependencies of the elements during learning-to-read and reading-to-learn instructional opportunities. (Dickey, 2022)

In addition, the following elements are critical to address access via literacy.

- **A safe, supportive reading culture:** Creating safe and supportive reading environments is essential. Learners must feel comfortable expressing their thoughts and emotions related to the texts they encounter. Because critical media literacy is crucial, that involves analyzing and discussing various media sources, such as news articles, advertisements, and social media posts. Students need a classroom that provides that expression. This involves establishing a classroom culture that values diversity, respects individual experiences, and encourages open dialogue (Emdin, 2016; Hammond, 2015). Teachers can cultivate a supportive reading environment by incorporating diverse literature that reflects students' backgrounds, experiences, and interests. Furthermore, educators should employ trauma-sensitive practices when designing reading and writing activities. This may mean providing trigger warnings, allowing students to choose some reading materials, and incorporating activities that encourage reflection and self-expression (Dickey, 2022; Gay, 2018; Ginwright, 2022).
- **Cultivated, literacy-rich environments:** Schools can provide a literacy-rich environment and foster a love of reading by providing an array of engaging books, magazines, and digital resources and providing inviting reading spaces with comfortable seating or cozy corners. Teachers should encourage students to explore different genres. For example, graphic novels allow differentiation, "improve students' reading comprehension" (Falter, 2017, p. 145), and challenge "conceptions of literacy practices, critical engagement, [and] interdisciplinarity" (Marlatt & Dallacqua, 2019, p. 19). Celebrate their literacy accomplishments by showcasing students' written work, such as poems, stories, and essays, in prominent places throughout the school. Publicly acknowledging students' literacy accomplishments boosts their confidence and validates their voices. In addition, incorporating community engagement into literacy practices reinforces the flywheel approach to schooling because connecting students to the larger community through literacy strengthens their sense of belonging and fosters empathy and social awareness. Collaborating with community

partners, such as local libraries, authors, or literacy organizations, to provide authentic reading experiences for students is a powerful way to bring outside expertise and passion into school buildings (Dickey, 2022).

- **Literacy integrated across the curricula:** Cross-curricular integration means across topics as well as modes. It is vital that schools extend beyond traditional print-based literacy and embrace a multimodal approach to literacy. Literacy extends to being financially and technologically literate, which requires effectively engaging with visual, digital, and audio communication. By engaging with literacy in various modalities, students can strengthen their communication skills and express their ideas more creatively. Thus, integrating literacy across the curriculum is critical. Teachers can encourage students to create multimedia presentations, videos, podcasts, art, or graphic novels to express their ideas and knowledge about any topic.

Ensuring that teachers are well versed in teaching literacy and how learning to read works goes a long way toward equity. The same is true for teachers instructing students specifically about the essential literacy elements of print concepts, phonemic and phonological awareness, phonics, encoding, and fluency.

Foundational Reading Skills

Foundational skills are often simplified and informally referred to as *decoding*. These skills are the fundamental building blocks on which all subsequent literacy will be based. Because of this, most federal and state or provincial standards documents for grades K–5 directly address these skills.

Print Concepts

The first element of foundational reading skills is *print concepts*. For preK–2 students, this element entails students having access to books as early as possible and being able to orient a book top to bottom. Print concepts for students in this range also include understanding that information in English is delivered to them in a book from left to right, grasping that, on a two-page spread, readers always start on the left side and go to the right side, and extracting information from the front cover, title page, back cover, and spine.

For intermediate elementary (grades 3–5) and secondary (grades 6–12) students, print concepts are a bit more expansive. They should include building and assessing student knowledge and capacity relative to the following listed categories of text features, and students' understanding of an author's use of those features to fulfill their purpose and their impact on the reader.

- **Print features:** This refers to how the typefaces in a text are used to emphasize content, draw the reader's attention, or illustrate the importance of a particular word, phrase, or idea. Examples include boldface, italicization, underlining, color, and enlarged words.
- **Graphic aids:** This refers to visual representations of information designed to supplement words within a text. Graphic aids visualize concepts central to the text, which helps readers develop conceptual understanding, apply prior knowledge, analyze concepts, synthesize ideas, evaluate the author's choices, and create original texts themselves. Graphic aids might include a chart or a graph representing textual information, a labeled diagram of the systems of the human body, a map of a given region of the world, a photograph of the subject of an informational text, or an illustration of a major character in a literary text.
- **Informational aids:** This refers to content that helps the reader gain information about the topic that the primary text did not communicate to the reader. Examples include captions, footnotes, labels, glossed words, pronunciation keys, sidebars, appendixes, and keys. Striving readers often ignore these aid, so be sure to point them out.
- **Organizational aids:** This refers to features of a text that help the reader locate information essential to a full understanding of the content. These aids include, but are not limited to, a table of contents, indexes, headings, subheadings, footnotes, bulleted lists, and glossaries.

Next, we cover phonemic awareness.

Phonemic Awareness

The second element of foundational reading skills is phonemic awareness (Castles et al., 2018; Snowling & Hulme, 2005). This element is not about seeing words in print, but about what students hear; it is the runway from which students can successfully take off in phonics. *Phonemic awareness* is concerned with students' ability to "hear and manipulate individual [phonemes] (sounds)" in words (Yopp, 1992). For example, preK–12 pupils possess adequate levels of phonemic awareness when they can do the following, using the word *cat* as an example.

- Hear and tally the three distinct phonemes in the word *cat*
- Orally segment, distinguish between and among, and repeat each phoneme in the word *cat*: [/k/ /a/ /t/]

- Orally manipulate the order of the phonemes in the word *cat* by changing initial phoneme to /b/ to create a different word: *bat* [/b/ /a/ /t/]; orally changing the vowel in *cat* to /u/ to create a different word: *cut* [/k/ /u/ /t/], and orally changing the final sound in *cat* to /n/ to create a different word: *can* [/k/ /a/ /n/]

When students fail to reach mastery levels of phonemic awareness in preK–2, upper-elementary grade reading instruction is especially difficult for them (Smith, Simmons, & Kame'enui, 1998). Students who are not reading at grade level by fourth grade "are more likely to struggle academically and eventually drop out of school" (Annie E. Casey Foundation, n.d.). Furthermore, secondary students without mastery levels of phonemic awareness may appear unmotivated, disengaged, and unwilling to participate in literacy and core content instruction when, in fact, they are drowning in a sea of prerequisite deficits. Let us refrain from blaming the victim. They were underserved. Instead of highlighting the symptoms of underservice (in phrases such as "These kids can't read" or "These kids are low"), let us focus on what they can do while addressing the root of their inability—a lack of access to systematic foundational skill instruction.

Phonological Awareness

The third element of foundational reading skills is phonological awareness (Gentry & Ouellette, 2019; Snowling & Hulme, 2005). Like phonemic awareness, phonological awareness is a body of knowledge and ability necessary for someone to successfully navigate and master phonics. *Phonological awareness* is the ability to hear, identify, and manipulate units of oral language, including words, syllables, and word parts.

As with phonemes, phonological awareness is not about students seeing words in print, but about what they *hear*. For example, preK–12 pupils who possess adequate levels of phonological awareness can do the following, using the word *happy* as an example.

- Hear and tally the two distinct syllables in the word *happy*
- Orally segment, distinguish between and among, and repeat each syllable in /hap-ē/
- Orally manipulate the base word *happy* by adding a prefix like *un-* to create the word *unhappy* and a suffix like *-est* to *unhappy* to create *unhappiest*
- Orally distinguish the four syllables in *unhappiest* /un-hap-ē-est/ from the combination of three words and word parts in *unhappiest*—the prefix, base word, and suffix [un-happy-est]

Budding readers need plenty of time practicing this skill. In this strength-based schooling model, systematic instruction to build student capacity to hear, identify, and manipulate units of oral language with automaticity is critical. It is critical to ensuring a student's ability to speak words, phrases, and sentences, and engage in oral dialogue for the purpose of ultimately composing original informational and literary texts.

Phonics

Phonics relates to understanding the relationship between the smallest unit of sound and the smallest use of writing. The concept is the extent to which someone understands the relationship between and among the twenty-six letters that make up the English alphabet, the forty-four phonemes, sounds, and symbols that comprise the language, and the 144 ways that letters can represent those sounds in writing (Gentry & Ouellette, 2019; Snowling & Hulme, 2005). Phonics, also referred to as *decoding*, is about what students should know and be able to do with their phonemic and phonological awareness when they encounter individual letters, double-letter combinations, and triple letter combinations (*graphemes*).

When students understand phonics, they can accurately associate a letter with the corresponding sound or sounds it makes (which they heard while acquiring phonemic and phonological awareness). For example, when a student encounters the words *cat*, *kite*, *duck*, *school*, *occur*, and *antique* in a text, they are consciously aware that the grapheme *c* in *cat*, *k* in *kite*, *ck* in *duck*, *ch* in *school*, *cc* in *occur*, and *que* in *antique* are different representations of the same phoneme: /k/. Students in preK–2 and beginning English learners need explicit help understanding that most phonemes have more than one grapheme.

Encoding

The fifth element of foundational reading skills is informally known as spelling, and formally known as *encoding* (Gentry & Ouellette, 2019; Snowling & Hulme, 2005). Though they are opposites, a student's ability to successfully encode (spell) is predicated on their ability to decode (comprehend phonics). Plainly stated, encoding and decoding are interdependent. Students must accurately and quickly draw on their knowledge of the letters, phonemes, and correlated graphemes to encode at developmentally appropriate levels. For example, when a student is writing (whether for personal gratification or class), it is helpful for them to know that the phoneme /f/ in *elephant* could be represented in writing with several graphemes, including *f*, *ff*, *ph*, *gh*, and *lf*. If the student did not acquire this knowledge base through systematic phonics instruction with phonemic and phonological awareness instruction as the backdrop, they cannot be expected to know this information.

Fluency

The sixth and final element of foundational reading skills is fluency (Gentry & Ouellette, 2019; Snowling & Hulme, 2005). Once students have begun a well-established journey toward phonemic awareness, phonological awareness, phonics, and encoding mastery, they should be able to navigate a developmentally appropriate text with *fluency*—smoothly, accurately, and with expression. Direct instruction by trained professionals is necessary for gauging fluency, as said earlier. Further, students need regularly scheduled opportunities to sit one to one with an educator to read aloud while the educator assesses the extent to which they can read fluently with developmentally appropriate word count pacing (Hasbrouck & Tindal, 2006).

In isolation or in any combination, none of these foundational skills can be classified as reading. To the contrary, they are essential, independent bodies of knowledge and ability with profound interdependencies that are necessary to help students whose native language is English as well as those new to the language, become readers.

The foundational literacy strategies focus on reading mechanics and are crucial to education at the beginning levels. It is also true that literacy instruction at the more proficient levels should include those same skills for many older students, as literacy remains a global challenge.

Knowledge-Based Competencies

Knowledge-based competencies are rooted in overall language comprehension and are often thought of as a combination of the awareness and cognition necessary to accurately and efficiently create meaning from a variety of informational and literary texts. Knowledge-based competencies are dynamic, continually developed over one's lifespan. Thus, these four competencies are important in deepening cognition and helping to build lifelong learners.

Any educational model that can provide unfettered access to high-quality preK–12 literacy skills must include excellent instruction that is planned, delivered, and supported by strong educators who can firmly grasp the transformational power of the relationship between foundational skills and knowledge-based competencies. Teachers must also be able to provide timely feedback to monitor student growth and be able to access any available tools to impact the most valuable resource for public education: effective initial whole-class instruction and targeted remediation. The knowledge-based competencies include vocabulary, background knowledge, oral language, and comprehension.

Vocabulary

The first element of knowledge-based competencies is *vocabulary*. High-level vocabulary instruction may be the most vital area of focus for every school at every level. In fact, research clearly indicates that after third grade, the greatest limiting factor in literacy development is vocabulary rather than reading mechanics (Biemiller, 2005; Marzano, 2020). We strongly assert that the impact of direct vocabulary instruction across the educational spectrum for all learners cannot be underestimated and is one of the most vital elements to increasing access to the standards and curriculum, as well as skills and knowledge. Consider, for instance, that technological literacy, financial literacy, media literacy, health literacy, social literacy, numeracy, and digital literacy have specific vocabulary words, and are important constructs for young people to become familiar with.

Vocabulary development should be considered in the context of a formula for bolstering reading capacity: *decoding + creating meaning = reading*. As discussed earlier, *decoding* refers to the ability to break the code between the letters encountered on a page and the sounds that one needs to produce orally based on their placement in a word. In other words, the byproduct of decoding in the absence of an ability to create meaning is just word calling and there is no meaning. Moreover, some grappling readers have decoding issues and other grappling readers have comprehension issues, while some preliterate students have difficulty with both.

Unfortunately, the task of intertwining vocabulary instruction with phonics has been made more complicated than it must be. Part of this issue revolves around the fact that the vast majority of teachers will, naturally, teach vocabulary in the same manner they learned it. This typically entails traditional practices like providing vocabulary lists, directing students to find word definitions and use the words in sentences, and giving students regular vocabulary assessments.

However, research on vocabulary instruction has evolved. Strength-based schools use the following models of vocabulary instruction: (1) transdisciplinary instruction and (2) tiered words.

Transdisciplinary instruction: High-level vocabulary instruction entails transdisciplinary instruction characterized by explicit access to the following.

- The 1,315 sight words (also known as *high-frequency words*) that make up 80 percent of the words that students will encounter while reading (tier 1 words)
- A firm understanding of the thirty most commonly occurring Latin and Greek prefixes, root words, and suffixes in the English

language, which are especially impactful for multilingual learners, students with disabilities, and students who struggle to read

- An understanding of terms that transcend grades and discipline, such as *identify, determine, inference, main idea, central idea, summary, analyze, argument, compare, contrast, text feature, tone,* and *point of view* (tier 2 words)
- A deep conceptual understanding of terms in a specific discipline or content area (sometimes referred to as *academic vocabulary*), such as *characterization* in English language arts, *coordinate plane* in mathematics, *metamorphosis* in science, *democracy* in social studies, or *gestalt* in art (tier 3 words; Dolch, 1936; Fry, 2004)

Tiered words: Marzano (2020) presents an even more comprehensive and innovative model of vocabulary instruction to increase vocabulary skills. He asserts that there are over eight thousand identified words—referred to as tier 1 (basic) and tier 2 (advanced)— that every student should be able to demonstrate a working knowledge of by the end of fifth grade. *Tier 1* words are general terms and phrases that students will encounter throughout their lives through reading and conversation. Examples of tier 1 words are *book, baby, river, tall, over,* and *dog. Tier 2* words are general terms that build on and relate to basic vocabulary but tend to be more advanced. These are words that students will typically encounter in reading more than in general conversation but are still considered essential to English language proficiency. Tier 2 words also include cognitive verbs that students use to process information and often encounter in standardized assessments, such as *analyze, evaluate,* and *generate.* Examples of tier 2 words are *fumble, extract, engage, penicillin, robust, detective,* and *notch.*

Students are commonly exposed to tier 1 and 2 words in their daily life experience and, therefore, do not usually require direct instruction to have a working knowledge of such terms. In this case, students typically gain a working knowledge of these words through regular exposure. Thus, providing ways in which schools can consciously and continuously provide that exposure is an important strategy for teacher teams to consider (Blachowicz & Fisher, 2012; Marzano, 2020).

Tier 3 words are academic vocabulary critical to an academic subject area. This includes content-specific words as well as cognitive verbs that are important for students' higher-level academic success. Examples of tier 3 words include *fission, antagonist, transversal, convey, variability, algorithm, authoritarian,* and *peripatetic.* As such, tier 3 words require more in-depth knowledge and must be directly taught.

A powerful teaching strategy to ensure deeper vocabulary knowledge uses the following six-step method (Marzano, 2020).

1. Provide a description, explanation, or example of the new term.
2. Direct students to restate the description, explanation, or example in their own words.
3. Ask students to construct a picture, symbol, or graphic representing the term or phrase.
4. Engage students periodically in activities that help them add to their knowledge of vocabulary terms.
5. Engage students periodically to discuss the terms they are learning.
6. Involve students periodically in wordplay games.

In mastery-based learning, academic vocabulary words (tier 3 words) are clearly listed at level 2 in proficiency scales.

Background Knowledge

The second element of knowledge-based competencies is *background knowledge*. Proficient readers organically and progressively accumulate background knowledge through reading opportunities and the visual and auditory world. A student who lacks unrestricted access to a wide array of reading and discovery opportunities—travel, summer camps, museums, conversations with adults about their occupation, apprenticing—is exponentially less likely and more challenged to encounter and store knowledge.

Many students may find a significant percentage of the individuals, events, ideas, and phenomena they encounter in texts while learning to read and reading to learn unfamiliar. When educators actively build access bridges by consciously and consistently unearthing the unfamiliar and backfilling individual gaps in general knowledge, more students will meet or exceed expectations. However, in a strength-based model, teachers tap into students' experiences to make connections to content rather than assume students have the same experiences reflected in the content.

Oral Language Skills

The third element of knowledge-based competencies is *oral language skills*, which includes vocabulary, grammatical knowledge, and listening comprehension (Kim, 2017). Of course, listening comprehension is an inherent part of these skills, which are intertwined with the phonemic awareness, phonological awareness, phonics, encoding, fluency, vocabulary development, and background knowledge imperatives discussed earlier in this chapter. Though helpful, simply integrating turn-and-talk opportunities into lessons is insufficient. Reading aloud to students improves their oral language skills prior to their being able to perform on their own (Napoli & Johnson, 2019). Dialogic reading is a research-backed strategy that promotes vocabulary and aligns with strength-based teaching and student agency. The teacher lets students take the lead and tell the story, asking questions, "encouraging the child to talk, and using modeling and expanding strategies. When used while considering the child's abilities and interests, dialogic reading can assist in the development of prereading skills" (Napoli & Johnson, 2019).

Reading Comprehension

The fourth and final element of knowledge-based competencies is *reading comprehension*. Widely oversimplified and misunderstood, this element is often erroneously thought of as a student's ability to understand an author's language. More accurately, reading comprehension is about what a reader can do intellectually and independently with what they have extracted. For example, a student with reading comprehension skills can successfully and without prompting or support determine the central message. Students use this skill across disciplines—for example, graphing and describing the relationship between the dependent and independent variable in mathematics, describing an author's text structures in writing about the law of the conservation of energy in science, and reading multiple texts on several forms of art and subsequently expressing an opinion in favor of or against one medium over another in a visual arts class—and the list goes on.

Academic Press

The second critical component of a strength-based approach to schooling is *academic press*, or holding every learner to mastery of high-level expectations. Students perform in ways that teachers expect, and a teacher's expectations—either high or low—become a self-fulfilling prophecy. There is a subtle yet important difference between expectations and academic press. A teacher having high expectations is one thing, but pressing every student to meet those expectations and then coupling them with ample support is what academic press is all about (Murphy & Torre, 2014). Providing learners with pathways, supports, and strategies to meet their academic goals is a part of academic fitness.

Consistently using quality proficiency scales directly relates to high expectations because scales identify and communicate a learning goal based on an identified-level standard. Proficiency scales should align with state, provincial, or national standards, with the expectation that learners will meet those standards.

Meaning and Motivation

The third critical component of a strength-based approach to schooling is providing personal meaning and motivation for every learner. In the best-selling book *Drive: The Surprising Truth About What Motivates Us*, Daniel Pink (2011) asserted that the keys to motivation are as follows.

- **Autonomy:** Being in control of what we do and how we do it (which relates to student voice and choice)
- **Mastery:** Improving our skills and selves (which relates to mastery-based learning)
- **Purpose:** Working toward something worthwhile (which relates to voice and choice, mastery-based learning, and agency)

Teachers can enhance meaning and motivation by instilling a sense of hope in learners, connecting academic curriculum to students' real-world experiences, and guiding students to embrace their role as global citizens.

Hope

Facilitating hope is a powerful element of a strength-based teaching model of schooling that can have a profound impact on meaning and motivation. The American psychologist Charles Richard Snyder developed a powerful research base on hope as a cognitive construct comprising the following three critical components.

1. **Goals:** A desired future state to aim for
2. **Agency:** Believing in one's ability to succeed
3. **Pathways**: Believing in one's ability to create avenues for reaching one's goals (Snyder, 1995, 2009; Snyder et al., 2002)

With the removal of any one component, hope is diminished. However, higher levels of hope consistently correlate with better outcomes in areas such as academics, athletics, physical health, psychological adjustment, and psychotherapy (Feldman & Kubota, 2015; Snyder, 2009). Mastery-based learning models are directly related to higher levels of hope in that learning goals, learning progressions articulated as proficiency scales, and student autonomy over their own success are fundamental elements. Furthermore, increasing meaning and the subsequent impact on student motivation are critical components of strength-based teaching (Hammond, 2015; Ladson-Billings, 2021a, 2021b). This is another example of how the segments of the school fitness flywheel continually interact with each other.

An additional element to consider here is *teacher hope.* If teachers don't have hope, they don't have belief in students' ability to learn, which is a clear impediment to growth. Continued growth in this area can show how low-performing students have untapped capabilities, which can give teachers confidence that their students can succeed.

Intrinsic motivation, the inner drive to learn and excel, plays a vital role in creating meaning in the classroom. Teachers can nurture intrinsic motivation by providing opportunities for students to pursue their interests within the curriculum. Offering choices in assignments, allowing students to explore topics they are passionate about, and acknowledging their achievements can all contribute to a sense of purpose and meaning in the learning process.

Curricula Linked to Real-World Relevance

A meaningful learning environment is one where students not only grasp the subject matter but also engage with it on a deeper level, connecting it to their lives and the world around them. The pursuit of meaning in the classroom is a multifaceted endeavor that involves connecting the curriculum to real-world relevance as well as nurturing intrinsic motivation. By implementing these strategies, educators can create classrooms where learning transcends mere grades and becomes a meaningful and transformative experience for students.

One of the key elements in creating meaning in the classroom is demonstrating the real-world relevance of the subject matter. Whether it's algebra, chemistry, or history, students are more likely to engage when they can see how they can apply the knowledge and skills they are acquiring in their lives. Teachers can achieve this by providing practical examples, inviting guest speakers from relevant fields, and encouraging discussions about how the curriculum relates to current events or everyday situations.

Teachers can also encourage students to write letters to local leaders, create persuasive arguments on issues of interest to them, or attend local events. Providing opportunities for student choice in reading materials, such as book clubs, literature circles, or independent reading projects, can also empower learners to make connections between academic content and their own lives, allowing them to develop a deeper connection to the literature and fostering a sense of ownership over their learning.

In a high school in Kansas City, first-year students used a combination of their research findings on local business partners and their personal interests to create an individual service project pitch. Students then were grouped based on common interests to collaboratively develop pitches tailored specifically for business partners. These pitches highlighted the collaborative plans between students and the business partners to improve the community.

In one of these community service projects, Let's Play Ball, students collected, refurbished, and cleaned gently used sports equipment. They then donated all the refurbished items to a local thrift store supporting people who are unhoused or insecurely housed achieve sustainable independence. In another service project through the Giving Back donation drive, students created thirty-seven care packages containing dog food for homeless pets and donated them to a local animal shelter for distribution.

A fundamental component of the strength-based teaching perspective is encouraging student agency during classroom discussion. These discussions align with strength-based teaching by activating students' prior knowledge and interests to guide their learning. Grouping learners to collaborate and providing small-group instruction increases motivation and engagement as students are able to embrace the concepts in a way that is more meaningful. Further, connecting with others helps facilitate academic, mental, and psychological fitness.

Global Citizenship

In a world characterized by interconnectedness and global challenges, the purpose of schooling extends beyond individual development to the collective well-being of humanity. Schools should strive to foster a sense of global citizenship among students, encouraging them to recognize their roles as responsible members of a diverse and interdependent world. This global perspective emphasizes the importance of cultural sensitivity, environmental stewardship, and social justice. Purpose-driven education equips students with the knowledge, skills, and attitudes necessary to address pressing global issues, fostering a sense of empathy and a commitment to positive change.

Achieving purpose-driven education requires a collective effort from educators, institutions, and communities. Teachers play a pivotal role in inspiring students to discover their purpose and guiding them on their educational journeys. Meaningful learning is not limited to the content of the curriculum; it also involves the relationships formed within the classroom. Teachers can create a supportive, inclusive culture where students feel valued. When students know that their opinions matter and that they are part of a community of learners, they are more likely to engage with the subject matter and find meaning in their educational journey. Thus, the teacher serves an important role as a learning partner—not simply someone who delivers content. Schools must create environments that encourage exploration, curiosity, and the pursuit of passions.

Educational institutions should also collaborate with communities to ensure that education aligns with the needs and aspirations of society. When schools and communities work together, they can create educational experiences that are not only purposeful but also relevant and meaningful.

Teacher as Facilitator

The fourth critical component of a strength-based approach to schooling is facilitating learning. Though this concept aligns with mastery-based learning in that teachers personalize instruction, it's also critical in strength-based teaching in that teachers assume the job of helping students learn rather than teaching students. It's a subtle but important distinction. This concept fits well in schools with mastery-based learning, where students consistently express how teaching looks and feels different than in traditional school models (Ruyle et al., 2019, 2022). However, teachers helping every student master important content and skills rather than simply serving as oracles of knowledge can happen in every classroom—mastery based or traditional.

Skillfully using proficiency scales and aligning all assessments and assignments to those scales gives learners constant feedback regarding their growth. This means teachers are better able to diagnose where student strengths and deficiencies lie, communicate those concepts to learners, and coach them to mastery. This is strength based in that it empowers learners to take ownership of their own learning and practice agency to achieve success. Growth is celebrated just as much as final success.

Proficiency scales extend beyond traditional academic subjects to encompass engagement, self-regulation, resilience, and cultural competency. Various students reported the following thoughts:

> Kids are more independent, but teachers are still there to help and push us to be better. They are always there for us. In this program, you actually have to learn and understand concepts. There is no way to mess around. You have to work because you need to understand that there are no Cs or Ds. You have to give evidence that you really know the standards and do good work.
>
> —Travis, high school student, California

> Now that we have been using proficiency scales for everything, school makes more sense. My teachers here teach me and explain things way better. They help me more here, and it is so much better.
>
> —Sara, middle school student, Arkansas

> Just doing mindfulness and learning goals with proficiency scales was a big deal for us. I like school and my teachers so much more. Why didn't we do this earlier?
>
> —Maria, high school student, California

In our experience in these schools, students regularly report higher levels of connection with their teachers and come to see the student-teacher dynamic as more of a learning partnership rather than the teacher simply directing learning activities. The one-to-one time between students and teachers and connectedness due to immediate feedback are two other reasons mastery-based learning promotes closer relationships (McGraw-Hill, 2023).

By focusing on individual competency rather than time-bound benchmarks, mastery-based learning creates the space and flexibility to tailor instruction to the unique needs of each student. In our experience, students consistently identify the individualized attention they experience in mastery-based learning systems as the most important factor in their engagement and ultimate success (Ruyle et al., 2019). This is largely due to the constant use of proficiency scales and aligned assessments, which provide teachers and students with evidence of student learning, and result in teachers using their increased instructional expertise to target strategies specific to student needs (Ruyle et al., 2019). Although teacher face time in mastery-based classrooms is rarely different than in traditional classrooms, students strongly expressed to us that they were more engaged in class based on their perception that instructors in the mastery-based model teach differently and respect their individual styles of learning more effectively than they had experienced in their traditional classes (Ruyle et al., 2019).

One of the key tenets of facilitating learning is recognizing that students have diverse learning needs and progress at different rates. (This is also fundamental to the other two core pieces of the flywheel.) When teachers have a clear picture of students' cognitive variability, they have clearer insight as to why some students have not yet achieved mastery and which targeted interventions will be most beneficial. Teachers can assess students' prior knowledge and skills and provide targeted interventions or remediation when needed. When teachers know which intervention will work best, it builds teacher confidence in themselves and in their students' capabilities. When mastery comes more easily, students see the benefits of persistence. This positively reinforces the growth mindset that a strength-based approach to schooling creates, thus positively reinforcing the overall school culture.

By tailoring instruction to meet students' diverse learning needs and incorporating activities that align with their strengths, teachers can focus on instruction and students can reach more advanced levels of skill and knowledge. For instance, allowing students with strong spatial abilities to use 3-D modeling to explore their understanding while letting students with stronger verbal skills read and discuss their conceptualization are ways to personalize education to meet the needs of all learners. This connection and mentoring lead to consciously creating learning partnerships—a fundamental component of culturally responsive teaching and mastery-based learning.

Education is most effective when it caters to the unique needs, backgrounds, interests, and abilities of individual learners. By personalizing instruction based on student needs, mastery-based learning creates a more inclusive and equitable learning environment, allowing all students to access and engage with the curriculum at their own pace and level of understanding. Mastery-based learning aligns seamlessly with personalized instruction, as it emphasizes individual competency mastery, student agency, and flexible pacing.

Culture and Community

The fifth critical component of a strength-based model of schooling is cultural and community appreciation. The importance of culture and community in schools cannot be overstated. As such, we address culture in this section by discussing cultural affirmation, culturally responsive teaching, and cultural resilience. All three are critical to enhance strength-based teaching in a mental, psychological, and academic-centered school model.

Cultural Affirmation

Cultural affirmation plays a vital role in a mental, psychological, and academic-centered learning environment. A strong culture of inclusivity and belonging is essential for the well-being and success of all students. This goes beyond celebrating diversity by consciously recognizing and valuing the cultural strengths students bring to the classroom. Mental, psychological, and academic-centered schools provide opportunities for students to see themselves reflected in their education, which empowers them with a stronger sense of belonging, confidence, and pride in who they are. In this way, students are more likely to be engaged in their learning, become curious, form positive relationships with peers and teachers, develop a strong self-identity, and think deeply on topics such as culture and equity in the world. Thus, culturally responsive practices serve *all* students and school communities (Ladson-Billings, 2009, 2021a; Paris & Alim, 2017).

Educators can foster cultural affirmation among students by incorporating diverse perspectives, histories, and experiences into the curriculum. This includes selecting instructional materials, resources, and literature that reflect the rich tapestry of cultures represented in the student body (Nieto & Bode, 2018). By doing so, students gain a broader understanding of the world and develop the skills needed to thrive in an increasingly globalized society. Furthermore, strong teacher-student relationships are at the core of an academic, mental, and psychological fitness-centered school's culture. When students have positive connections with their teachers, they are more likely to seek help when needed, participate actively in class, and develop a love for learning. These relationships provide an academic and emotional safety net for students (Ladson-Billings, 2014).

Furthermore, teachers and leaders can enhance cultural affirmation by reflecting on their own cultures to consider their beliefs about their students and how that may impact their expectations, instructional practices, and relationships with both the student and parents. Educators should also examine and regularly reflect on how they reinforce concepts such as belonging, transparency, flexibility, and equitable practices (Gay, 2018; Hammond, 2015).

To foster cultures of belonging that were both culturally affirming and academically challenging, a high school in Kansas City adopted author Susie Wise's (2022) indicators of belonging as a guiding framework in their building. Those indicators offer staff tools to create a deep and meaningful sense of belonging. The school's version encompasses those six indicators.

- **Welcoming:** Entrance and lobby, classroom setup, and routines and traditions
- **Validating:** Validate, affirm, and justice
- **Accepting:** Culture-building events, acceptance of identity, and restorative practices
- **Including:** Equity, inclusion, and access to opportunities
- **Contributing:** Student leadership, student voice, and supports and interventions
- **Growing:** Goal setting, independent learners, and connecting

Working as teams, staff members delved into the questions listed under each indicator, conducting a self-assessment to gauge their collective position as a team, department, or building. Then, they identified the specific components they were willing to commit to and implement.

Culturally Responsive Teaching

Culturally responsive teaching recognizes that ineffective instruction for marginalized students is an equity issue that educators must address. It is not a simply talking to students about racism, leading implicit-bias training, or adding authors of color to the curriculum resources. Rather, it is a deep, intentional approach to education that focuses on the assets all students bring to the classroom rather than what students can't do.

Our brains are wired to make connections. Our brains can better learn and store information if they are connected to the background knowledge that students bring to the classroom every day. All students come from communities with traditions of learning, including those coming from other countries as refugees and those from low-income neighborhoods. Thus, culturally responsive teaching supports the use of students' prior knowledge and draws from their cultural background and experiences to connect what they know and what they need to learn (Hammond, 2015). These connections help students access rigorous academic curriculum and develop higher-level academic skills. They also raise expectations and make learning relevant for all students. Even at the post-high school and college levels, culturally responsive teaching influences student satisfaction, socialization, retention, and graduation rates (Hutchison & McAlister-Shields, 2020). A school leader in Montana shared that their school used the local community's traditional name rather than the historically newer English name and adopted the local tribal community song as their school song. Rather than view the community norms from a deficit model, the school worked hard to become a place where the community could live out their values, which helped build great support and pride in the school. The principal was happy when she overheard some older students calmly informing a rather rambunctious new student, "Hey, we don't do that here."

Another school where most of the students are Indigenous respectfully and authentically used local tribal music in their music program, working with community members and obtaining permission and support. Although the school used the community's music rather than mainstream music, they still met district and state standards of musical concepts. Parents and community members were in awe after the winter school performance, some in tears when they heard the students singing songs from their youth and speaking the language that was previously forbidden in the same school.

These two schools have started to move toward becoming places of culturally sustaining practices (Mackey, Faircloth, & Cummins, 2020) and places of empowerment and growth rather than perpetuating culturally harmful assimilative practices.

Cultural Resilience

The connection between culture and academic, mental, and psychological fitness is clear and profound. As such, an emerging yet solid base of research focused on the concept of *cultural resilience* speaks to the important role culture can play in building resilience (Masten, 2018; Sanders, Munford, & Liebenberg, 2016; Seligman & Csikszentmihalyi, 2014). This cultural resilience means possessing a sense of belonging to one's culture and community. Seeing one's historical trajectory, culture and larger community, as well as one's current reality and why things are the way they are, is deeply empowering.

Cultural resilience is positively correlated to improved mental health functioning in that it can serve as one protective factor against mental illness (Fleming & Ledogar, 2008; Holtorf, 2018). In fact, the notion of cultural resilience suggests that individuals and communities can confront and overcome adversity based on individual strengths as well as support of the larger social community (Bulger, Schultz, & Schultz, 2020).

Schools can also act as powerful agents of change and address deep recesses of intergenerational and community trauma by providing educational experiences that empower the unique community where the school is located (Malone, Rizkalla, & Bartlett, n.d.). *Place-based education* is a concept that honors a school's location and the unique histories that the community holds (Yemini, Engel, & Simon, 2023). Embracing the cultural strengths of the surrounding community can benefit both, since viewing the community through an asset-based perspective can assist schools. For example, if a school is in a predominantly blue-collar neighborhood, it may be a good idea to emphasize the tradition of a strong work ethic and tie that into the ethos of the school culture. As another example, an educator whose early career was in rural Alaska noted that most of the staff were from the lower forty-eight states and disconnected from the community. The students' rich culture was not reflected in the schools when it could have been celebrated. In fact, many staff members viewed the students' culture negatively and saw it as a deficit. The school principal viewed himself as a military general on a mission in a foreign land; this educator said, "He was the general, the teachers were the officers, the students were the troops in training . . . and the community? The community was the enemy" (as cited in Khalifa, 2018, p. xi). This harms both students and the community, and makes educators' jobs more difficult.

Creating proficiency scales to deepen cultural identity is a powerful strategy for building cultural resilience. Doing so can increase student motivation, because the scales identify specific actions that represent each teaching. Teams discussed examples and nonexamples of each quality and held each member to proficiency in daily actions.

Teachers and students who have delved into cultural components of their own tribe reported this as one of the most empowering activities they've engaged in and said the clarity provided direction for the entire organization moving forward.

Summary

Simply defined, strength-based teaching means identifying student assets in the classroom. Doing so boosts well-being, engagement, perseverance, and achievement (Seligman et al., 2009; Waters, Loton, & Jach, 2019). As such, in a healing- and resilience-centered school, strength-based teaching can lead to increased levels of equity and cultural affirmation through personalized learning experiences, inclusive curriculum design, and strong partnerships with families and communities. By embracing and valuing the unique assets and identities of each student, these schools provide a foundation for academic success, personal growth, and social empowerment for every student, regardless of their cultural backgrounds or individual circumstances.

The "Professional Development in Strength-Based Teaching: Proficiency Scale" (page 116) is a way for schools to monitor their progress toward mastery of strength-based teaching, as defined in level 3.

We advise these three next steps as most important from this chapter for school leaders.

1. Deepen professional learning focused on how literacy takes on many forms and how your school is impacted by literacy challenges.
2. Engage in professional development to understand how close connections to personal culture can facilitate healing and growth.
3. Examine the difference between academic press and high expectations and consider what that means in your school context.

We advise these three next steps as most important from this chapter for teachers and other classroom staff.

1. Embed a schoolwide vocabulary program to address literacy and access to content and curriculum.
2. Consider how to engage with the larger community to bring community values into the school as well as examine how the school can serve as a center of healing, strength, and growth.
3. Use collaborative teams to deepen understanding of how proficiency scales can enhance motivation and hope, and discuss strategies to make the scales a commonly used tool in daily practices.

Professional Development in Strength-Based Teaching: Proficiency Scale

<table>
<tr><th colspan="4">Teachers</th></tr>
<tr><td>Score 4.0</td><td colspan="2">In addition to score 3.0, in-depth inferences and applications that go beyond what was taught.
The teacher:
• Can create and utilize proficiency scales on schoolwide initiatives focused on delivering instruction from a lens of culture and belonging</td><td>Sample Resources and Activities</td></tr>
<tr><td></td><td>3.5</td><td>In addition to score 3.0 performance, in-depth inferences and applications with partial success</td><td></td></tr>
<tr><td>Score 3.0</td><td colspan="2">The teacher:
• Is skilled at using learning goals and proficiency scales in their daily classroom practice to increase academic press
• Can demonstrate quality literacy practices to ensure access to the curriculum as well as resources for learning
• Can use an array of strategies to tailor instruction to meet individual learning needs
• Can utilize information from a learner profile to better help that learner connect new content to their prior knowledge
• Clearly communicates and presents the foundational elements of strength-based teaching to a wide variety of stakeholders
The teacher exhibits no major errors or omissions.</td><td>• Humanized Education (Ruyle, Awachíikaate, Child, & Dickey, 2025)
• District- or school-created proficiency scales
• The New Art and Science of Teaching (Marzano, 2017)</td></tr>
<tr><td></td><td>2.5</td><td>No major errors or omissions regarding 2.0 content and partial knowledge of the 3.0 content</td><td></td></tr>
<tr><td>Score 2.0</td><td colspan="2">The teacher will recognize or recall specific vocabulary (for example, academic press, agency, equity, fluency, inclusivity, learning partnerships, literacy, meaning, motivation, phonics, science of reading, and tier 1, 2, and 3 vocabulary words,) and perform basic processes such as the following.
• Explain that a student's background knowledge is a critical component to further learning and new content.
• Explain that culture can be defined as the collective beliefs, values, attitudes, traditions, and behaviors that shape the climate and interactions within a school.
• Describe how cultural resilience can be defined as possessing a sense of belonging to one's culture and community, and how it positively correlates to improved mental health functioning.
• Foster cultural affirmation by incorporating diverse perspectives, histories, and experiences into the curriculum.</td><td>• The School Wellness Wheel (Ruyle, Child, & Dome, 2021)
• Culturally Responsive Teaching: Theory, Research, and Practice, Third Edition (Gay, 2018)
• Culturally Responsive Teaching and the Brain: Promoting Authentic Engagement and Rigor Among Culturally and Linguistically Diverse Students (Hammond, 2015)
• The Dreamkeepers: Successful Teachers of African American Children (Ladson-Billings, 2022)</td></tr>
</table>

	1.5	Partial knowledge of the 2.0 content but major errors or omissions regarding the 3.0 content	
Score 1.0	With help, a partial understanding of some of the simpler details and processes and some of the more complex ideas and processes		
	0.5	With help, a partial understanding of the 2.0 content but not the 3.0 content	
Score 0.0	Even with help, no understanding or skill demonstrated		

5

Initiated Flywheel

Life is really simple, but we insist on making it complicated.

—CONFUCIUS

The school fitness flywheel is the only framework that specifically links the powerful research behind growth-based schooling, strength-based teaching, and mastery-based learning to enhance student mental, psychological, and academic fitness. As stated in the introduction, we strongly assert that true equity, cultural affirmation, inclusion, healing, and resilience can only be fully realized in a mastery-based school. Merely sprinkling some social-emotional work or cultural affirmation into the traditional educational model is ineffective. It is vital that all three elements of (1) mastery-based learning, (2) growth-based schooling, and (3) strength-based teaching all operate at peak efficiency—hence the flywheel metaphor that once in motion it can power itself. This is the way schools can become places where not only students but families go for connection, guidance, wisdom, and healing in addition to mastering vital skills and standards that will be necessary for their full participation and success in the world beyond school.

By themselves, mastery-based learning, growth-based schooling, or strength-based teaching are insufficient to shift the existing educational paradigm. Their combined force in a comprehensive system, however, can present a clear, new model of schooling that is ultimately transformational. Until we create schools that actively focus on the overall health of the brains, bodies, and psyches of the humans in the building, the quality of the curriculum, instruction, and assessments is irrelevant. Thus, there is a critical responsibility for educators and other stakeholders to adjust their orientation *away* from only delivering curriculum, providing instruction, and maintaining traditional grading systems and *toward* growing within a humanized educational model that recognizes individuality. Fitness in the realms of academics, mentality, and psychology is a collective concern. The consequences of leaving these issues unaddressed are profound and far reaching, impacting various aspects of an individual's life and society's collective well-being. Let us not risk squandering the potential of an entire generation and undermining the future prosperity of society as a whole.

In the following sections, we explore the practical strategies to implement the school fitness flywheel framework, the critical leadership qualities necessary to shift the educational paradigm, and ideas on how to monitor progress.

Implementation

The paradigm shift to an updated model of schooling calls for an enormous amount of cognitive energy from a vast array of stakeholders and requires great collaboration to evolve from the traditional, industrialized system of schooling most of us endured. The burden must not fall solely on the shoulders of schools; instead, it requires comprehensive partnerships that leverage the expertise, perspectives, and resources of multiple stakeholders. Addressing the array of challenges demands robust and strategic collaborations among schools, families, communities, healthcare experts, and legislative agencies. As a principal from St. Louis, Missouri, said, "This is truly a revolution. Unfortunately, revolutionaries usually end up dead. So, we need to embrace a revolutionary mindset, but use evolutionary practices" (A. Washington, personal communication, May, 2023).

For an array of possible steps for implementing a healing- and resilience-centered system, consult *The School Wellness Wheel* (Ruyle et al., 2022), which suggests and explains such steps in depth. In this book, we focus specifically on evolutionary practices that impact the state, province, district, school, and classroom levels of the educational system. These evolutionary practices are the first steps in building a coalition of all stakeholders and include embracing the Portrait of a Graduate model, generating a localized visual representation of the school fitness flywheel, creating learner profiles specific to every student in the classroom, and providing cohesive, coherent professional development along with sufficient planning and collaboration time for educators to bring the efforts to fruition.

Create a Portrait of a Graduate

One of the most critical tasks facing educators is the necessity of balancing a clear, comprehensive vision of high academic expectations with the flexibility to allow multiple pathways for success. A fully formed Portrait of a Graduate serves that purpose by providing broad skills goals for students and requirements for high school graduation. The earliest iterations of the Portrait of a Graduate model began with a strategic partnership between an array of educational agencies such as Battelle for Kids, CASEL, the Aurora Institute, ExcelinEd, and KnowledgeWorks (Cline, 2023). These portraits attempt to define the skills, competencies, and dispositions that a community believes students should embody and exemplify by graduation. The intention and hope is that those skills, competencies, and dispositions will directly contribute to a life of well-being, fulfillment, and economic security.

Although most Portraits of a Graduate are visual graphics for ease of understanding, the words and content are critical. Usually, students must demonstrate mastery in traditional literacies (reading, writing, speaking) as well as digital and media literacy, along with academic skills such as communication, critical thinking, creativity, and problem solving. In addition, students should demonstrate mastery of attributes that contribute to community and society such as acting responsibly, engaging effectively, and working with people while practicing empathy, collaboration, and cultural sensitivity so that they can be people of global competence, citizenship, stewardship, and service. As such, the school fitness flywheel framework relates well to a Portrait of a Graduate as both embrace students as whole people with a vast array of experiences, abilities, and challenges that inform their learning. In our experience, many districts and state agencies have created and adopted the process and customized their own Portrait of a Graduate.

As the process of creating the vision evolves, it is important for educators to identify key attributes that represent the core knowledge, skills, and dispositions that their students should possess and be able to demonstrate by graduation. These attributes must be broad enough to accommodate diverse learners, so educators must consider evolving educational priorities based on larger societal needs. These are the skills that they will directly teach and assess in schools as students will be held to proficiency or mastery of them. As such, the larger focus of assessment shifts from merely quantifying academic achievements to measuring the learner profile attributes that truly matter for long-term success. Continually developing teacher assessment literacy, as well as adopting assessment tools and practices that can capture evidence of students' growth across a wide range of skills and competencies (including critical thinking, creativity, communication, and collaboration), are important. This approach not only provides a more accurate picture of student progress but also encourages educators to prioritize meaningful learning experiences.

Figure 5.1 (page 122) is a Profile of a Graduate from North Kansas City, Missouri.

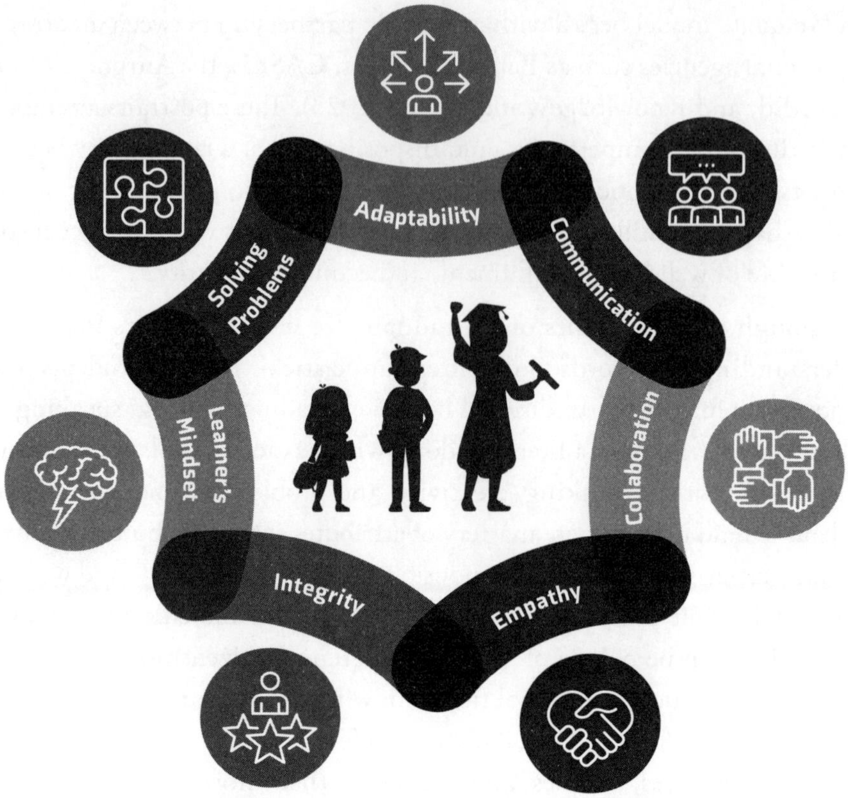

Source: © *2024 by North Kansas City High School. Adapted with permission.*

FIGURE 5.1: North Kansas City Portrait of a Graduate.

While many districts often agree that these skill sets are essential for learners, they also face challenges in operationalizing them. It can be difficult to connect universal dispositions to curricular and pedagogical goals, especially since they do not directly correlate to current methods of assessment and grading, nor are they included on standardized tests. Thus, it is important to make them actionable—and be able to ensure students are meeting them. Teachers must also be able to measure and understand student variability (cognitive and SEL) to support students with appropriate tools and pathways to reach proficiency.

A powerful way to monitor progress and assess levels of mastery is by building proficiency scales aligned to the identified skills, competencies, and dispositions. To accomplish this, each school or district should use collaborative practices common to their own specific situation. We suggest, however, that in building proficiency scales around the Portrait of a Graduate competencies, it is important to utilize the expertise of the educators who are already doing the work of using proficiency scales in practice. The following steps outline a potential process.

1. A select group of educational leaders, board members, and teachers collaborates to articulate the goal of the identified competency.

2. The same group of educational experts collaborates to identify critical vocabulary and simpler content to create the learning progression and proficiency scales in which students will demonstrate proficiency. Guiding questions for the educational team entail some iteration of the following.
    - What does this competency (such as being a critical thinker or having empathy) look like in a good citizen in the community and the world?
    - What are the important terms, knowledge, and skills we expect a citizen to master around this competency?
3. Educators invite representatives from local business groups, higher education, families, the larger educational community, and students to provide feedback. The educator group can explain the competency goal and describe the pathway. If teachers and schools have been using proficiency scales in common practice, the explanation and creation of new proficiency scales become much more straightforward.

Purposeful engagement in a process such as this provides a way to cultivate a culture of reflection and growth by encouraging students, teachers, parents, and community members to regularly examine the portrait and use it as a guide for learner growth, continuous improvement, and goal setting. By making reflection and continuous improvement parts of the school culture, school leaders can foster a sense of ownership and shared commitment to the Portrait of a Graduate. In addition, doing so provides a way for collaborative teams to focus their efforts on learning and the brain, mastery-based learning elements, and continued professional learning. Figure 5.2 (page 124) shows an example proficiency scale for students in grades 6–8 working in groups. The proficiency scale in figure 5.3 (page 124) works with the collaboration and communication components of the North Kansas City Portrait of a Graduate.

Having Portrait of a Graduate visuals like those in figures 5.1 and 5.2 posted in buildings and on websites is an important step in identifying the purpose and vision of a school system. But placing proficiency scales in the hands of the learners as well as their families is even more vital. This is one of the most critical steps a school can take in the paradigm shift to becoming a healing and resilient organization and sends the message that schools exist not simply to provide students with curriculum, but rather to grow healthy citizens that contribute to a healthy community.

4.0	**The student will:** • **Evaluate how well** the class in general works in groups and offer useful suggestions for whole-class improvement
3.5	In addition to score 3.0 performance, partial success at score 4.0 content
3.0	**WG1—The student will:** • **Help the group stay on task** (for example, working cooperatively to determine attainable goals as a group, identify tasks that each group member can complete to fulfil those stated goals, and monitor completion of each task) • **Try to understand contrary opinions expressed in the group instead of immediately rejecting them** (for example, making attempts to honestly evaluate opposing opinions by listing pros and cons for each viewpoint)
2.5	No major errors or omissions regarding score 2.0 content and partial success at score 3.0 content
2.0	**WG1—The student will:** • **Explain the characteristics of helping the group stay on task** (for example, describing the different tactics group members can use to stay on task, such as any group member courteously reminding others when a discussion goes off topic) • **Understand the characteristics of trying to evaluate contrary opinions** (for example, describing what it looks like to consider contrary opinions, such as by evaluating the strengths and weaknesses of each opinion)
1.5	Partial success at score 2.0 content and major errors or omissions regarding score 3.0 content
1.0	With help, partial success at score 2.0 content and score 3.0 content
0.5	With help, partial success at score 2.0 content but not at score 3.0 content
0.0	Even with help, no success

Source: © 2016 by Julia A. Simms. Adapted with permission.

FIGURE 5.2: Working in groups, grades 6–8 life skills.

4.0	**The student will:** • **Analyze the positive effect on their learning when they work in groups and the negative effect on their learning when they do not**
3.5	In addition to score 3.0 performance, partial success at score 4.0 content
3.0	**WG1—The student will:** • **Take on a role—recorder, information gatherer, information synthesizer, and so on—that furthers the efforts of the group even though they might prefer a different role** (for example, volunteering for a role no one else wants) • **Help to solve group problems and reconcile differences among group members** (for example, creating a positive environment by suggesting rules that encourage group members to respect each other, such as by identifying inappropriate behaviors that would inhibit a cooperative environment and offering procedures to courteously address the behaviors)
2.5	No major errors or omissions regarding score 2.0 content and partial success at score 3.0 content
2.0	**WG1—The student will:** • **Be aware of the roles within a group and their various functions** (for example, describing the specific functions of each role within a group) • **Understand the characteristics of trying to reconcile differences among group members** (for example, describing different tactics that group members can use to reconcile differences of opinion, such as finding commonalities between seemingly conflicting ideas)

1.5	Partial success at score 2.0 content and major errors or omissions regarding score 3.0 content
1.0	With help, partial success at score 2.0 content and score 3.0 content
0.5	With help, partial success at score 2.0 content but not at score 3.0 content
0.0	Even with help, no success

Source: © 2016 by Julia A. Simms. Adapted with permission.

FIGURE 5.3: Working in groups, grades 9–12 life skills.

Create a Version of the School Fitness Flywheel

Once the Portrait of a Graduate is complete, customizing a visual of the school fitness flywheel utilizing a school's specific and common language is appropriate and necessary. This visual can provide a clear, comprehensive vision of the way a school or district will carry out its mission of fulfilling the vision embodied in the original portrait. Different schools will utilize different, more localized language or terms to communicate their mission, goals, values, and vision. For example, in our experience, some schools have adopted the term *standards-based learning* to describe the educational philosophy they have adopted. In other schools, those words have a negative connotation and they can more easily adopt a term such as *personalized, competency-based education* or *mastery-based education*. The important element is that whatever terms the school adopts should be clearly articulated and defined in the visual.

This critical step helps all stakeholders make more sense of the overarching framework and provides clear direction for all collaborative teams, professional development, and progress reporting. Linking the larger Portrait of a Graduate with a school's vision of the school fitness flywheel helps clarify for all stakeholders what is occurring with the evolving school. Figures 5.4 (page 126), 5.5 (page 127), and 5.6 (page 128) show examples of customized school fitness flywheels.

In all three cases, the overwhelming feedback from leaders who led the process was that the visual made all the district or school initiatives clearer and more understandable.

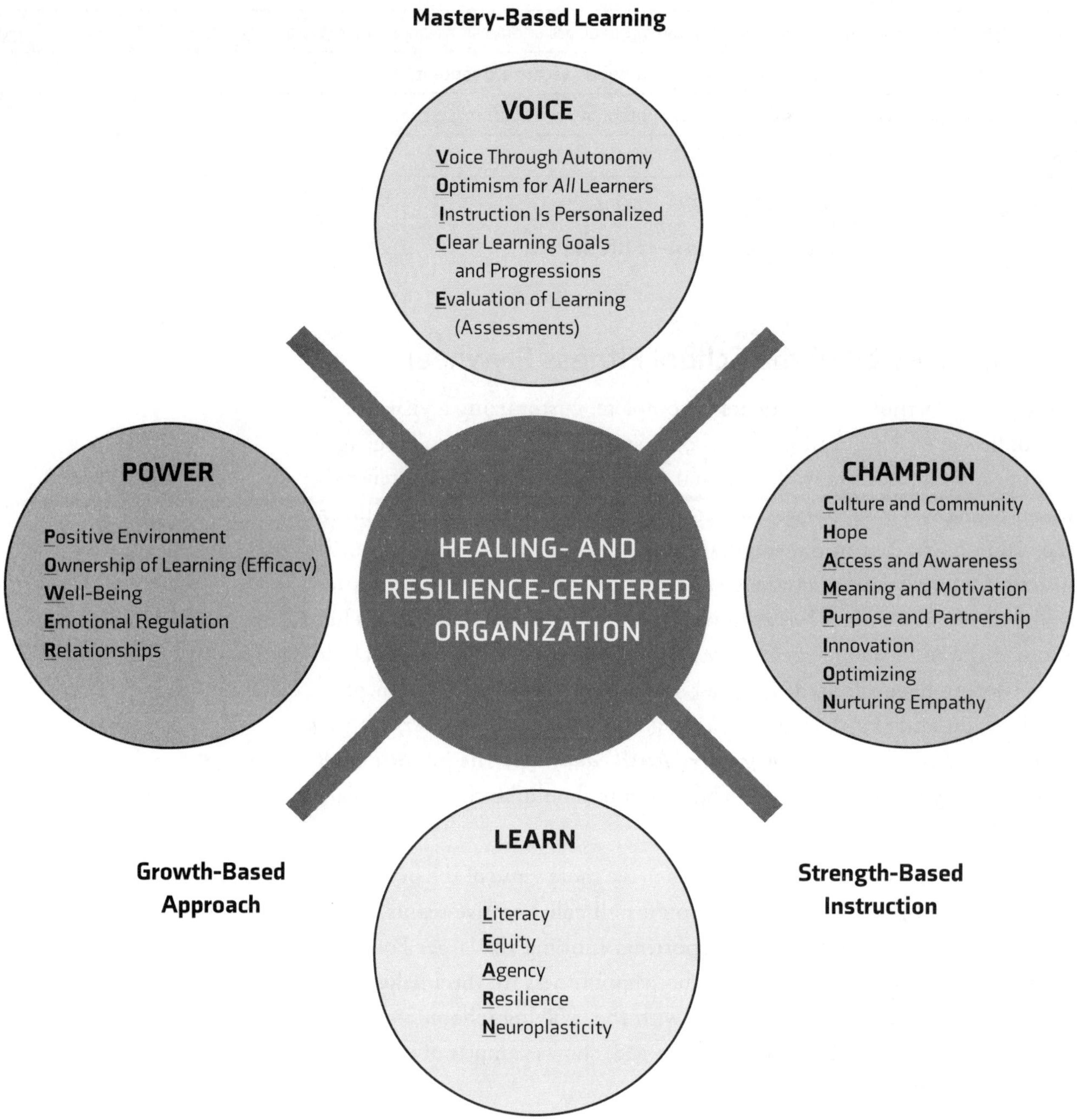

Source: © *2024 by Little Rock School District, Little Rock, Arkansas. Adapted with permission.*

FIGURE 5.4: Example one of customized school fitness flywheel.

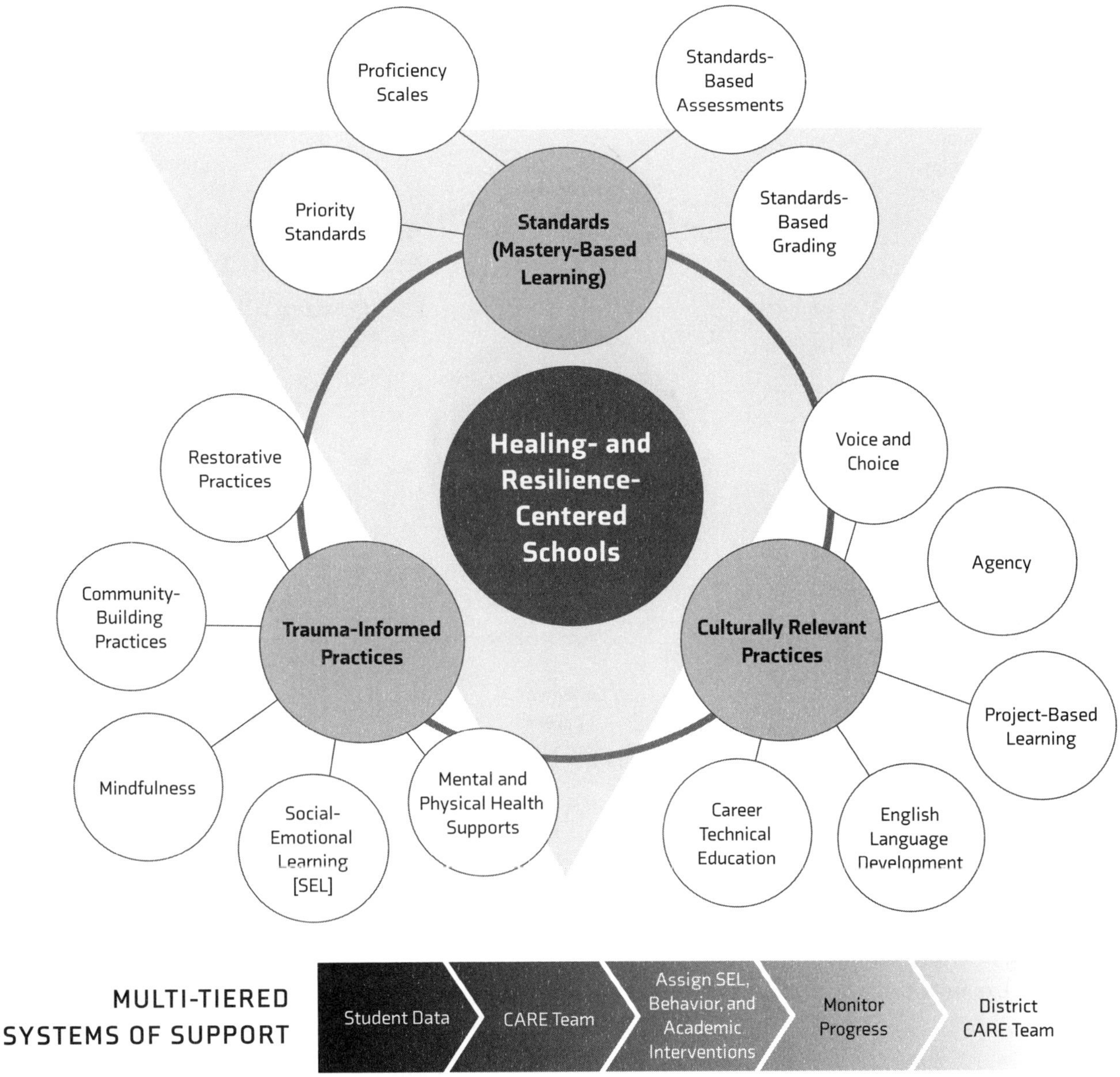

Source: © 2024 *by Antioch School District, Antioch, California. Adapted with permission.*

FIGURE 5.5: Example two of customized school fitness flywheel.

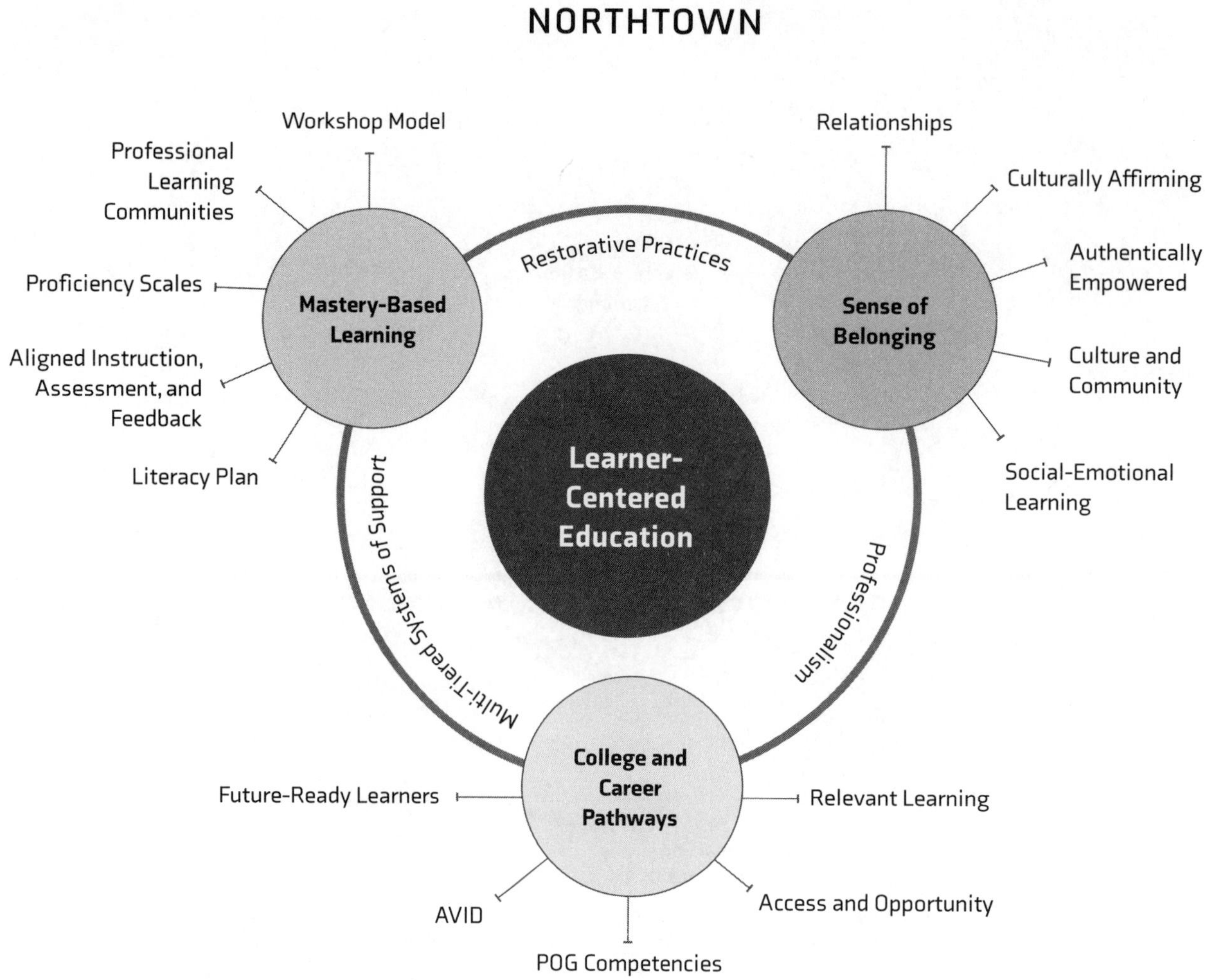

Source: © 2024 by Northtown High School, Kansas City, Missouri. Adapted with permission.

FIGURE 5.6: Example three of customized school fitness flywheel.

Build Learner Profiles

After a district or school has established an overarching Portrait of a Graduate and created a visual of the school fitness flywheel based on the community's accepted language, it is important to become more granular. A *learner profile* is a comprehensive and holistic representation of a student's individual development, addressing each human's three core parts—(1) cognitive, (2) academic, and (3) social-emotional—with which the flywheel aligns.

Learner profiles can help students and teachers consider who they are as learners, their strengths, their interests, their passions, and the ways that they might struggle or need support. By creating learner profiles, schools can align their practices with a shared vision of success for every student. Moreover, these profiles provide valuable insights into each student's unique strengths, challenges, and aspirations, helping educators to tailor their approach and ensure that every learner reaches their full potential. Profiles should do the following.

- Delve deeper than simply uncovering students' interests.
- Determine why students have those interests.
- Determine how their experiences have shaped who they are and what new experiences could shape who they might become.
- Go beyond student self-perception to include objective and third-party insights into students' capacities.

When teachers have a solid understanding of the learners in their classroom, they can design instruction and materials that are more engaging and within a student's zone of proximal development. In turn, learners develop their own agency because they become increasingly aware of their own strengths, how they learn best, and what they need to do to succeed. In this sense, teachers can incorporate mastery-based learning as well as growth-based schooling and strength-based teaching into their regular classroom practice; thus, they enhance academic, psychological, and mental fitness for their learners.

Building learner profiles is the next critical step in evolving educational programs into mental, psychological, and academic fitness-centered schools. As a school administrator from Arkansas said:

> I would compare the value of a learner profile to going to the eye doctor. You go in because everything is fuzzy. Sure, you can see but it's all fuzzy. And then the doctor puts on those lenses: Is it 1 or 2, 1 or 2, 1 or 2? And then, "Boom, it's all clear." It's like that with a learner profile. You wonder about your kids and then you get the learner profile and it's like putting on the perfect pair of glasses. "Boom, it's all clear." Seriously folks, this is game changing. (Crystal B., personal communication, April, 2021)

It is not only adult educators who struggle to see a bigger picture. Students notoriously miscalculate their actual strengths and needs, a phenomenon known as the Dunning Kruger effect (Kruger & Dunning, 1999; Murphy, 2017). The best learner profiles become a tool for self-awareness and self-reflection so students develop a better understanding of the effort required to meet their goals and make the best choices to achieve them.

The following resources can help guide teams as they create learner profiles.

- Developing Learner Profiles (https://tinyurl.com/2awa2jwn)
- Personalized Learning Plan for Success (https://tinyurl.com/5n7d9tbd)

Educators can easily compile academic data by generating grade reports from assignments and assessments. They can gather behavior data through disciplinary data or metacognitive proficiency scales. As an example, *The Critical Concepts* (Marzano Resources, n.d.) provides metacognitive learning goals that can help identify where students currently are in their progression toward mastery in an array of soft skills. Figure 5.7 lists sample critical concepts in proficiency scale form.

4.0	**The student will:** • Provide rudimentary self-evaluations of how well they participate in class
3.5	In addition to score 3.0 performance, partial success at score 4.0 content
3.0	**P1—The student will:** • **Attempt to answer direct questions asked by the teacher** (for example, trying to answer a question when called on by the teacher) • **Wait for an appropriate amount of time to ask a question or make a comment** (for example, waiting to ask a question, raising a hand, and not speaking until called on by the teacher)
2.5	No major errors or omissions regarding score 2.0 content and partial success at score 3.0 content
2.0	**P1—The student will:** • **Explain how answering direct questions asked by the teacher might be helpful to the teacher and other students** (for example, explaining that answering direct questions can help the teacher determine what a student knows) • **Explain how raising a hand when wishing to ask a question or make a comment is helpful to the teacher and other students** (for example, explaining that raising a hand can help the teacher pick different students so that each question is answered in turn)
1.5	Partial success at score 2.0 content and major errors or omissions regarding score 3.0 content
1.0	With help, partial success at score 2.0 content and score 3.0 content
0.5	With help, partial success at score 2.0 content but not at score 3.0 content
0.0	Even with help, no success

Source: © 2016 by Julia A. Simms. Adapted with permission.

FIGURE 5.7: Proficiency scale for metacognitive learning.

Other surveys from reliable sources are available; recommended examples follow.

- OECD Survey on Social and Emotional Skills
- Panorama Social-Emotional Learning Questionnaire Measures
- Student Survey: How I Feel About My Classroom and School

Surveys such as these enable students to rate their feelings and emotional reactions, which in turn helps educators see trends over time in cohorts. That helps focus efforts.

Cognitive screeners can simultaneously identify student strengths and needs across the neurological domains that drive learning success: complex reasoning, memory, executive functioning, and processing. An array of screening tools is becoming more common, largely due to the recognition that emotions, culture, and cognition are all inextricably linked. Some of the available tools follow.

- Cognifit (www.cognifit.com/school-test)
- MindPrint (https://mindprintlearning.com)
- National Center for Education Statistics (https://nces.ed.gov/ecls/assessments2011.asp)
- Pearson Assessments (http://tinyurl.com/49jjc9kx)
- Psychological Assessment Resources (www.parinc.com/Products/intelligence-cognitive)

The best cognitive assessments go beyond numerical scoring on individual cognitive skills and integrate academic, mental, and psychological skills data to provide a comprehensive view of the whole person. They provide insight into *why* students might be struggling academically or behaviorally and thus make it easier to identify the most effective pathways for success. Whole-person insights such as this can deepen teacher empathy for a student's learning challenges and increase their interest in personalizing and differentiating a student's instruction and assessment.

While these objective data can be incredibly valuable to teachers in identifying who needs supports and why, *it is important that these results are used to empower every student.* All learners have variability, and everyone experiences learning challenges at times (Rose, 2016). As an example, a MindPrint Profile provides a corresponding student version of the profile, without any numerical scores. Removing the numerical scoring changes the focus from the test performance to the metacognitive process of why they enjoy some learning tasks while others feel much harder. Allowing students to comfortably reflect on relative strengths and needs creates an environment where students can celebrate their successes while also being more open to discussing their challenges and the reasons for them. Such environments also encourage students to problem solve and identify pathways and strategies that will help them succeed.

Once students have a learner profile and can understand where they are in a progression of learning, teachers can better identify specific strategies to meet individual student needs. The clarity of outcomes and goals provided by learner profiles can promote individual flexibility and creativity. When students, educators, and parents have a clear understanding of the desired outcomes, they can more effectively tailor their efforts to support the unique needs and aspirations of each learner. A well-defined learner profile offers a road map for success, allowing stakeholders to take creative approaches and make informed decisions in achieving the established goals. By fostering a shared understanding of what success looks like, learner profiles ultimately empower students and educators to be more flexible, adaptive, and innovative in their pursuit of excellence.

Provide Cohesive, Coherent Professional Learning Planning and Collaboration

In our experience, once schools have adopted their specific version of the school fitness flywheel, all their initiatives, professional learning needs, and collaborative efforts become clear. Ultimately, by providing educators insights on the diverse, complex developmental pathways through which students develop, engage, and learn, the school fitness flywheel can help align schools and instructional design with students' individual capacities and needs. Thus, continued learning for educators on neurophysiology is vital as they take on a new role in the future. Deepening professional development in brain development along with continued discussion and practice via collaboration, walkthroughs, and instructional coaching are nonnegotiable elements for evolving and growing as teachers.

Equity and cultural affirmation in a mastery-based learning model also require ongoing professional development for teachers. Educators should receive training on cultural competency, anti-bias practices, and strategies for creating inclusive classrooms. By continuously expanding their knowledge and understanding of different cultures, teachers can better support and engage students from diverse backgrounds, ensuring that no student is left behind.

Cloverdale Middle School in Little Rock, Arkansas, engaged in extensive and focused professional development around understanding the science of learning. Some of the testimonials from teachers follow:

> "I get it now. Yes, some of my students need 'glasses.' They will all be able to see, but they will need different prescriptions." —Middle school English language arts teacher
>
> "I will use this information to plan and implement instruction and assignments. I have all I need to get started." —Middle school mathematics teacher

Implementing a healing- and resilience-centered education starting from the state, province, or district level (via Portrait of a Graduate) to the school level (via the school fitness flywheel) to the individual classroom (via learner profile creation) is a big job. But all three parts are necessary to transform education on a systemic level. Once schools have addressed and adopted those three areas, they can much more effectively drive and measure continued growth in the new paradigm.

Leadership

Nothing in education will ever effectively evolve—especially a massive paradigm shift such as moving to a more humanized model of schooling—unless it is led well, with focus, commitment, and energy. Teachers in the classroom do the heavy lifting every day with the learners. But equally important is the effort of the leadership to help raise the model with the teachers, families, and larger community.

School leaders who have successfully shifted to a new model of schooling are fully aware of the anxiety, frustration, fear, and pushback that are all part of the discussion. It's critical for leaders to never take those challenges personally because they should anticipate the issues arising. There are a wide range of difficulties that are part of bringing updated knowledge and research. Change is hard for people because it's uncomfortable.

Figure 5.8 identifies some specific actions that are important for leadership teams to consider during the change process, especially in the early stages.

- ☐ Building and communicating a collective reason for all components of academic, mental, and psychological fitness-centered schooling
- ☐ Ensuring a common focus on achieving a shared vision for mastery-based learning and academic, mental, and psychological fitness-centered schooling
- ☐ Creating a common language and framework in the school and community
- ☐ Helping teachers increase learner agency, as well as voice and choice in their daily practice in all classrooms
- ☐ Leveraging professional and community partnerships and technologies that align with personalized learning and mental, psychological, and academic-centered education
- ☐ Growing access to personalized learning experiences from a few classrooms to all learners
- ☐ Communicating and ensuring sustainable, equitable change

FIGURE 5.8: Leadership teams actions.

Visit ***MarzanoResources.com/reproducibles*** *for a free reproducible version of this figure.*

Finally, the following traits and actions are pivotal to shifting to mastery-based teaching, growth-based schooling, and strength-based teaching.

- New leader development
- Transformational instructional leadership
- Ethical leadership
- Mindful leadership
- Extreme ownership

New Leader Development

One of the most important tasks for a leader implementing change is identifying and cultivating their replacements or the people who will carry the load to ensure that growth is sustainable and the organization can continue to evolve. In our experience, leaders who can successfully engage in school evolution—especially those who are able to successfully implement mastery-based learning mindsets in schools—are often called on to replicate their efforts elsewhere or are moved into higher level organizational roles to empower more people to follow and engage with the vision. Thus, cultivating successors is a critical element for leaders to embrace.

In addition, sharing leadership responsibilities during the change process is important for leaders to be able to maintain their mental and emotional health by not carrying the mantle of leadership by themselves. Furthermore, cultivating future leaders is a way for educators to continually model lifelong learning and helps them engage with the research and new learning at a deeper, more profound level. Building a leadership team of people pulling in the same direction can come from teachers, instructional coaches, and other administrators. Also, collaborating with other school leadership teams on the same journey is a refreshing and empowering way to keep the momentum during the challenging times and mounting obstacles inherent in the change process.

Transformational Instructional Leadership

Great teachers are essential, but great principals are necessary to help guide, grow, and advocate for the teachers in the building. If we are asking and expecting teachers to grow their practices to truly be experts in learning rather than be simply people who deliver content, we need to provide them with goals, learning progressions, and feedback to improve. Our leaders must model for teachers what needs to happen in the classrooms. Consider the four leadership qualities that Jason Grissom, Anna Egalite, & Constance Lindsay (2021, as cited in Gold, 2024) suggested produce transformative school outcomes:

> **Engaging in instructionally focused interactions** with teachers, including structured classroom observations with specific, actionable feedback and professional learning opportunities aligned with school goals.
>
> **Building a productive climate** through empowering teachers, providing teachers with autonomy and being engaged with the local community.
>
> **Facilitating collaboration and professional learning communities** by leading effective data use and creating explicit protocols and time for collaboration.
>
> **Managing personnel and resources strategically**, including protecting teacher time and scheduling for common planning time.

Clearly, professional learning, focused feedback, data-based assessment, and collaboration are foundational to helping teachers employ updated practices to evolve their classrooms. Simply delegating responsibilities to teachers or teams under the guise of shared leadership rather than leading the paradigm shift is no longer acceptable. Leaders who want to successfully adopt the school fitness flywheel as their instructional model are educational visionaries who must offer expertise and guidance to staff. They serve as teachers to the teachers, and they also recognize that every adult in the building can serve as a teacher to young people. As such, professional development includes support staff as well.

As a middle school teacher from California stated when speaking about her principal:

> There is a lot of front-end loading with this. We need to identify the goals, communicate the scales, and change the purpose of grading. It's exhausting — but my life is so much easier now. I was going to leave teaching, but now I love my job. There is such a different energy and culture now. If my principal left and we went back to the old way, I'd retire instantly. (J. Courtney, personal communication, March, 2022)

This leads to ethical leadership.

Ethical Leadership

Modern school leaders carry the tremendous ethical responsibility to lead courageously and evolve traditional educational paradigms into more potent, relevant models. Transforming school systems requires leaders who are deeply committed and possess the skill, will, energy, and expertise to rectify inadequacies within the existing system. Thus, continuing to remain informed, engaged, and connected with evolutionary colleagues is the best way to nurture the ethical leadership that is nonnegotiable and necessary to build the momentum until the flywheel effect can come to fruition. To help accomplish this and keep stakeholders' eyes on the prize, ethical leaders constantly deepen their knowledge and commitment through reading, collaboration, and professional social networking. They also reach out to leading innovative school districts to learn from educators on the same journey—almost in a clinical model—to grow intellectually as well as in practice.

Mindful Leadership

School leaders are trying to evolve systems in an era where many people are experiencing increased stress levels due to the massive foundational, social, and economic shifts brought about by what Thomas Friedman (2016) has proclaimed *the age of accelerations.* As the respected educational thinker Sir Ken Robinson (2001) stated near the turn of the century:

> There are forces at work now for which there are no precedents. . . . New technologies are revolutionizing the nature of work everywhere. . . . What is certain is that in the next 50 to 100 years, our children will need to confront challenges that are unique in human history. (pp. 5–6)

This level of stress, anxiety, and general unrest impacts people in all segments of society, and in schools it has manifested in a variety of behavioral and academic challenges (Weinstein & Tsai, 2023). The onslaught of interruptions, stress, violence, staff shortages, and resultant increased anxiety, and the disruption of an entire educational structure create an environment that can push leaders over the edge. Thus, just as leaders need to attend to the mental fitness of their students and teachers, it is critical that leaders also lead and exemplify this quality in themselves. A quieter mind enables a school leader to purposefully direct attention for the benefit of all. In terms of practical ways to strengthen their internal capacity for mindfulness, leaders can consciously engage in deepening their knowledge and enhancing their personal practice through mindfulness practices like those mentioned in chapter 3 (page 59).

When mindful leaders are aware of their own thoughts, actions, emotions, and expressions, they can help create a more positive environment in the larger school setting; they have improved metacognitive and self-awareness skills, which improves decision making (Future Education Magazine, n.d.). Just as teachers can co-regulate the students in their classrooms, so can school leaders co-regulate with those around them to cultivate a culture of healing and resilience. Simply, leaders can influence positive emotional states in staff and students. If leaders can learn to communicate in ways that inspire and motivate others, it is likely followers will mimic those positive emotions (Grissom et al., 2021).

An elementary teacher from Iowa spoke about her principal being always present:

> We are willing and encouraged to try anything—whatever could work—and we have no fear of failure or change. But leadership is not just flying by the seat of their pants. It's all research based and solid with data. Our principal isn't afraid of offending people. She'll call it like it is and work to keep us focused on the main thing. You can't have second-order change without risk and focus. But she makes sure we are all in a good and strong place emotionally and physically to take on the work. And we now do mindfulness practices before every meeting, which is a great strategy to bring us all together and get us on the same page. (V. Coleen, personal communication, February, 2023)

A useful resources that provides a focused plan is *Mindfulness First: A Nine-Week Leadership Plan for Supporting Yourself and Your School* (Iberlin, 2023).

Extreme Ownership

The final trait that is fundamental for leaders to exhibit in shifting a school to a healing- and resilience-centered model is extreme ownership. This construct entails cultivating the internal choice to move ahead boldly and assume personal responsibility for the success or failure of the school mission. The brainchild of former Navy SEALs and cofounders of Echelon Front Jocko Willink and Leif Babin (2015), *extreme ownership* asserts that leadership is the single most important factor in whether any worthwhile endeavor flourishes or fades.

The educational leader must be a true believer in the mission of creating a healing- and resilience-centered organization that can nurture the mental, academic, and psychological fitness of all stakeholders. Leaders must continually assess how they lead and what they can control and improve. They must acknowledge and assert that their school's performance needs to improve, and they don't blame, make excuses, or wait for others to come in and fix the problems. Rather, they own the situation and they psychologically invest in a plan to own the solution. For example, rather than asking, "Why is attendance so bad and retention so low?" they own the situation and ask, "What will I do to improve the school so that students and teachers want to come to school?"

A high school teacher from Arkansas spoke to his principal's level of commitment:

> Our principal was the driving force behind this [change] in the beginning. She had to work with the teachers and the kids and downtown. Everyone by herself. Now though, we are all on the same team and are the driving force ourselves. It's all of us now and we are leaping higher every month. But she needed to lead us in the beginning and during the tough times. It takes courage and energy—and not many people have that! This is the first time I've had an administrator willing to learn new stuff with us and make sure every teacher is able to get the job done. (J. Clope, personal communication, September, 2022)

The crucial traits of extreme ownership, along with instructional, ethical, and mindful leadership, are about leaders making the personal choice to do the work.

Tools to Monitor Progress

The last step to ensure effective implementation of a school focused on healing and resilience is monitoring its own progress toward mastery. Educators can accomplish this by creating proficiency scales aligned to implementation goals and gathering evidence. Just as teachers would use a proficiency scale in the classroom to provide the pathway to mastery, teachers should have the same tool to guide their own learning.

One school personalized the "Professional Development in Mastery-Based Learning: Proficiency Scale" (page 57) and created the version in figure 5.9 using language specific to their culture, location, and individual dynamic. Level 2 of the scale in figure 5.9, being skilled at using the proficiency scales necessary in mastery-based learning, identifies some critical vocabulary as well as the simpler skills and knowledge teachers will need to progress toward mastery. Level 3 of the scale is articulated via three high-level skills.

1. Teachers use learning goals and proficiency scales in their daily practice.
2. Teachers deepen and evolve their assessment practices to provide valid and reliable feedback for student growth.
3. Teachers are fluent in the language of mastery-based learning and can discuss it with a variety of people in any setting.

In any case, springboarding off a vision as articulated in the preceding proficiency scale provides clarity and direction for schools to focus their efforts. Schools can engage in a process by themselves if they have a clear vision of how to implement a healing- and resilience-centered school framework along with tools to monitor progress.

I can systematically design and integrate curriculum, instruction, assessment, and feedback in alignment with proficiency scales.	
4.0	I can: ☐ Empower students to self-monitor their learning needs based on the data from proficiency scales and assessments ☐ Create and utilize an array of proficiency scales in all courses at all levels ☐ Capture and collect various pieces of evidence of mastery from all learners ☐ Empower students to provide evidence to show their personal growth or further need for enrichment
3.5	I can independently meet the learning target and demonstrate in-depth applications beyond what was taught with partial success.
3.0	I can systematically design and integrate curriculum, instruction, assessment, and feedback in alignment with proficiency scales by: ☐ Integrating learning goals and proficiency scales in my daily classroom practice ☐ Creating lessons and activities directly aligned with proficiency scales and explicitly teaching each indicator at level 2 and 3 of the scale ☐ Creating valid and reliable assessments aligned with proficiency scales ☐ Creating proficiency scales for constructive student feedback and making them available to both students and parents
2.5	I can demonstrate partial understanding of most concepts and the skills of the level 3 content.

FIGURE 5.9: Customized mastery-based learning proficiency scale.

continued →

2.0	I can use **learning goals and proficiency scales** in my classroom practice by: ☐ Identifying the difference between an activity and a learning outcome ☐ Recognizing or recalling specific mastery-based learning vocabulary (such as *aligned assessments, collaborative teams*, *learning targets*, *priority standard*, and *proficiency scale*) ☐ Describing the structure of a proficiency scale ☐ Explaining that standards are designed to provide a pathway to learning in our classrooms I can use proficiency scales to plan for **instruction** by: ☐ Comparing scales and rubrics ☐ Clarifying learning goals that state what students will know or be able to do at the end of the lesson or unit ☐ Using proficiency scales as the basis of instruction ☐ Describing how professional learning teams can operationalize mastery-based learning in every classroom I can clarify how having **valid and reliable assessments** aligned with proficiency scales influences students' learning by: ☐ Describing why a proficiency scale provides for an accurate picture of student learning performance ☐ Explaining how gathering more evidence can provide a more reliable understanding of students' learning ☐ Using assessments directly aligned to the scale I can use proficiency scales that provide **constructive feedback** to students by: ☐ Centering student feedback around the criteria of the proficiency scale ☐ Aligning comments with specific scale indicators, highlighting their strength and areas for growth, and tracking their progress toward mastery ☐ Communicating clear proficiency scales that help students understand the progression of knowledge they are expected to master ☐ Using student-friendly scales and getting them into the hands of learners
1.5	I can demonstrate partial knowledge of level 2.0 content.
1.0	With help, I can demonstrate partial understanding of some of the simpler details and processes.
0.0	There is no evidence of learning. Even with help, no understanding or skill demonstrated.

Source: © 2024 by Dr. Marian G. Lacey K-8 Academy. Adapted with permission.

Summary

By themselves, any one of the three keys to the school fitness flywheel are insufficient to shift the educational paradigm. Combined, however, they are a new education model. That kind of transformation requires comprehensive partnerships that leverage the expertise, perspectives, and resources of multiple stakeholders. With those stakeholders, a district can create clear, comprehensive expectations in a Portrait of a Graduate and a customized school fitness flywheel that incorporates each school's intentions visually. Learner profiles allow educators to get more granular with comprehensive, holistic student development in three parts—(1) cognitive, (2) academic, and

(3) social-emotional; attending to educators' professional learning helps fill gaps once these goals are outlined. All this, of course, requires ethical, mindful leadership the kind of which that takes radical ownership.

We advise these three next steps as most important from this chapter for school leaders.

1. Identify a Portrait of a Graduate as adopted by your state, province, or other agency and consider how to adapt it based on local language and norms (for district- or building-level implementation).
2. Create a team of innovators to engage with the concepts behind healing- and resilience-centered schools who can then begin building a visual representation to drive all school efforts moving forward (for district- or school-level implementation).
3. Identify possible learner profiles to identify student strengths and weaknesses to be better able to help students demonstrate mastery of identified academic and citizenship standards (for classroom-level implementation).

We advise these three next steps as most important from this chapter for teachers and other classroom staff.

1. Examine how your course- or grade-level curricula fit with the Portrait of a Graduate.
2. Consider the visual school fitness flywheel representation to deeply understand how all school initiatives fit together and determine specific areas where you can immediately engage.
3. Discuss with colleagues how you could use a learner profile to help guide students on their paths to mastery.

Epilogue

Addressing the array of challenges facing society and the people in it demands robust, strategic collaborations between schools, families, communities, healthcare experts, and legislative agencies. In addition, tackling school evolution to humanize the experience requires a multidimensional approach that encompasses the growth-based schooling, strength-based teaching, and mastery-based learning that are necessary for cultivating academic, mental, and psychological fitness.

Through collaborative efforts, schools and communities can build a culture within this robust framework that prioritizes mental health, ensures equitable access to services, and supports the holistic development of students.

It takes committed administrators and teachers to accomplish this evolution. For true well being, strong school-community-business partnerships create an ecosystem of support that nurtures the *whole* well-being of *all* students. The school fitness flywheel combines knowledge and capacities of educational institutions, mental health professionals, community organizations, and families that can build a comprehensive support network to effectively addresses students' mental, emotional, and physical needs. This is the right work and will empower teachers and administrators to embrace the reason they, hopefully, entered the field to begin with: to help build stronger, healthier communities by growing stronger, healthier young people.

References and Resources

Abelson, S., Lipson, S. K., & Eisenberg, D. (2022). Mental health in college populations: A multidisciplinary review of what works, evidence gaps, and paths forward. In L. W. Perna (Ed.), *Higher education: Handbook of theory and research* (Vol. 37, pp. 133–238). New York: Springer.

Abrams, Z. (2023). *Teaching social-emotional learning is under attack.* Accessed at www.apa.org/monitor/2023/09/social-emotional-learning-under-fire on March 11, 2024.

Acevedo-Vigo, M. (2022, January 27). *School start times and the impact on teen mental health.* Accessed at https://stnonline.com/news/school-start-times-and-the-impact-on-teen-mental-health on March 16, 2024.

Ackerman, C. E. (2018). *Self determination theory and how it explains motivation.* Accessed at https://positivepsychology.com/self-determination-theory on June 3, 3024.

Ahrnsbrak, R., Bose, J., Hedden, S. L., Lipari, R. N., & Park-Lee, E. (2017, September). *Key substance use and mental health indicators in the United States: Results from the 2016 National Survey on Drug Use and Health.* Rockville, MD: Author. Accessed at www.samhsa.gov/data/sites/default/files/NSDUH-FFR1-2016/NSDUH-FFR1-2016.htm on January 13, 2023.

Allen, A., Scott, L. M., & Lewis, C. W. (2013). Racial microaggressions and African American and Hispanic students in urban schools: A call for culturally affirming education. *Interdisciplinary Journal of Teaching and Learning, 3*(2), 117–129.

Altman, D. (2016). *101 mindful ways to build resilience: Cultivate calm, clarity, optimism and happiness each day.* Eau Claire, WI: PESI.

American Academy of Pediatrics. (n.d.). *AAP-AACAP-CHA declaration of a national emergency in child and adolescent mental health.* Accessed at www.aap.org/en/advocacy/child-and-adolescent-healthy-mental-development/aap-aacap-cha-declaration-of-a-national-emergency-in-child-and-adolescent-mental-health on February 12, 2024.

American Psychiatric Association. (2013). *Diagnostic and statistical manual of mental disorders* (5th ed.). Washington, DC: Author.

American Psychological Association. (n.d.). *Teaching tip sheet: Self-efficacy.* Accessed at www.apa.org/pi/aids/resources/education/self-efficacy on February 16, 2024.

Andersen, S. C., & Nielsen, H. S. (2016). Reading intervention with a growth mindset approach improves children's skills. *PNAS, 113*(43), 12111–12113.

Annie E. Casey Foundation. (n.d.). *Grade-level reading.* Accessed at www.aecf.org /topics/grade-level-reading on March 14, 2024.

Arhin, D., & Opoku, W. B. (2020). A meta-analysis on effects of mastery learning strategy (MLS) on academic achievements of learners. *International Journal of Research and Innovation in Social Science, 5*(7), 102–106.

Aspen Institute. (n.d.). *From a nation at risk to a nation at hope: Recommendations from the National Commission on Social, Emotional, and Academic Development.* Washington, DC: Author. Accessed at https://files.eric.ed.gov /fulltext/ED606337.pdf on January 23, 2024.

Australian Psychological Society. (2022). *Position statement: Psychologists in schools.* Accessed at https://psychology.org.au/getmedia/3478fa00-0a90-43ff-8d90 -99a42ea53981/22aps-ps-psysch-p1.pdftarget= on June 2, 2204.

Avallone, A. (2022). *An educator's guide to learner profiles for students.* Accessed at www.nextgenlearning.org/articles/getting-to-know-you-learner-profiles-for -personalization on January 23, 2024.

Awachíikaate (Cummins, J. D.), & Chang, E. (2020). Safe zones, dangerous leadership: Decolonial leadership in settler-colonial school contexts. *Journal of School Leadership, 30*(6), 519–540. https://doi.org/10.1177/1052684620 951723

Bai, B., & Wang, J. (2023). The role of growth mindset, self-efficacy and intrinsic value in self-regulated learning and English language learning achievements. *Language Teaching Research, 27*(1), 207–228.

Bandura, A. (1977). Self-efficacy: Toward a unifying theory of behavioral change. *Psychological Review, 84*(2), 191–215.

Bandura, A. (1986). *Social foundations of thought and action: A social cognitive theory.* Hoboken, NJ: Prentice Hall.

Bandura, A. (1990). Perceived self-efficacy in the exercise of personal agency. *Journal of Applied Sport Psychology, 2*(2), 128–163.

Bandura, A. (1997). *Self-efficacy: The exercise of control.* New York: W. H. Freeman.

Bartlett, J. D., & Vivrette, R. (2020, April). *Ways to promote children's resilience to the COVID-19 pandemic.* Accessed at https://cms.childtrends.org/wp-content /uploads/2020/04/COVIDProtectiveFactors_ChildTrends_April2020.pdf on January 23, 2024.

Basile, K. C., Clayton, H. B., DeGue, S., Gilford, J. W., Vagi, K. J., Suarez, N. A., et al. (2020). Interpersonal violence victimization among high school students—Youth Risk Behavior Survey, United States, 2019. *Morbidity and Mortality Weekly Report Supplements 69*(1), 28–37.

Bastos, J. L., Harnois, C. E., & Paradies, Y. C. (2018). Health care barriers, racism, and intersectionality in Australia. *Social Science and Medicine, 199*, 209–218.

Bath, H. (2010, March). *Calming together: The pathway to self-control.* Accessed at https://cyc-net.org/cyc-online/cyconline-mar2010-bath.html on January 23, 2024.

Bauer, C. C. C., Caballero, C., Scherer, E., West, M. R., Mrazek, M. D., Phillips, D. T., et al. (2019). Mindfulness training reduces stress and amygdala reactivity to fearful faces in middle-school children. *Behavioral Neuroscience, 133*(6), 569–585.

Bavarian, N., Lewis, K. M., DuBois, D. L., Acock, A., Vuchinich, S., Silverthorn, N., et al. (2013). Using social-emotional and character development to improve academic outcomes: A matched-pair, cluster-randomized controlled trial in low-income, urban schools. *Journal of School Health, 83*(11), 771–779. https://doi.org/10.1111/josh.12093

Beers, L. S., Szilagyi, M., Seigel, W. M., Davis, W. S., Fukuda, Y., Joseph, M., et al. (2021). Immunizing against hate: Overcoming Asian American and Pacific Islander racism. *Pediatrics, 148*(1), Article e2021051836.

Belcourt, A. (2018, January 25). *The hidden health inequalities that American Indians and Alaskan Natives face.* Accessed at https://theconversation.com/the-hidden-health-inequalities-that-american-indians-and-alaskan-natives-face-89905 on February 8, 2021.

Berg, J., Osher, D., Same, M. R., Nolan, E., Benson, D., & Jacobs, N. (2017). *Identifying, defining, and measuring social and emotional competencies.* Accessed at www.air.org/sites/default/files/2021-06/Identifying-Defining-and-Measuring-Social-and-Emotional-Competencies-December-2017-rev.pdf on January 23, 2024.

Berger, K. S. (2011). *The developing person through the life span* (8th ed.). New York: Worth Publishers.

Bergstrom, A., Cleary, L. M., & Peacock, T. D. (2003). *The seventh generation: Native students speak about finding the good path.* Charleston, WV: ERIC Clearinghouse on Rural Education and Small Schools.

Berkes, F., & Ross, H. (2013). Community resilience: Toward an integrated approach. *Society and Natural Resources, 26*(1), 5–20.

Berkowitz, R., Moore, H., Astor, R. A., & Benbenishty, R. (2017). A research synthesis of the associations between socioeconomic background, inequality, school climate, and academic achievement. *Review of Educational Research, 87*(2), 425–469.

Bernert, R. A., & Joiner, T. E. (2007). Sleep disturbances and suicide risk: A review of the literature. *Neuropsychiatric Disease and Treatment, 3*(6), 735–743.

Best, J. R., Miller, P. H., & Naglieri, J. A. (2011). Relations between executive function and academic achievement from ages 5 to 17 in a large, representative national sample. *Learning and Individual Differences, 21*(4), 327–336.

Bezdek, K. G., & Telzer, E. H. (2017, December). Have no fear, the brain is here! How your brain responds to stress. *Frontiers for Young Minds, 5*, Article 71.

Bhushan, D., Kotz, K., McCall, J., Wirtz, S., Gilgoff, R., Dube, S. R., et al. (2020, December 9). *Roadmap for resilience: The California Surgeon General's report on adverse childhood experiences, toxic stress, and health.* Sacramento, CA: Office of the California Surgeon General.

Biemiller, A. (2005). Size and sequence in vocabulary development: Implications for choosing words for primary grade vocabulary instruction. In E. H. Hiebert & M. L. Kamil (Eds.), *Teaching and learning vocabulary: Bringing research to practice* (pp. 223–242). Mahwah, NJ: Lawrence Erlbaum Associates.

Biemiller, A., & Boote, C. (2006). An effective method for building meaning vocabulary in primary grades. *Journal of Educational Psychology, 98*(1), 44–62.

Biesta, G., & Tedder, M. (2007). Agency and learning in the lifecourse: Towards an ecological perspective. *Studies in the Education of Adults, 39*, 132–149.

Bill & Melinda Gates Foundation. (2014, November). *Early progress: Interim research on personalized learning.* Seattle, WA: Author. Accessed at https://usprogram.gatesfoundation.org/news-and-insights/usp-resource-center/resources/early-progress-interim-research-on-personalized-learning--report on July 2, 2024.

Bjork, R. A., & Bjork, E. L. (2020). Desirable difficulties in theory and practice. *Journal of Applied Research in Memory and Cognition*, *9*(4), 475–479.

Blachowicz, C. L. Z., & Fisher, P. (2012). Keep the "fun" in fundamental: Encouraging word consciousness and incidental word learning in the classroom through word play. In E. J. Kame'enui & J. F. Baumann (Eds.), *Vocabulary instruction: Research to practice* (2nd ed., pp. 189–209). New York: Guilford Press.

Black, D. S., & Fernando, R. (2014). Mindfulness training and classroom behavior among lower-income and ethnic minority elementary school children. *Journal of Child and Family Studies, 23*(7), 1242–1246.

Black, P., & Wiliam, D. (1998). Assessment and classroom learning. *Assessment in Education: Principles, Policy & Practice, 5*(1), 7–74.

Blackwell, L. S., Trzesniewski, K. H., & Dweck, C. S. (2007). Implicit theories of intelligence predict achievement across an adolescent transition: A longitudinal study and an intervention. *Child Development, 78*(1), 246–263.

Bloom, B. S. (1968). Learning for mastery. *Evaluation Comment, 1*(2), 1–10.

Bloom, B. S. (1971). Mastery learning. In J. H. Block (Ed.), *Mastery learning: Theory and practice* (pp. 47–63). New York: Holt, Rinehart and Winston.

Bloom, B. S. (1977). Favorable learning conditions for all. *Teacher, 95*(3), 22–28.

Bloom, B. S. (Ed.). (1984). *Taxonomy of educational objectives: Book 1—Cognitive domain* (2nd ed.). Boston: Addison Wesley Longman. (Original work published 1956)

Bloom, S. L. (2020). Creating healthy biocratic organizations. In K. R. Ginsburg & Z. B. R. McClain (Eds.), *Reaching teens: Strength-based, trauma-sensitive, resilience-building communication strategies rooted in positive youth development* (2nd ed., pp. 800–816). Itasca, IL: American Academy of Pediatrics.

Bloom, S. L., & Farragher, B. (2013a). *Destroying sanctuary: The crisis in human service delivery systems.* New York: Oxford University Press.

Bloom, S. L., & Farragher, B. (2013b). *Restoring sanctuary: A new operating system for trauma-informed systems of care.* New York: Oxford University Press.

Bonanno, G. A. (2004). Loss, trauma, and human resilience: Have we underestimated the human capacity to thrive after extremely aversive events? *American Psychologist*, *59*(1), 20–28.

Bonanno, G. A., Westphal, M., & Mancini, A. D. (2011). Resilience to loss and potential trauma. *Annual Review of Clinical Psychology, 7*, 511–535.

Boogren, T. H. (2021). *Coaching for educator wellness: A guide to supporting new and experienced teachers*. Bloomington, IN: Solution Tress Press.

Bradley, D. (2021, October 7). *Justice Department to address threats against teachers, school board members* [Video file]. Accessed at www.wrtv.com/news/education/justice-department-to-address-threats-against-teachers-school-board-members on January 24, 2024.

Branova, S. (2023). *The asset model: An approach to teaching and education*. Accessed at https://asm.org/articles/2023/december/the-asset-model-an-approach-to-teaching-and-educat on April 15, 2024.

Bray, B. (2019). *Maslow's hierarchy of needs and Blackfoot (Siksika) Nation beliefs*. Accessed at https://barbarabray.net/2019/03/10/maslows-hierarchy-of-needs-and-blackfoot-nation-beliefs on August 13, 2021.

Brett, B., Hill-Mead, L., & Wu, S. (2000). Perspectives on evaluation use and demand by users: The case of city year. *New Directions for Evaluation*, (88), 71–83.

Brez, C., Hampton, E. M., Behrendt, L., Brown, L., & Powers, J. (2020). Failure to replicate: Testing a growth mindset intervention for college student success. *Basic and Applied Social Psychology*, *42*(6), 460–468.

Brod, G. (2021). *Toward an understanding of when prior knowledge helps or hinders learning*. Accessed at www.nature.com/articles/s41539-021-00103-w on March 16, 2024.

Brookhart, S. M. (2011). Educational assessment knowledge and skills for teachers. *Educational Management: Issues and Practice*, *30*(1), 3–12.

Brooks, J. S., & Theoharis, G. (Eds.). (2019). *Whiteucation: Privilege, power, and prejudice in school and society*. New York: Routledge.

Brown, B. (2015). *Rising strong: How the ability to reset transforms the way we live, love, parent, and lead*. New York: Random House.

Brown, B. (2017). *Braving the wilderness: The quest for true belonging and the courage to stand alone*. New York: Random House.

Buchanan, M., Walker, G., Boden. J. M., Mansoor, Z., & Newton-Howes, G. (2023). Protective factors for psychosocial outcomes following cumulative childhood adversity: Systematic review. *BJPsych Open*, *9*(6): e197.

Buchanan-Rivera, E. (2022). *Identity affirming classrooms: Spaces that center humanity*. New York: Routledge.

Buchmann, M., & Steinhoff, A. (2017). Co-development of student agency components and its impact on educational attainment—Theoretical and methodological considerations. *Research in Human Development*, *14*(2), 96–105.

Buckman, D. G., Hand, N. W. J., & Johnson, A. (2021). Improving high school graduation through school climate. *NASSP Bulletin*, *105*(1), 5–24.

Bulger, C. A., Schultz, D. P., & Schultz, S. E. (2020). *Psychology and work today* (11th ed.). Abingdon, United Kingdom: Routledge.

Bull, R., Espy, K. A., & Wiebe, S. A. (2008). Short-term memory, working memory, and executive functioning in preschoolers: Longitudinal predictors of mathematical achievement at age 7 years. *Developmental Neuropsychology, 33*(3), 205–228.

Bull, R., & Johnston, R. S. (1997). Children's arithmetical difficulties: Contributions from processing speed, item identification, and short-term memory. *Journal of Experimental Child Psychology, 65*(1), 1–24.

Burden, K., Younie, S., & Leask, M. (2013). Translational research principles applied to education: The mapping educational specialist knowhow (MESH) initiative. *Journal of Education for Teaching, 39*(4), 459–463. https://doi.org/10.1080/02607476.2013.801216

Burgdorf, V., Szabó, M., & Abbott, M. J. (2019). *The effect of mindfulness interventions for parents on parenting stress and youth psychological outcomes: A systematic review and meta-analysis.* Accessed at www.frontiersin.org/journals/psychology/articles/10.3389/fpsyg.2019.01336/full on February 16, 2024.

Caballero, C., Scherer, E., West, M. R., Mrazek, M. D., Gabrieli, C. F. O., & Gabrieli, J. D. E. (2019). Greater mindfulness is associated with better academic achievement in middle school. *Mind, Brain, and Education, 13*(3), 157–166.

Calgary Board of Education. (2014). *Create safety and routines.* Accessed at www.teachingrefugees.com/docs/Create-Safety-and-Routines-Tips-for-Teachers.pdf on March 17, 2024.

California State Department of Education. (1986). *Beyond language: Social and cultural factors in schooling language minority students.* Los Angeles: Evaluation, Dissemination and Assessment Center.

Call, C., Purvis, K., Parris, S. R., & Cross, D. (2014, September 2). *Creating trauma-informed classrooms.* Accessed at https://adoptioncouncil.org/publications/adoption-advocate-no-75 on February 8, 2021.

Campbell, J. (1991). *The power of myth.* New York: Anchor Books.

Canadian Mental Health Association. (n.d.). *Social determinants of health.* Accessed at https://ontario.cmha.ca/provincial-policy/social-determinants on January 24, 2024.

Cantor, P., Osher, D., Berg, J., Steyer, L., & Rose, T. (2019). Malleability, plasticity, and individuality: How children learn and develop in context. *Applied Developmental Science, 23*(4), 307–337.

Card, D. (1999). The causal effect of education on earnings. In O. C. Ashenfelter & D. Card (Eds.), *Handbook of labor economics* (Vol. 3, pp. 1801–1863). Amsterdam: Elsevier.

Caron, C. (2022, July 8). Before heading to college, make a mental health checklist. *The New York Times.* Accessed at www.nytimes.com/2022/07/08/well/mind/mental-health-college-students.html on January 24, 2024.

Carter, P. L., Skiba, R., Arredondo, M. I., & Pollock, M. (2017). You can't fix what you don't look at: Acknowledging race in addressing racial discipline disparities. *Urban Education, 52*(2), 207–235.

Cásedas, L., Pirruccio, V., Vadillo, M. A., & Lupiáñez, J. (2020). Does mindfulness meditation training enhance executive control? A systematic review and meta-analysis of randomized controlled trials in adults. *Mindfulness, 11*, 411–424.

Castles, A., Rastle, K., & Nation, K. (2018). Ending the reading wars: Reading acquisition from novice to expert. *Psychological Science in the Public Interest, 19*(1), 5–51.

Center for Collegiate Mental Health. (n.d.). *2015 annual report*. University Park, PA: Author.

Center for Teaching Innovation. (n.d.). *Collaborative learning*. Accessed at https://teaching.cornell.edu/teaching-resources/active-collaborative-learning/collaborative-learning on March 17, 2024.

Center for the Study of Social Policy. (n.d.). *Primary health partners: Promoting children's health and resiliency: A Strengthening Families approach*. Washington, DC: Author. Accessed at https://cssp.org/wp-content/uploads/2019/01/Messaging-at-the-Intersections_Primary-Health.pdf on January 30, 2024.

Center on Child Wellbeing and Trauma. (n.d.). *Principle 2: Transparency and trust*. Accessed at https://childwellbeingandtrauma.org/becoming-trauma-informed-and-responsive/guiding-principles/principle-2-transparency-and-trust on January 24, 2024.

Center on Innovations in Learning. (2015, February 4). *High school competency-based education and post-secondary success*. Accessed at www.compcenternetwork.org/sites/default/files/archive/2015_02.04HSCompetencyBasedEducationAndPostSecondarySuccess.pdf on January 24, 2024.

Center on Reinventing Public Education. (2022). *The state of the American student: Fall 2022: A guide to pandemic recovery and reinvention*. Tempe, AZ: Mary Lou Fulton Teachers College. Accessed at https://crpe.org/wp-content/uploads/CRPE-%E2%80%94-Profile-of-a-Student-Report.pdf on January 24, 2024.

Center on the Developing Child. (n.d.). *Executive function and self-regulation*. Accessed at https://developingchild.harvard.edu/science/key-concepts/executive-function on January 25, 2024.

Center on the Developing Child. (2007). *A science-based framework for early childhood policy: Using evidence to improve outcomes in learning, behavior, and health for vulnerable children*. Cambridge, MA: Harvard University.

Centers for Disease Control and Prevention. (n.d.a). *About teen dating violence*. Accessed at www.cdc.gov/intimate-partner-violence/about/about-teen-dating-violence.html on June 2, 2024.

Centers for Disease Control and Prevention. (n.d.b). *About the CDC-Kaiser ACE study*. Accessed at www.cdc.gov/violenceprevention/aces/about.html on February 9, 2021.

Centers for Disease Control and Prevention. (n.d.c). *School connectedness*. Accessed at www.cdc.gov/healthyschools/school_connectedness.htm on May 5, 2024

Centers for Disease Control and Prevention. (2019). *Preventing adverse childhood experiences (ACEs): Leveraging the best available evidence*. Accessed at https://stacks.cdc.gov/view/cdc/82316 on March 19, 2024.

Centers for Disease Control and Prevention. (2022). *Protective factors in schools*. Accessed at www.cdc.gov/healthyschools/protective_factors_schools.htm on March 15, 2024.

Centers for Disease Control and Prevention. (2023). *Youth risk behavior survey: Data summary and trends report.* Accessed at www.cdc.gov/healthyyouth/data/yrbs/pdf/yrbs_data-summary-trends_report2023_508.pdf on June 2, 2024.

Cepeda, N. J., Vul, E., Rohrer, D., Wixted, J. T., & Pashler, H. (2008). Spacing effects in learning: A temporal ridgeline of optimal retention. *Psychological Science, 19*(11), 1095–1102.

Chamberlin, K., Yasué, M., & Chiang, I. A. (2018). The impact of grades on student motivation. *Active Learning in Higher Education, 24*(2), 1–16.

Chen, L., Chang, H., Rudoler, J., Arnardottir, E., Zhang, Y., de los Angeles, C., et al. (2022). Cognitive training enhances growth mindset in children through plasticity of cortico-striatal circuits. *npj Science of Learning, 7*(1), 30.

Child Welfare Information Gateway. (2017). *Supporting brain development in traumatized children and youth.* Washington, DC: U.S. Department of Health and Human Services, Children's Bureau. Accessed at https://oaesv.org/wp-content/uploads/2021/04/braindevtrauma.pdf on February 14, 2024.

Chrona, J. (2022). *Wayi Wah! Indigenous pedagogies: An act for reconciliation and anti-racist education.* Winnipeg, Manitoba, Canada: Portage & Main Press.

Cline, N. (2023). *Portrait of a Graduate: The story behind state-designed student sameness.* Accessed at https://higherground.work/portrait-of-a-graduate-the-story-behind-state-designed-student-sameness on June 2, 2024.

Cochrane, S. V., Chhabra, M., Jones, M. A., & Spragg, D. (Eds.). (2017). *Culturally responsive teaching and reflection in higher education: Promising practices from the Cultural Literacy Curriculum Institute.* New York: Routledge.

Cole-Lewis, Y. C. O., Hope, E. C., Mustafaa, F. N., & Jagers, R. J. (2021). Incongruent impressions: Teacher, parent, and student perceptions of two Black boys' school experiences. *Journal of Adolescent Research, 38*(3), 391–422.

Coleman, S. T., & Davis, J. (2020). Using asset-based pedagogy to facilitate STEM learning, engagement, and motivation for Black middle school boys. *Journal of African American Males in Education, 11*(2), 76–94.

Collaborative for Academic, Social, and Emotional Learning. (n.d.). *Fundamentals of SEL.* Accessed at https://casel.org/fundamentals-of-sel on January 25, 2024.

Collaborative for Academic, Social, and Emotional Learning. (2017). *What is the CASEL framework?* Accessed at https://casel.org/fundamentals-of-sel/what-is-the-casel-framework on May 5, 2024.

Collins, J. (2001). *Good to great: Why some companies make the leap and others don't.* New York: HarperBusiness.

Committee for Children. (2016). *Why social and emotional learning and employability skills should be prioritized in education.* Seattle, WA: Author. Accessed at www.cfchildren.org/wp-content/uploads/policy-advocacy/sel-employability-brief.pdf on January 25, 2024.

Committee on Psychosocial Aspects of Child and Family Health, Committee on Early Childhood, Adoption, and Dependent Care, & Section on Developmental and Behavioral Pediatrics. (2012). Early childhood adversity, toxic stress, and the role of the pediatrician: Translating developmental science into lifelong health. *Pediatrics, 129*(1), 224–231.

Conley, D. T., & French, E. M. (2014). Student ownership of learning as a key component of college readiness. *American Behavioral Scientist*, *58*(8), 1018–1034. https://doi.org/10.1177/0002764213515232

Cooper, E. (2022). Brave spaces: Indigenous children in Canada plan for a different tomorrow. *Applied Physiology, Nutrition, and Metabolism*, *47*(6), 659–670.

Costa, A., & Faria, L. (2018). Implicit theories of intelligence and academic achievement: A meta-analytic review. *Frontiers in Psychology*, *9*, Article 829.

Craft, S. (2021, October 4). *College dropout rates*. Accessed at www.thinkimpact.com/college-dropout-rates on January 30, 2024.

Crepelle, A. (2023, January 6). *Federal policies trap tribes in poverty*. Accessed at www.americanbar.org/groups/crsj/publications/human_rights_magazine_home/wealth-disparities-in-civil-rights/federal-policies-trap-tribes-in-poverty on January 25, 2024.

Cronholm, P. F., Forke, C. M., Wade, R., Bair-Merritt, M. H., Davis, M., Harkins-Schwarz, M., et al. (2015). Adverse childhood experiences: Expanding the concept of adversity. *American Journal of Preventive Medicine*, *49*(3), 354–361.

Crottaz-Herbette, S., & Menon, V. (2006). Where and when the anterior cingulate cortex modulates attentional response: Combined fMRI and ERP evidence. *Journal of Cognitive Neuroscience*, *18*(5), 766–780.

Csikszentmihalyi, M. (1997). *Finding flow: The psychology of engagement with everyday life*. New York: Basic Books.

Csikszentmihalyi, M., Rathunde, K., & Whalen, S. (1996). *Talented teenagers: The roots of success and failure*. New York: Cambridge University Press.

Cuncic, A. (2023). *How to develop and practice self-regulation*. Accessed at www.verywellmind.com/how-you-can-practice-self-regulation-4163536 on March 17, 2024.

Darling-Hammond, L. (2002). *10 features of good small schools: Redesigning high schools, what matters and what works*. Stanford, CA: School Redesign Network.

Darling-Hammond, L. (2007). Race, inequality and educational accountability: The irony of "No Child Left Behind." *Race Ethnicity and Education*, *10*(3), 245–260.

Darling-Hammond, L., & Cook-Harvey, C. M. (2018, September). *Educating the whole child: Improving school climate to support student success*. Palo Alto, CA: Learning Policy Institute. Accessed at https://learningpolicyinstitute.org/sites/default/files/product-files/Educating_Whole_Child_REPORT.pdf on January 25, 2024.

Davis, B. R. (2023). *A generation at-risk: The dire need for effective mental health counseling*. Accessed at www.k12digest.com/a-generation-at-risk-the-dire-need-for-effective-mental-health-counseling on February 16, 2024.

Davis, N. O., & Carter, A. S. (2008). Parenting stress in mothers and fathers of toddlers with autism spectrum disorders: Associations with child characteristics. *Journal of Autism and Developmental Disorders*, *38*(7), 1278–1291.

Deal, T. E., & Peterson, K. D. (2009). *Shaping school culture: Pitfalls, paradoxes, and promises* (2nd ed.). San Francisco: Jossey-Bass.

Dean, S. (2023, July 13). *"If students don't feel safe, they can't learn"* [Blog post]. Accessed at https://itgetsbetter.org/if-students-dont-feel-safe-they-cant-learn on March 16, 2024.

Deater-Deckard, K., Li, M., & Bell, M. A. (2016). Multifaceted emotion regulation, stress and affect in mothers of young children. *Cognition and Emotion*, *30*(3), 444–457.

De Bellis, M. D., & Zisk, A. (2014). The biological effects of childhood trauma. *Child and Adolescent Psychiatric Clinics in North America*, *23*(2), 185–222.

de Boer, H., Timmermans, A. C., & van der Werf, M. P. C. (2018). The effects of teacher expectation interventions on teachers' expectations and student achievement: Narrative review and meta-analysis. *Educational Research and Evaluation*, *24*(3–5), 180–200.

de Brey, C., Snyder, T. D., Zhang, A., & Dillow, S. A. (2021). *Digest of education statistics 2019 (NCES 2021-009).* Washington, DC: National Center for Education Statistics, Institute of Education Sciences, U.S. Department of Education. Accessed at https://nces.ed.gov/pubs2021/2021009.pdf on September 28, 2023.

Dekel, S., Ein-Dor, T., & Solomon, Z. (2012). Posttraumatic growth and posttraumatic distress: A longitudinal study. *Psychological Trauma: Theory, Research, Practice, and Policy*, *4*(1), 94–101. https://doi.org/10.1037/a0021865

del Carmen Salazar, M., & Lerner, J. (2019). *Teacher evaluation as cultural practice: A framework for equity and excellence*. New York: Routledge.

DeLorenzo, R. A., Battino, W. J., Schreiber, R. M., & Carrio, B. G. (2009). *Delivering on the promise: The education revolution*. Bloomington, IN: Solution Tree Press.

Delpit, L. (1993). The silenced dialogue: Power and pedagogy in educating other people's children. In L. Weis, & M. Fine (Eds.), *Beyond silenced voices: Class, race, and gender in United States schools* (pp. 119–139). Albany: State University of New York Press.

Delpit, L. (2006). *Other people's children: Cultural conflict in the classroom*. New York: The New Press.

Delpit, L. (2013). *"Multiplication is for White people": Raising expectations for other people's children*. New York: The New Press.

Demirbas-Celik, N. (2018). Happiness in high school students: Autonomy, relatedness, competence and meaning in life. *Cypriot Journal of Educational Sciences*, *13*(3), 422–430.

Desautels, L. L. (2023). *Intentional neuroplasticity: Moving our nervous systems and educational system toward post-traumatic growth*. Deadwood, OR: Wyatt-Mackenzie.

Dewey, J. (1916). *Democracy and education*. New York: Macmillan.

Diaz, M. J., Wolfersteig, W., Moreland, D., Yoder, G., Dustman, P., et al. (2020). Teaching youth to resist abuse: Evaluation of a strengths-based child maltreatment curriculum for high school students. *Journal of Child and Adolescent Trauma*, *14*(1), 141–149.

Dickey, D. D. (2022). *An integrated approach to student achievement* (4th ed.). Randallstown, MD: Educational Epiphany.

Dolch, E. W. (1936). A basic sight vocabulary. *The Elementary School Journal, 36*(6), 456–460.

Dong, S. (2021, June 2). *The history and growth of the diversity, equity, and inclusion profession*. Accessed at https://insights.grcglobalgroup.com/the-history-and-growth-of-the-diversity-equity-and-inclusion-profession on January 25, 2024.

Dost, R. (2023). *Modern science and self-love*. Accessed at https://ralphdost.medium.com/modern-science-and-self-love-ed1577df27d2 on July 2, 2024.

Dray, J., Bowman, J., Freund, M., Campbell, E., Wolfenden, L., Hodder, R. K., et al. (2014). Improving adolescent mental health and resilience through a resilience-based intervention in schools: Study protocol for a randomised controlled trial. *Trials, 15*, Article 289.

Dubinski, K. (2023). *Teachers, principals seeing more outbursts and less self-regulation, survey finds*. Accessed at www.cbc.ca/news/canada/london/teachers-principals-seeing-more-outbursts-and-less-self-regulation-survey-finds-1.6767674 on March 15, 2024.

Ducharme, J. M., & Shecter, C. (2011). Bridging the gap between clinical and classroom intervention: Keystone approaches for students with challenging behavior. *School Psychology Review, 40*(2), 257–274.

Duckworth, A. L., Kim, B., & Tsukayama, E. (2013). Life stress impairs self-control in early adolescence. *Frontiers in Psychology, 3*, Article 608.

Duckworth, A. L., Quirk, A., Gallop, R., Hoyle, R. H., Kelly, D. R., & Matthews, M. D. (2019). Cognitive and noncognitive predictors of success. *Proceedings of the National Academy of Sciences of the United States of America, 116*(47), 23499–23504.

Duckworth, A. L., & Seligman, M. E. P. (2005). Self-discipline outdoes IQ in predicting academic performance of adolescents. *Psychological Science, 16*(12), 939–944.

Duffy, M. E., Twenge, J. M., & Joiner, T. E. (2019). Trends in mood and anxiety symptoms and suicide-related outcomes among U.S. undergraduates, 2007–2018: Evidence from two national surveys. *Journal of Adolescent Health, 65*(5), 590–598.

Durlak, J. A., Weissberg, R. P., Dymnicki, A. B., Taylor, R. D., & Schellinger, K. B. (2011). The impact of enhancing students' social and emotional learning: A meta-analysis of school-based universal interventions. *Child Development, 82*(1), 405–432. https://doi.org/10.1111/j.1467-8624.2010.01564.x

Dweck, C. S. (2008). *Mindsets and math/science achievement*. New York: Carnagie Corporation of New York.

Dweck, C. S., & Yeager, D. S. (2019). Mindsets: A view from two eras. *Perspectives on Psychological Science, 14*(3), 481–496.

EAB. (2023). *Building a better behavior management strategy for students* and *teachers: Key findings from EAB's student behavior survey* [Executive briefing]. Accessed at https://pages.eab.com/rs/732-GKV-655/images/Student%20Behavior%20Executive%20Briefing.pdf on January 25, 2024.

Edwards, A. (2017). The dialectic of person and practice: How cultural-historical accounts of agency can inform teacher education. In D. J. Clandinin & J. Husu (Eds.), *The SAGE handbook of research on teacher education* (pp. 269–285). London: SAGE.

Egger, F., Benzing, V., Conzelmann, A, & Schmidt, M. (2019). *Boost your brain, while having a break! The effects of long-term cognitively engaging physical activity breaks on children's executive functions and academic achievement.* Accessed at https://journals.plos.org/plosone/article?id=10.1371/journal.pone.0212482 on March 17, 2024.

Eisenberg, D., Ketchen Lipson, S., & Heinze, J. (2021). *The healthy minds study.* Accessed at https://healthymindsnetwork.org/wp-content/uploads/2022/01/HMS_nationalwinter2021_-update1.5.21.pdf on January 25, 2024.

Emdin, C. (2016). *For White folks who teach in the hood . . . and the rest of y'all too: Reality pedagogy and urban education.* Boston: Beacon Press.

Enlow, M. B., Blood, E., & Egeland, B. (2013). Sociodemographic risk, developmental competence, and PTSD symptoms in young children exposed to interpersonal trauma in early life. *Journal of Traumatic Stress, 26*(6), 686–694.

Eteläpelto, A., Vähäsantanen, K., Hökkä, P., & Paloniemi, S. (2013). What is agency? Conceptualizing professional agency at work. *Educational Research Review, 10*, 45–65.

Evans, G. W., Farah, M. J., & Hackman, D. A. (2021). Early childhood poverty and adult executive functioning: Distinct, mediating pathways for different domains of executive functioning. *Developmental Science, 24*(5), Article e13084.

Evans, G. W., & Kim, P. (2013). Childhood poverty, chronic stress, self-regulation, and coping. *Child Development Perspectives, 7*(1), 43–48.

Evans-Campbell, T. (2008). Historical trauma in American Indian/Native Alaska communities: A multilevel framework for exploring impacts on individuals, families, and communities. *Journal of Interpersonal Violence, 23*(3), 316–338.

Exner-Cortens, D., Baker, E., & Craig, W. (2021). The national prevalence of adolescent dating violence in Canada. *Journal of Adolescent Health, 69*(3), 495–502.

Ezarik, M. (2022, April 18). *Student mental health status report: Struggles, stressors and supports.* Accessed at www.insidehighered.com/news/2022/04/19/survey-college-students-reflect-mental-health-and-campus-help on January 25, 2024.

Fain, P. (2019, May 22). *Wealth's influence on enrollment and completion.* Accessed at www.insidehighered.com/news/2019/05/23/feds-release-broader-data-socioeconomic-status-and-college-enrollment-and-completion on January 25, 2024.

Fallot, R. D., & Harris, M. (2008). Trauma-informed services. In G. Reyes, J. D. Elhai, & J. D. Ford (Eds.), *The encyclopedia of psychological trauma* (pp. 660–662). Hoboken, NJ: Wiley.

Fallot, R. D., & Harris, M. (2011). *Creating cultures of trauma-informed care (CCTIC): A self- assessment and planning protocol.* Accessed at https://children.wi.gov/Documents/CCTICSelf-AssessmentandPlanningProtocol0709.pdf on February 14, 2024.

Falter, M. M. (2017). The power and potential of graphic novels in the classroom. *Anthropology Now*, *9*(3), 144–146.

Farrington, C. A., Roderick, M., Allensworth, E., Nagaoka, J., Keyes, T. S., Johnson, D. W., et al. (2012). *Teaching adolescents to become learners: The role of noncognitive factors in shaping school performance—A critical literature review.* Chicago: University of Chicago Consortium on Chicago School Research.

Federal Student Aid. (n.d.). *What are graduation, retention, and transfer rates?* Accessed at https://studentaid.gov/help/graduation-retention-transfer-rates on January 26, 2024.

Feldman, D. B., & Kubota, M. (2015). Hope, self-efficacy, optimism, and academic achievement: Distinguishing constructs and levels of specificity in predicting college grade-point average. *Learning and Individual Differences*, *37*, 210–216.

Feldman, J. (2023). *Grading for equity: What it is, why it matters, and how it can transform schools and classrooms.* Thousand Oaks, CA: Corwin.

Felitti, V. J., Anda, R. F., Nordenberg, D., Williamson, D. F., Spitz, A. M., Edwards, V., et al. (1998). Relationship of childhood abuse and household dysfunction to many of the leading causes of death in adults: The Adverse Childhood Experiences (ACE) Study. *American Journal of Preventive Medicine*, *14*(4), 245–258.

Fell, B., & Hewstone, M. (2015, June 4). *Psychological perspectives on poverty.* Accessed at www.jrf.org.uk/report/psychological-perspectives-poverty on January 26, 2024.

Ferguson, R. F. (2003). Teachers' perceptions and expectations and the Black-White test score gap. *Urban Education*, *38*(4), 460–507.

Ferguson, R. F. (2015, October). *The influence of teaching beyond standardized test scores: Engagement, mindsets, and agency—A study of 16,000 sixth through ninth grade classrooms.* Accessed at www.aitsl.edu.au/docs/default-source/general/the-influence-of-teaching-(2015).pdf on January 26, 2024.

Ferlazzo, L. (2022, September 18). *How attacks on critical race theory are affecting teachers.* Accessed at www.edweek.org/leadership/opinion-how-attacks-on-critical-race-theory-are-affecting-teachers/2022/09 on January 26, 2024.

Feter, N., Caputo, E. L., Smith, E. C., Doring, I. R., Cassuriaga, J., Leite, J. S, et al. (2021). Association between physical activity and subjective memory decline triggered by the COVID-19 pandemic: Findings from the PAMPA cohort. *Preventive Medicine*, *145*, Article 106415.

First Nations Education Steering Committee. (n.d.). *First peoples principles of learning.* Accessed at www.fnesc.ca/wp/wp-content/uploads/2020/09/FNESC-Learning-First-Peoples-poster-11x17-hi-res-v2.pdf on January 26, 2024.

Fleming, J., & Ledogar, R. J. (2008). Resilience, an evolving concept: A review of literature relevant to Aboriginal research. *Pimatisiwin*, *6*(2), 7–23.

Ford, E. (2023). *Benches in the bathroom: Leading a physically, emotionally, and socially safe school culture.* Bloomington, IN: Solution Tree Press.

Fortner, K. M., Lalas, J., & Strikwerda, H. (2021). Embracing asset-based school leadership dispositions in advancing true equity and academic achievement for students living in poverty. *Journal of Leadership, Equity, and Research, 7*(1), n1.

Frazier, A. D., Cross, J. R., Cross, T. L., & Kim, M. (2021). "The spirit is willing": A study of school climate, bullying, self-efficacy, and resilience in high-ability low-income youth. *Roeper Review, 43*(1), 7–20.

Freedman, J. (2000, June 25). *What are emotions?* Accessed at www.6seconds.org/2000/06/25/what-are-emotions on January 26, 2024.

Freud, A. (1967). Normality and pathology in childhood: Assessments of development. *Social Work, 12*(1), 110–111.

Frey, N., Nagel, D., Fisher, D., Faddis, T., & Allen-Rotell, A. (2024). *PLC+: A playbook for instructional leaders.* Thousand Oaks, CA: Corwin.

Friedman, T. L. (2016). *Thank you for being late: An optimist's guide to thriving in the age of accelerations.* New York: Farrar, Straus, & Giroux.

Fry, E. (2004). *The vocabulary teacher's book of lists.* San Francisco: Jossey-Bass.

Fullan, M. (2023). *The principal 2.0: Three keys to maximizing impact.* San Francisco: Jossey-Bass.

Fullan, M., Hill, P., & Rincón-Gallardo, S. (2017). *Deep learning: Shaking the foundations* [White paper]. Accessed at www.researchgate.net/publication/316044370_Deep_Learning_Shaking_the_Foundations on February 12, 2024.

Future Education Magazine. (n.d.). *Self-awareness: The power of metacognition in education.* Accessed at https://futureeducationmagazine.com/metacognition-in-education on July 2, 2024.

Galla, C. K., & Goodwill, A. (2017). Talking story with vital voices: Making knowledge with Indigenous language. *Journal of Indigenous Wellbeing, 2*(3), Article 6.

Galloway, M., Conner, J., & Pope, D. (2013). Nonacademic effects of homework in privileged, high-performing high schools. *The Journal of Experimental Education, 81*(4), 490–510.

Gallup. (n.d.). *State of the global workplace: 2023 report.* Accessed at www.gallup.com/workplace/349484/state-of-the-global-workplace.aspx on January 26, 2024.

Gallup. (2014, December 11). *Gallup student poll 2014 U. S. overall report.* Accessed at www.gallup.com/services/180029/gallup-student-poll-2014-overall-report.aspx on January 26, 2024.

Gay, G. (2002). Preparing for culturally responsive teaching. *Journal of Teacher Education, 53*(2), 106–116.

Gay, G. (2018). *Culturally responsive teaching: Theory, research, and practice* (3rd ed.). New York: Teachers College Press.

Gentry, J. R., & Ouellette, G. P. (2019). *Brain words: How the science of reading informs teaching.* Portsmouth, NH: Stenhouse.

Gieryn, T. F. (2000). A space for place in sociology. *Annual Review of Sociology, 26*, 463–496.

Ginwright, S. (2016). *Hope and healing in urban education: How urban activists and teachers are reclaiming matters of the heart.* New York: Routledge.

Ginwright, S. (2022). *The four pivots: Reimagining justice, reimagining ourselves.* Berkeley, CA: North Atlantic Books.

Gleason, S. C., & Gerzon, N. (2013). *Growing into equity: Professional learning and personalization in high-achieving schools.* Thousand Oaks, CA: Corwin.

Goddard, R. D., Hoy, W. K., & Hoy, A. W. (2004). Collective efficacy: Theoretical developments, empirical evidence, and future directions. *Educational Researcher, 33*(3), 3–13.

Goddard, R. D., Sweetland, S. R., & Hoy, W. K. (2000). Academic emphasis of urban elementary schools and student achievement in reading and mathematics: A multilevel analysis. *Educational Administration Quarterly, 36*(5), 683–702.

Godman, H., & Howley, E. K. (2023). A patient's guide to mental health. *U.S. News and World Report.* Accessed at https://health.usnews.com/conditions/mental-health on August 5, 2024.

Goetz, J. L., Keltner, D., & Simon-Thomas, E. (2010). Compassion: An evolutionary analysis and empirical review. *Psychological Bulletin, 136*(3), 351–374.

Gold, M. (2024). *The right school principals can boost teacher retention, student outcomes.* Accessed at www.ncsl.org/state-legislatures-news/details/the-right-school-principals-can-boost-teacher-retention-student-outcomes on March 19, 2024.

Goldberg, H. (2022). Growing brains, nurturing minds—Neuroscience as an educational tool to support students' development as life-long learners. *Brain Sciences, 12*(12), Article 1622.

Goleman, D. (2005). *Emotional intelligence* (10th ed.). New York: Bantam Books.

Goleman, D. (2017). What is empathy? In Harvard Business Review (Ed.), *Empathy* (pp. 1–4). Brighton, MA: Harvard Business Review.

Gone, J. P. (2021). The (post)colonial predicament in community mental health services for American Indians: Explorations in alter-Native psy-ence. *American Psychologist, 76*(9), 1514–1525. https://doi.org/10.1037/amp0000906

Goodwill, J. R., & Zhou, S. (2020). Association between perceived public stigma and suicidal behaviors among college students of color in the U.S. *Journal of Affective Disorders, 262*, 1–7.

Gough, P. B., & Tunmer, W. E. (1986). Decoding, reading, and reading disability. *Remedial and Special Education, 7*(1), 6–10.

Grady, C. (2020). *Do the soaring sales of anti-racism books signal a true cultural shift?* Accessed at www.vox.com/culture/2020/6/11/21288021/anti-racism-books-reading-list-sales-figures on January 26, 2024.

Greater Good Magazine. (n.d.). *What is empathy?* Accessed at https://greatergood.berkeley.edu/topic/empathy/definition on June 3, 2024.

Green, R. L., White, G., & Green, K. K. (2012). The expectations factor in Black male achievement: Creating a foundation for educational equity. In S. Lewis, M. Casserly, C. Simon, R. Uzzell, & M. Palacios (Eds.), *A call for change: Providing solutions for Black male achievement* (pp. 21–46). Washington, DC: Council of the Great City Schools.

Greenberg, J., Romero, V. L., Elkin-Frankston, S., Bezdek, M. A., Schumacher, E. H., & Lazar, S. W. (2019). Reduced interference in working memory following mindfulness training is associated with increases in hippocampal volume. *Brain Imaging and Behavior, 13*(2), 366–376.

Greenberg, M. T., Domitrovich, C. E., Weissberg, R. P., & Durlak, J. A. (2017). Social and emotional learning as a public health approach to education. *The Future of Children, 27*(1), 13–32.

Grisham, M. L., Steinhaus, K., Bannerman, V., Valtierrez, M., & El-Atwani, K. (2022, June). *Culturally and linguistically responsive guidance handbook.* Santa Fe: New Mexico Public Education Department. Accessed at https://webnew.ped.state.nm.us/wp-content/uploads/2022/07/CLR-Guidance-Handbook-Review.pdf on January 29, 2024.

Grissom, J. A., Egalite, A. J., & Lindsay, C. A. (2021). *How principals affect students and schools: A systematic synthesis of two decades of research.* Accessed at https://wallacefoundation.org/sites/default/files/2023-09/How-Principals-Affect-Students-and-Schools.pdf on March 19, 2024.

Guskey, T. R. (1997). *Implementing mastery learning* (2nd ed.). Belmont, CA: Wadsworth.

Guskey, T. R. (2007). Closing achievement gaps: Revisiting Benjamin S. Bloom's "Learning for mastery." *Journal of Advanced Academics, 19*(1), 8–31.

Guskey, T. R. (2008). Mastery learning. In T. L. Good (Ed.), *21st century education: A reference handbook* (vol. 1, pp. 194–202). Thousand Oaks, CA: SAGE.

Guskey, T. R. (2015). Mastery learning. In J. D. Wright (Ed.), *International encyclopedia of the social and behavioral sciences* (vol. 14, 2nd ed., pp. 752–759). Amsterdam: Elsevier.

Halliday, A. J., Kern, M. L., Garrett, D. K., & Turnbull, D. A. (2019). The student voice in well-being: A case study of participatory action research in positive education. *Educational Action Research, 27*(2), 173–196. doi: 10.1080/09650792.2018.1436079

Hallinger, P. (2012). *School leadership that makes a difference: Lessons from 30 years of international research.* Accessed at www.utsbasilicata.it/attachments/article/810 /03a_Leadership_21st_century_schools[1].pdf on January 19, 2018.

Hallinger, P., & Murphy, J. (1985). Assessing the instructional management behavior of principals. *The Elementary School Journal, 86*(2), 217–247.

Hammond, Z. (2015). *Culturally responsive teaching and the brain: Promoting authentic engagement and rigor among culturally and linguistically diverse students.* Thousand Oaks, CA: Corwin.

Hanh, T. N. (1991). *Peace is every step: The path of mindfulness in everyday life.* New York: Bantam Books.

Hanover Research. (2022). *Best practices for elevating student voice.* Accessed at https://wasa-oly.org/WASA/images/WASA/6.0%20Resources/Hanover/Best-Practices-for-Elevating-Student-Voice.pdf on March 19, 2024.

Hanson, M. (2021). *College dropout rates.* Accessed at https://educationdata.org/college-dropout-rates#:~:text=In%20the%20United%20States%2C%20the,college%20dropout%20rate%20at%2054%25 on January 26, 2024.

Hardy, K. V. (2013). Healing the hidden wounds of racial trauma. *Reclaiming Children and Youth*, *22*(1), 24–28.

Harris, N. B. (2021). *The deepest well: Healing the long-term effects of childhood trauma and adversity.* Boston: Mariner Books.

Harris, N. B., Marques, S. S., Oh, D., Bucci, M., & Cloutier, M. (2017). Prevent, screen, heal: Collective action to fight the toxic effects of early life adversity. *Academic Pediatrics*, *17*(7), S14–S15.

Harvard Health Publishing. (2013). *Positive psychology: Harnessing the power of happiness, mindfulness, and inner strength.* Boston: Author.

Harvard Health Publishing. (2020). *Understanding the stress response.* Accessed at www.health.harvard.edu/staying-healthy/understanding-the-stress-response on July 22, 2021.

Hasbrouck, J., & Tindal, G. (2006). *Oral reading fluency: 90 years of measurement.* Eugene, OR: Behavioral Research and Teaching. Accessed at https://eric.ed.gov/?id=ED531458 on June 17, 2024.

Hattie, J. (2009). *Visible learning: A synthesis of over 800 meta-analyses relating to achievement.* New York: Routledge.

Hattie, J. (2015a, June). *What doesn't work in education: The politics of distraction.* London: Pearson.

Hattie, J. (2015b, June). *What works best in education: The politics of collaborative expertise.* London: Pearson.

Hierck, T., & Weber, C. (2024). *Positive behaviors start with positive mindsets: Twenty-eight actions to motivate students and boost achievement.* Bloomington, IN: Solution Tree Press.

Hollowood, T. (2017). *Negative self-talk gets in the way of finding help for PTSD.* Accessed at www.healthyplace.com/blogs/traumaptsdblog/2017/07/negative-self-talk-gets-in-the-way-of-finding-help-for-ptsd on March 17, 2024.

Holtorf, C. (2018). Embracing change: How cultural resilience is increased through cultural heritage. *World Archaeology*, *50*(4), 639–650. https://doi.org/10.1080/00438243.2018.1510340

Hoover, W. A., & Tunmer, W. E. (2018). The simple view of reading: Three assessments of its adequacy. *Remedial and Special Education*, *39*(5), 304–312. https://doi.org/10.1177/0741932518773154

Horn, M. B. (2023). *Moving to mastery learning class by class, teacher by teacher.* Accessed at https://michaelbhorn.substack.com/p/moving-to-mastery-learning-class on March 19, 2024.

Hough, L. (2019). *Grade expectations: Why we need to rethink grading in our schools.* Accessed at www.gse.harvard.edu/ideas/ed-magazine/19/05/grade-expectations on January 26, 2024.

Houston, D. M., Peterson, P. E., & West, M. R. (2023). Partisan rifts widen, perceptions of school quality decline: Results from 2022 *Education Next* survey of public opinion. *Education Next*, *23*(1), 8–19.

Hoy, W. K. (n.d.a). *About Wayne Hoy.* Accessed at www.waynekhoy.com on February 9, 2021.

Hoy, W. K. (n.d.b). *School AO.* Accessed at www.waynekhoy.com/school-ao on March 19, 2024.

Hoy, W. K., Tarter, C. J., & Bliss, J. R. (1990). Organizational climate, school health, and effectiveness: A comparative analysis. *Educational Administration Quarterly, 26*(3), 260–279.

Hoy, W. K., Tarter, C. J., & Hoy, A. W. (2006a). Academic optimism of schools: A force for student achievement. *American Educational Research Journal, 43*(3), 425–446.

Hoy, W. K., Tarter, C. J., & Hoy, A. W. (2006b). Academic optimism of schools: A second-order confirmatory factor analysis. In W. K. Hoy & C. Miskel (Eds.), *Contemporary issues in educational policy and school outcomes* (pp. 135–157). Greenwich, CT: Information Age.

Hoy, W. K., Tarter, C. J., & Kottkamp, R. B. (1991). *Open schools/healthy schools: Measuring organizational climate.* Thousand Oaks, CA: SAGE.

Hughes, J. M., Bigler, R. S., & Levy, S. R. (2007). Consequences of learning about historical racism among European American and African American children. *Child Development, 78*(6), 1689–1705. https://doi.org/10.1111/j.1467-8624.2007.01096.x

Hunn, L., Teague, B., & Fisher, P. (2023). Literacy and mental health across the globe: A systematic review. *Mental Health and Social Inclusion, 27*(4), 392–406.

Hutchison, L., & McAlister-Shields, L. (2020). Culturally responsive teaching: Its application in higher education environments. *Education Sciences, 10*(5), 124.

Iberlin, J. M. (2023). *Mindfulness first: A nine-week leadership plan for supporting yourself and your school.* Bloomington, IN: Marzano Resources.

Iberlin, J. M., & Ruyle, M. (2017). *Cultivating mindfulness in the classroom.* Bloomington, IN: Marzano Resources.

Immordino-Yang, M. H. (2016a). *Emotions, learning, and the brain: Exploring the educational implications of affective neuroscience.* New York: Norton.

Immordino-Yang, M. H. (2016b). Emotion, sociality, and the brain's default mode network: Insights for educational practice and policy. *Policy Insights from the Behavioral and Brain Sciences, 3*(2), 211–219.

Immordino-Yang, M. H., & Damasio, A. (2007). We feel, therefore we learn: The relevance of affective and social neuroscience to education. *Mind, Brain, and Education, 1*(1), 3–10.

Immordino-Yang, M. H., Darling-Hammond, L., & Krone, C. (2018). *The brain basis for integrated social, emotional, and academic development: How emotions and social relationships drive learning.* Washington, DC: Aspen Institute.

Irish, L. A., Kline, C. E., Gunn, H. E., Buysse, D. J., & Hall, M. H. (2015). The role of sleep hygiene in promoting public health: A review of empirical evidence. *Sleep Medicine Reviews, 22*, 23–36.

Irwin, V., Wang, K., Tezil, T., Zhang, J., Filbey, A., Jung, J., et al. (2023). *Report on the condition of education 2023 (NCES 2023-144rev).* Accessed at https://nces.ed.gov/pubsearch/pubsinfo.asp?pubid=2023144rev on June 3, 2024.

Iuculano, T., Rosenberg-Lee, M., Richardson, J., Tenison, C., Fuchs, L., Supekar, K., et al. (2015). Cognitive tutoring induces widespread neuroplasticity and remediates brain function in children with mathematical learning disabilities. *Nature Communications, 6*, Article 8453.

Jacobsen, W. C., Pace, G. T., & Ramirez, N. G. (2019). Punishment and inequality at an early age: Exclusionary discipline in elementary school. *Social Forces, 97*(3), 973–998.

Jensen, E. (2008). *Brain-based learning: The new paradigm of teaching* (2nd ed.). Thousand Oaks, CA: Corwin.

Jensen, E. (2009). *Teaching with poverty in mind: What being poor does to kids' brains and what schools can do about it.* Alexandria, VA: ASCD.

Jones, S. E., Ethier, K. A., Hertz, M., DeGue, S., Le, V. D., Thornton, J., et al. (2022). Mental health, suicidality, and connectedness among high school students during the COVID-19 pandemic: Adolescent behaviors and experiences survey, United States, January–June 2021. *Morbidity and Mortality Weekly Report, 71*(3), 16–21.

Jones, S. M., Bailey, R., & Jacob, R. (2014). Social-emotional learning is essential to classroom management. *Phi Delta Kappan, 96*(2), 19–24.

Jones, S. M., Brush, K., Ramirez, T., Mao, Z. X., Marenus, M., Wettje, S., et al. (2021). *Navigating SEL from the inside out: Looking inside and across 33 leading SEL programs: A practical resource for schools and OST providers* (2nd ed.). Accessed at https://wallacefoundation.org/sites/default/files/2023-08/navigating-social-and-emotional-learning-from-the-inside-out-2ed.pdf on January 29, 2024.

Joseph, M. X. (2021). *9 ways to promote equity in our schools.* Accessed at www.edutopia.org/article/9-ways-promote-equity-our-schools on March 16, 2024.

Jowkar, B., Kojuri, J., Kohoulat, N., & Hayat, A. A. (2014). Academic resilience in education: The role of achievement goal orientations. *Journal of Advances in Medical Education and Professionalism, 2*(1), 33–38.

Juneau, D., & Broaddus, M. S. (2006). And still the waters flow: The legacy of Indian education in Montana. *Phi Delta Kappan, 88*(3), 193–197.

Jung, N., Wranke, C., Hamburger, K., & Knauff, M. (2014). How emotions affect logical reasoning: Evidence from experiments with mood-manipulated participants, spider phobics, and people with exam anxiety. *Frontiers in Psychology, 5*, Article 570. https://doi.org/10.3389/fpsyg.2014.00570

Kabat-Zinn, J. (1990). *Full catastrophe living: Using the wisdom of your body and mind to face stress, pain, and illness.* New York: Delacorte Press.

Kabat-Zinn, J. (2005a). *Coming to our senses: Healing ourselves and the world through mindfulness.* New York: Hyperion.

Kabat-Zinn, J. (2005b). *Full catastrophe living: Using the wisdom of your body and mind to face stress, pain, and illness.* New York: Delta Trade Paperbacks.

Kairuz, C. A., Casanelia, L. M., Bennet-Brook, K., Coombes, J., & Yadav, U. N. (2021). *Impact of racism and discrimination on physical and mental health among Aboriginal and Torres Strait islander peoples living in Australia: A systematic scoping review.* Accessed at https://bmcpublichealth.biomedcentral.com/articles/10.1186/s12889-021-11363-x on March 11, 2024.

Kaler-Jones, C. (2020, May 7). *When SEL is used as another form of policing.* Accessed at https://medium.com/@justschools/when-sel-is-used-as-another-form-of-policing-fa53cf85dce4 on January 29, 2024.

Kanaan, R. (2023, October 26). *Learner profiles: What are they, why are they important and how can you get started co-creating them?* Accessed at https://knowledgeworks.org/resources/learner-profiles-what-why-how on October 26, 2023.

Kang, Y. H., & Shaw, S. (2024). The school psychology shortage in Canada: The role of university training programs. *Psynopsis, 46*(1), 14-15.

Karpicke, J. D., & Roediger, H. L. (2008). The critical importance of retrieval for learning. *Science, 319*(5865), 966–968.

Kearns, D. M., Hancock, R., Hoeft, F., Pugh, K. R., & Frost, S. J. (2019). The neurobiology of dyslexia. *Teaching Exceptional Children, 51*(3), 175–188. https://doi.org/10.1177/0040059918820051

Kellezi, B., Coupland, C., Morriss, R., Beckett, K., Joseph, S., Barnes, J., et al. (2017). The impact of psychological factors on recovery from injury: A multicentre cohort study. *Social Psychiatry and Psychiatric Epidemiology, 52*(7), 855–866. doi:10.1007/s00127-016-1299-z

Khalifa, M. (2018). *Culturally responsive school leadership*. Cambridge, MA: Harvard Education Press.

Khalifa, M. A., Gooden, M. A., & Davis, J. E. (2016). Culturally responsive school leadership: A synthesis of the literature. *Review of Educational Research, 86*(4), 1272–1311.

Kim, Y-S. G. (2017). Why the simple view of reading is not simplistic: Unpacking component skills of reading using a direct and indirect effect model of reading (DIER). *Scientific Studies of Reading, 21*(4), 310–333.

KnowledgeWorks Foundation. (2016). *Recommendations for advancing personalized learning under the Every Student Succeeds Act (ESSA)*. Accessed at https://knowledgeworks.org/wp-content/uploads/2018/01/personalized-learning-essa-recommendations.pdf on March 13, 2023.

Komariah, M., Ibrahim, K., Pahria, T., Rahayuwait, L., & Somantri, I. (2022). Effect of mindfulness breathing meditation on depression, anxiety, and stress: A randomized controlled trial among university students. *Healthcare, 11*(1), 26.

Konrath, S. (2019, December). *Speaking of psychology: Episode 95—The decline of empathy and the rise of narcissism* [Podcast episode]. Accessed at www.apa.org/news/podcasts/speaking-of-psychology/empathy-narcissism on June 3, 2024.

Konrath, S. H., O'Brien, E. H., & Hsing, C. (2011). Changes in dispositional empathy in American college students over time: A meta-analysis. *Personality and Social Psychology Review, 15*(2), 180–198.

Koskela, T. (2021). *Promoting well-being of children at school: Parental agency in the context of negotiating for support*. Accessed at www.frontiersin.org/articles/10.3389/feduc.2021.652355/full on April 5, 2024.

Krenzke, T., Mohadjer, L., Li, J., Erciulescu, A., Fay, R., Ren, W., et al. (2020). *Program for the International Assessment of Adult Competencies (PIAAC): State and county estimation methodology report*. Washington, DC: Institute of Education Sciences. Accessed at https://nces.ed.gov/pubsearch/pubsinfo.asp?pubid=2020225 on March 28, 2023.

Kress, T. M., Emdin, C., & Lake, R. (Eds.). (2021). *Critical pedagogy for healing: Paths beyond "wellness," toward a soul revival of teaching and learning*. New York: Bloomsbury.

Kruger, J., & Dunning, D. (1999). Unskilled and unaware of it: How difficulties in recognizing one's own incompetence lead to inflated self-assessments. *Journal of Personality and Social Psychology, 77*(6), 1121–1134. https://doi .org/10.1037/0022-3514.77.6.1121

Kumar, M. B., & Tjepkema, M. (2019). *Suicide among First Nations people, Métis and Inuit (2011–2016): Findings from the 2011 Canadian Census Health and Environment Cohort (CanCHEC)*. Accessed at https://www150.statcan.gc.ca /n1/pub/99-011-x/99-011-x2019001-eng.htm on March 11, 2024.

Lacoe, J. (2020). Too scared to learn? The academic consequences of feeling unsafe in the classroom. *Urban Education, 55*(10), 1385–1418.

Ladson-Billings, G. (1995). Toward a theory of culturally relevant pedagogy. *American Educational Research Journal, 32*(3), 465–491.

Ladson-Billings, G. (2009). *The dreamkeepers: Successful teachers of African American children* (2nd ed.). San Francisco: Jossey-Bass.

Ladson-Billings, G. (2014). Culturally relevant pedagogy 2.0: a.k.a. the remix. *Harvard Educational Review, 84*(1), 74–84.

Ladson-Billings, G. (2021a). *Culturally relevant pedagogy: Asking a different question*. New York: Teachers College Press.

Ladson-Billings, G. (2021b). Three decades of culturally relevant, responsive, and sustaining pedagogy: What lies ahead? *The Educational Forum, 85*(4), 351–354.

Ladson-Billings, G. (2022). *The dreamkeepers: Successful teachers of African American children* (3rd ed.). San Francisco: Jossey-Bass.

Larson, K. E., Pas, E. T., Bradshaw, C. P., Rosenberg, M. S., & Day-Vines, N. L. (2018). Examining how proactive management and culturally responsive teaching relate to student behavior: Implications for measurement and practice. *School Psychology Review, 47*(2), 153–166.

Lavretsky, H., & Newhouse, P. A. (2012). Stress, inflammation, and aging. *The American Journal of Geriatric Psychiatry, 20*(9), 729–733.

Lawrie, G., Marquis, E., Fuller, E., Newman, T., Qiu, M., Nomikoudis, M., et al. (2017). Moving towards inclusive learning and teaching: A synthesis of recent literature. *Teaching and Learning Inquiry, 5(1)*, 9–21.

Lawson, V., & Elwood, S. (Eds.). (2018). *Relational poverty politics: Forms, struggles, and possibilities*. Athens, GA: University of Georgia Press.

Lazar, S. W., Bush, G., Gollub, R. L., Fricchione, G. L., Khalsa, G., & Benson, H. (2000). Functional brain mapping of the relaxation response and meditation. *Neuroreport, 11*(7), 1581–1585.

Lazar, S. W., Kerr, C. E., Wasserman, R. H., Gray, J. R., Greve, D. N., Treadway, M. T., et al. (2005). Meditation experience is associated with increased cortical thickness. *Neuroreport, 16*(17), 1893–1897.

Lee, S., Kim, S., Suh, S., Han, H., Jung, J., Yang, S., et al. (2022). Relationship between screen time among children and lower economic status during elementary school closures due to the coronavirus disease 2019 pandemic. *BMC Public Health, 22*(1), 160.

Lei, H., Wang, X., Chiu, M. M., Du, M., & Xie, T. (2023). Teacher-student relationship and academic achievement in China: Evidence from a three-level meta-analysis. *School Psychology International, 44*(1), 68–101.

León-Jiménez, S., Villarejo-Carballido, B., López de Aguileta, G., & Puigvert, L. (2020). Propelling children's empathy and friendship. *Sustainability, 12*(18), 7288.

Letourneau, E. J., Schaeffer, C. M., Bradshaw, C. P., & Feder, K. A. (2017). Preventing the onset of child sexual abuse by targeting young adolescents with universal prevention programming. *Child Maltreatment, 22*(2), 100–111.

Levine, E., & Patrick, S. (2019). *What is competency-based education? An updated definition*. Arlington, VA: Aurora Institute. Accessed at https://aurora-institute.org/wp-content/uploads/what-is-competency-based-education-an-updated-definition-web.pdf on August 13, 2021.

Li, Y., Tang, J., Ma, X., Zhang, X., Xue, Y., & Zhao, X. (2023). Impact of metacognition on health-related behavior: A mediation model study. *Journal of Environmental and Public Health, 16*, 1–8.

Lilienfeld, S. O. (2017a). Microaggressions: Strong claims, inadequate evidence. *Perspectives on Psychological Science, 12*(1), 138–169.

Lilienfeld, S. O. (2017b, June 23). *The science of microaggressions: It's complicated* [Blog post]. Accessed at https://blogs.scientificamerican.com/observations/the-science-of-microaggressions-its-complicated on January 29, 2024.

Lin-Siegler, X., Dweck, C. S., & Cohen, G. L. (2016). Instructional interventions that motivate classroom learning. *Journal of Educational Psychology, 108*(3), 295–299.

Lipp, J. (2020, October 7). *Strengths-based teaching is about starting with the known* [Blog post]. Accessed at https://edublog.scholastic.com/post/strengths-based-teaching-about-starting-known on January 29, 2024.

Lipson, S. K., Kern, A., Eisenberg, D., & Breland-Noble, A. M. (2018). Mental health disparities among college students of color. *Journal of Adolescent Health, 63*(3), 348–356.

Lipson, S. K., Zhou, S., Abelson, S., Heinze, J., Jirsa, M., Morigney, J., et al. (2022). Trends in college student mental health and help-seeking by race/ethnicity: Findings from the national healthy minds study, 2013–2021. *Journal of Affective Disorders, 306*, 138–147.

Lombardi, E., Traficante, D., Bettoni, R., Offredi, I., Giorgetti, M., & Vernice, M. (2019). The impact of school climate on well-being experience and school engagement: A study with high-school students. *Frontiers in Psychology, 10*, Article 2482.

Lopez, S. J., & Louis, M. C. (2009). The principles of strengths-based education. *Journal of College and Character, 10*(4).

Love Is Respect. (n.d.a). *Relationship spectrum*. Accessed at www.loveisrespect.org/everyone-deserves-a-healthy-relationship/relationship-spectrum on June 2, 2024.Love Is Respect. (n.d.b). *Warning signs of abuse*. Accessed at https://www.loveisrespect.org/dating-basics-for-healthy-relationships/warning-signs-of-abuse/ on June 12, 2024.

Lupoli, C. (2018, April 20). *Deepening student voice and empowerment* [Blog post]. Accessed at www.ascd.org/blogs/deepening-student-voice-and-empowerment on March 19, 2024.

Luthar, S. S., Cicchetti, D., & Becker, B. (2000). The construct of resilience: A critical evaluation and guidelines for future work. *Child Development, 71*(3), 543–562. https://doi.org/10.1111/1467–8624.00164

Macey, W. H., Schneider, B., Barbera, K. M., & Young, S. A. (2009). *Employee engagement: Tools for analysis, practice, and competitive advantage.* Hoboken, NJ: Wiley.

Mackey, H. J., Faircloth, S., & Cummins, J. D. (2020). Special issue: Indigenous school leadership theorizing and practice. *Journal of School Leadership, 30*(6).

Macy, R. D., Behar, L., Paulson, R., Delman, J., Schmid, L., & Smith, S. F. (2004). Community-based, acute posttraumatic stress management: A description and evaluation of a psychosocial-intervention continuum. *Harvard Review of Psychiatry, 12*(4), 217–228.

Madda, M. J. (2019, May 15). *Dena Simmons: Without context, social-emotional learning can backfire.* Accessed at www.edsurge.com/news/2019-05-15-dena-simmons-without-context-social-emotional-learning-can-backfire on January 29, 2024.

Mader, J., & Butrymowicz, S. (2017, November 11). *The vast majority of students with disabilities don't get a college degree.* Accessed at https://hechingerreport.org/vast-majority-students-disabilities-dont-get-college-degree on January 29, 2024.

Malone, H.-L. S., Rizkalla, D., & Bartlett, E. (n.d.). *Interrogating, interrupting and eradicating disproportionality through youth voice and action: A guide for youth-adult partnership in pursuit of educational equity.* Accessed at https://steinhardt.nyu.edu/metrocenter/iesc/interrogating-interrupting-and-eradicating-disproportionality-through-youth-voice on January 29, 2024.

Malti, T., & Noam, G. G. (2009). A developmental approach to the prevention of adolescent's aggressive behavior and the promotion of resilience. *International Journal of Developmental Science, 3*(3), 235–246.

Marcovitch, S., & Zelazo, P. D. (2009). A hierarchical competing systems model of the emergence and early development of executive function. *Developmental Science, 12*(1), 1–18.

Margolis, H., & McCabe, P. P. (2006). Improving self-efficacy and motivation: What to do, what to say. *Intervention in School and Clinic, 41*(4), 218–227.

Marlatt, R., & Dallacqua, A. K. (2019). Loud and clear: Using the graphic novel to challenge the status quo in content area literacy. *Journal of Language and Literacy Education, 15*(1), 1–24.

Martin, A. J. (2011). Personal best (PB) approaches to academic development: Implications for motivation and assessment. *Educational Practice and Theory, 33*(1), 93–99.

Martin, A. J. (2012). The role of personal best (PB) goals in the achievement and behavioral engagement of students with ADHD and students without ADHD. *Contemporary Educational Psychology, 37*(2), 91–105.

Martin, A. J., & Liem, G. A. D. (2010). Academic personal bests (PBs), engagement, and achievement: A cross-lagged panel analysis. *Learning and Individual Differences, 20*(3), 265–270.

Martínez-Martí, M. L., & Ruch, W. (2017). Character strengths predict resilience over and above positive affect, self-efficacy, optimism, social support, self-esteem, and life satisfaction. *The Journal of Positive Psychology, 12*(2), 110–119.

Marzano, R. J. (2000). *Transforming classroom grading.* Alexandria, VA: ASCD.

Marzano, R. J. (2006). *Classroom assessment and grading that work.* Alexandria, VA: ASCD.

Marzano, R. J. (2009). Setting the record straight on "high-yield" strategies. *Phi Delta Kappan, 91*(1), 30–37.

Marzano, R. J. (2017). *The new art and science of teaching.* Bloomington, IN: Solution Tree Press.

Marzano, R. J. (2018). *Making classroom assessments reliable and valid.* Bloomington, IN: Solution Tree Press.

Marzano, R. J. (2020). *Teaching basic, advanced, and academic vocabulary: A comprehensive framework for elementary instruction.* Bloomington, IN.: Marzano Resources.

Marzano, R. J., & Hardy, P. (2023). *Leading a competency-based secondary school.* Bloomington, IN: Marzano Resources.

Marzano, R. J., & Heflebower, T. (2011). Grades that show what students know. *Educational Leadership, 69*(3), 34–39.

Marzano, R. J., Heflebower, T., Hoegh, J. K., Warrick, P., & Grift, G. (2016). *Collaborative teams that transform schools: The next steps in PLCs.* Bloomington, IN: Marzano Resources.

Marzano, R. J., & Kosena, B. (2022). *Leading a competency-based elementary school.* Bloomington, IN: Marzano Resources.

Marzano, R. J., & Marzano, J. S. (2015). *Managing the inner world of teaching: Emotions, interpretations, and actions.* Bloomington, IN: Marzano Resources.

Marzano, R. J., Norford, J. S., Finn, M., & Finn, D., III. (2017). *A handbook for personalized competency-based education.* Bloomington, IN: Marzano Resources.

Marzano, R. J., Norford, J. S., & Ruyle, M. (2019). *The new art and science of classroom assessment.* Bloomington, IN: Solution Tree Press.

Marzano, R. J., & Pickering, D. J. (2005). *Building academic vocabulary: Teacher's manual.* Alexandria, VA: ASCD.

Marzano, R. J., Scott, D., Boogren, T. H., & Newcomb, M. L. (2017). *Motivating and inspiring students: Strategies to awaken the learner.* Bloomington, IN: Marzano Resources.

Marzano, R. J., Warrick, P., & Simms, J. A. (2014). *A handbook for High Reliability Schools: The next step in school reform.* Bloomington, IN: Marzano Resources.

Marzano, R. J., & Waters, T. (2009). *District leadership that works: Striking the right balance.* Bloomington, IN: Solution Tree Press.

Marzano, R. J., Waters, T., & McNulty, B. A. (2005). *School leadership that works: From research to results.* Alexandria, VA: ASCD.

Marzano, R. J., Yanoski, D. C., Hoegh, J. K., & Simms, J. A. (2013). *Using Common Core standards to enhance classroom instruction and assessment.* Bloomington, IN: Marzano Resources.

Marzano Resources. (n.d.). *The critical concepts.* Accessed at www.marzano resources.com/educational-services/critical-concepts on September 9, 2021.

Maslow, A. H. (1943). A theory of human motivation. *Psychological Review, 50*(4), 370–396.

Masten, A. S. (2018). Resilience theory and research on children and families: Past, present, and promise. *Journal of Family Theory and Review, 10*(1), 12–31.

Masten, A. S., Fiat, A. E., Labella, M. H., & Strack, R. A. (2015). Educating homeless and highly mobile students: Implications of research on risk and resilience. *School Psychology Review, 44*(3), 315–330. https://doi.org/10.17105/spr-15-0068.1

Mayo Clinic Staff. (n.d.a). *Chronic stress puts your health at risk.* Accessed at www.mayoclinic.org/healthy-lifestyle/stress-management/in-depth/stress/art-20046037 on July 2, 2023.

Mayo Clinic Staff. (n.d.b). *Stress management.* Accessed at www.mayoclinic.org/tests-procedures/stress-management/basics/definition/prc-20021046 on July 2, 2023.

Mazzocco, M. M., & Kover, S. T. (2007). A longitudinal assessment of executive function skills and their association with math performance. *Child Neuropsychology, 13*(1), 18–45.

McCorry, L. K. (2007). Physiology of the autonomic nervous system. *American Journal of Pharmaceutical Education, 71*(4), 78. https://doi. org/10.5688/aj710478

McCrae, R. (2018). *The purpose statement in a TILTed assignment.* Accessed at www.usg.edu/teaching-and-learning-excellence/assets/facultydevelopment/documents/TILT-supplementalmaterials.pdf on January 29, 2024.

McGhee, H. C., & Ray, V. (2022, September 1). School is for making citizens. *The New York Times.* Accessed at www.nytimes.com/2022/09/01/opinion/us-school-citizenship.html on January 29, 2024.

McGrath J. J., Al-Hamzawi, A., Alonso, J., Altwaijri, Y., Andrade, L. H., Bromet, E. J., et al. (2023). Age of onset and cumulative risk of mental disorders: A cross-national analysis of population surveys from 29 countries. *Lancet Psychiatry, 10*(9), 668–681.

McGraw-Hill. (2023). *What is mastery-based learning?* Accessed at https://medium.com/inspired-ideas-prek-12/what-is-mastery-based-learning-eb6310f3a974#:~:text=Student%2Dteacher%20relationships%20also%20have,1%3A1%20time%20with%20students. on March 13, 2024.

Melli, G., Carraresi, C., Poli, A., & Bailey, R. (2016).The role of metacognitive beliefs in health anxiety. *Personality and Individual Differences, 89,* 80–85. doi:10.1016/j.paid.2015.10.006

Mental Health Commission of Canada. (2021). *Shining a light on mental health in Black communities.* Accessed at www.mentalhealthcommission.ca/wp-content/uploads/drupal/2021-02/covid_19_tip_sheet%20_health_in_black_communities_eng.pdf on March 11, 2024.

Mezzina, R., Gopikumar, V., Jenkins, J., Saraceno, B., & Sashidharan, S. P. (2022). Social vulnerability and mental health inequalities in the "syndemic": Call for action. *Frontiers in Psychiatry, 13*, Article 894370.

Michael, S. L., Merlo, C. L., Basch, C. E., Wentzel, K. R., & Wechsler, H. (2015). Critical connections: Health and academics. *Journal of School Health, 85*(11), 740–758.

Miller, D. I. (2019). When do growth mindset interventions work? *Trends in Cognitive Sciences, 23*(11), 910–912.

Miyake, A., Friedman, N. P., Emerson, M. J., Witzki, A. H., Howerter, A., & Wager, T. D. (2000). The unity and diversity of executive functions and their contributions to complex "frontal lobe" tasks: A latent variable analysis. *Cognitive Psychology, 41*(1), 49–100.

Moats, L. C. (2020). *Speech to print: Language essentials for teachers* (3rd ed.). Baltimore: Brookes.

Morsy, L., & Rothstein, R. (2019, May 1). *Toxic stress and children's outcomes: African American children growing up poor are at greater risk of disrupted physiological functioning and depressed academic achievement.* Washington, DC: Economic Policy Institute. Accessed at https://files.epi.org/pdf/164823.pdf on January 29, 2024.

Muppalla, S. K., Vuppalapati, S., Pulliahgaru, A. R., & Sreenivasulu, H. (2023). Effects of excessive screen time on child development: An updated review and strategies for management. *Cureus, 15*(6), Article e40608. https://doi.org/10.7759/cureus.40608

Murphy, J., & Torre, D. (2014). *Creating productive cultures in schools: For students, teachers, and parents.* Thousand Oaks, CA: Corwin.

Murphy, M. (2017, January 24). The Dunning-Kruger Effect shows why some people think they're great even when their work is terrible. *Forbes*. Accessed at www.forbes.com/sites/markmurphy/2017/01/24/the-dunning-kruger-effect-shows-why-some-people-think-theyre-great-even-when-their-work-is-terrible/?sh=23923d575d7c on January 29, 2024.

Murray, D. W., Rosanbalm, K., Christopoulos, C., & Hamoudi, A. (2015, January). *Self-regulation and toxic stress report 1: Foundations for understanding self-regulation from an applied perspective* [OPRE Report 2015–21]. Washington, DC: Office of Planning, Research and Evaluation, Administration for Children and Families, U.S. Department of Health and Human Services. Accessed at www.acf.hhs.gov/sites/default/files/documents/report_1_foundations_paper_final_012715_submitted_508_0.pdf on January 29, 2024.

Murray, D. W., Rosanbalm, K., Christopoulos, C., & Meyer, A. L. (2019). An applied contextual model for promoting self-regulation enactment across development: Implications for prevention, public health, and future research. *The Journal of Primary Prevention, 40*(4), 367–403. https://doi.org/10.1007/s10935-019-00556-1

Napoli, A. R., & Johnson, V. J. (2019). *Promoting young children's early language and prereading skills with dialogic reading.* Accessed at https://extensionpubs.unl.edu/publication/2032/html/view on June 4, 2024.

Naser, A. Y., Hameed, A. N., Mustafa, N., Alwafi, H., Dahmash, E. Z., Alyami, H. S., et al. (2021). Depression and anxiety in patients with cancer: A cross-sectional study. *Frontiers in Psychology, 12*, Article 585534. https://doi.org/10.3389/fpsyg.2021.585534

National Assessment of Educational Progress. (2022). *NAEP Report Card: Reading.* Accessed at www.nationsreportcard.gov/reading/nation/groups/?grade=4 on July 2, 2024.

National Association of School Psychologists. (n.d.). *Shortage of school psychologists.* Accessed at www.nasponline.org/research-and-policy/policy-priorities/critical-policy-issues/shortage-of-school-psychologists on January 29, 2024.

National Center for Education Statistics. (n.d.a). *International educational attainment.* Accessed at https://nces.ed.gov/programs/coe/indicator/cac on January 29, 2024.

National Center for Education Statistics. (n.d.b). *Undergraduate retention and graduation rates.* Accessed at https://nces.ed.gov/programs/coe/indicator/ctr on January 29, 2024.

National Center for Education Statistics. (2022, July 6). *More than 80 percent of U.S. public schools report pandemic has negatively impacted student behavior and socio-emotional development.* Accessed at https://nces.ed.gov/whatsnew/press_releases/07_06_2022.asp on January 29, 2024.

National Equity Project. (n.d.). *Educational equity means that each child receives what they need to develop to their full academic and social potential.* Accessed at www.nationalequityproject.org/education-equity-definition on June 3, 2024.

National Reading Panel. (2000). *Teaching children to read: An evidence-based assessment of the scientific research literature on reading and its implications for reading instruction* (NIH Publication No. 00-4769). Bethesda, MD: National Institute of Child Health and Human Development.

Native Hope. (2018, September 14). *How trauma gets passed down through generations* [Blog post]. Accessed at https://blog.nativehope.org/how-trauma-gets-passed-down-through-generations on August 13, 2021.

Nawaz, A., & Norris, C. (2023, May 10). States push for harsher school discipline practices to address student misbehavior. *PBS News Hour.* Accessed at www.pbs.org/newshour/show/states-push-for-harsher-school-discipline-practices-to-address-student-misbehavior on January 29, 2024.

Newland, B. (2022, May). *Federal Indian Boarding School Initiative investigative report.* Washington, DC: Bureau of Indian Affairs. Accessed at www.bia.gov/sites/default/files/dup/inline-files/bsi_investigative_report_may_2022_508.pdf on January 24, 2024.

New York State Education Department. (n.d.). *Culturally responsive-sustaining education framework.* Albany, NY: Author. Accessed at www.nysed.gov/common/nysed/files/programs/crs/culturally-responsive-sustaining-education-framework.pdf on September 28, 2021.

Nieto, S., & Bode, P. (2018). *Affirming diversity: The sociopolitical context of multicultural education* (7th ed.). New York: Pearson.

Noam, G. G., Allen, P. J., & Triggs, B. (2018). The measurement of youth social and emotional competencies in OST settings. In E. Devaney & D. A. Moroney (Eds.), *Social and emotional learning in out-of-school time* (pp. 245–264). Charlotte, NC: Information Age.

Noam, G. G., & Hermann, C. A. (2002). Where education and mental health meet: Developmental prevention and early intervention in schools. *Development and Psychopathology, 14*(4), 861–875.

Noam, G. G., & Malti, T. (2008). Responding to the crisis: RALLY's developmental and relational approach. *New Directions for Youth Development*, (120), 31–55. https://doi.org/10.1002/yd.284

Noam, G. G., Malti, T., & Guhn, M. (2012). From clinical-developmental theory to assessment: The Holistic Student Assessment tool. *International Journal of Conflict and Violence, 6*(2), 201–213. https://doi.org/10.4119/UNIBI/ijcv.276

Noam, G. G., Malti, T., & Karcher, M. J. (2014). Mentoring relationships in developmental perspective. In D. L. DuBois & M. J. Karcher (Eds.), *Handbook of youth mentoring* (2nd ed., pp. 99–115). Thousand Oaks, CA: SAGE.

Noam, G. G., & Triggs, B. (2015). Positive developments during the transition to adulthood. In R. A. Scott, S. M. Kosslyn, & M. Buchmann (Eds.), *Emerging trends in the social and behavioral sciences* (pp. 1–15). Hoboken, NJ: Wiley.

Noguera, P. A. (2008). *The trouble with Black boys: And other reflections on race, equity, and the future of public education.* San Francisco: Jossey-Bass.

Norford, J. S, & Marzano, R. J. (2016). *Personalized competency-based education: Creating a cohesive and coherent system.* Accessed at http://soltreemrls3.s3-website-us-west-2.amazonaws.com/marzanoresearch.com/media/documents/Personalized_CBE _Whitepaper_September_2016.pdf on May 5, 2021.

North Kansas City Schools. (n.d.). *Portrait of a Graduate.* Accessed at www.nkcschools.org/district/portrait-of-a-graduate on January 31, 2024.

Oberle, E., Schonert-Reichl, K. A., Hertzman, C., & Zumbo, B. D. (2014). Social-emotional competencies make the grade: Predicting academic success in early adolescence. *Journal of Applied Developmental Psychology, 35*(3), 138–147.

Olagaray, T. (2022). *Student survey #1.* Accessed at https://wpvip.edutopia.org/wp-content/uploads/2022/10/Student-Survey-created-by-Tara-Olagaray.pdf on June 3, 2024.

Organisation for Economic and Co-operation and Development. (2019). *Student agency for 2030.* Accessed at www.oecd.org/education/2030-project/teaching-and-learning/learning/student-agency/Student_Agency_for_2030_concept_note.pdf on June 2, 2024.

Organisation for Economic and Co-operation and Development. (2023). *PISA 2022 results (vol. I): The state of learning and equity in education*. Paris: OECD Publishing.

O'Rourke, M., & Addison, P. (2017). *What is the rationale and evidence base for student agency?* Accessed at www.edpartnerships.edu.au/file/388/I/What_is_the_rationale_and_evidence_base_for_student_agency_.pdf on February 12, 2024.

Osher, D., Cantor, P., Berg, J., Steyer, L., & Rose, T. (2020). Drivers of human development: How relationships and context shape learning and development. *Applied Developmental Science, 24*(1), 6–36.

Osher, D., Kidron, Y., Brackett, M., Dymnicki, A., Jones, S., & Weissberg, R. P. (2016). Advancing the science and practice of social and emotional learning: Looking back and moving forward. *Review of Research in Education, 40*(1), 644–681.

Oueder, M., & Abousaber, I. (2018). A study of the impact of social media usage on academic performance. *American Scientific Research Journal for Engineering, Technology, and Sciences, 40*(1), 77–88.

Paley, B., & Hajal, N. J. (2022). Conceptualizing emotion regulation and coregulation as family-level phenomena. *Clinical Child and Family Psychology Review, 25*(1), 19–43.

Palmer, M., Gravett, E., & LaFleur, J. (2016, November 9–13). *Measuring the transparency of assignment descriptions* [Conference presentation]. Professional and Organizational Development Network Conference, Louisville, KY, United States.

Pane, J. F., Steiner, E. D., Baird, M. D., & Hamilton, L. S. (2015). *Continued progress: Promising evidence on personalized learning.* Accessed at www.rand.org/content/dam/rand/pubs/research_reports/RR1300/RR1365/RAND_RR1365.pdf on January 30, 2024.

Pang, J. C., Aquino, K. M., Oldehinkel, M., Robinson, P. A., Fulcher, B. D., Breakspear, M., et al. (2023). Geometric constraints on human brain function. *Nature, 618*, 566–574.

Paris, D. (2012). Culturally sustaining pedagogy: A needed change in stance, terminology, and practice. *Educational Researcher, 41*(3), 93–97.

Paris, D. (2021). Culturally sustaining pedagogies and our futures. *The Educational Forum, 85*(4), 364–376.

Paris, D., & Alim, H. S. (2014). What are we seeking to sustain through culturally sustaining pedagogy? A loving critique forward. *Harvard Educational Review, 84*(1), 85–100.

Paris, D., & Alim, H. S. (Eds.). (2017). *Culturally sustaining pedagogies: Teaching and learning for justice in a changing world.* New York: Teachers College Press.

Park, N., & Peterson, C. (2008). Positive psychology and character strengths: Application to strengths-based school counseling. *Professional School Counseling, 12*(2), 85–92.

Patel, J. A., Nielsen, F. B. H., Badiani, A. A., Assi, S., Unadkat, V. A., Patel, B., et al. (2020). Poverty, inequality and COVID-19: The forgotten vulnerable. *Public Health, 183*, 110–111. https://doi.org/10.1016/j.puhe.2020.05.006

Paunesku, D., Walton, G. M., Romero, C., Smith, E. N., Yeager, D. S., & Dweck, C. S. (2015). Mind-set interventions are a scalable treatment for academic underachievement. *Psychological Science, 26*(6), 784–793.

Pawlo, E., Eichert, B., Lorenzo, A., & Elias, M. J. (2019). *All SEL should be trauma-informed.* Accessed at https://kappanonline.org/all-sel-should-be-trauma-informed-schools-pawlo-lorenzo-eichert-elias76390-2 on May 29, 2024.

Perry, A. M. (2014, July 7). Zero-tolerance policies are destroying the lives of Black children. *The Washington Post.* Accessed at www.washingtonpost.com/posteverything/wp/2014/07/07/zero-tolerance-policies-are-destroying-the-lives-of-black-children on January 30, 2024.

Perry, B. D. (n.d.). *Neurosequential network.* Accessed at www.neurosequential.com on March 19, 2024.

Perry, B. D. (2015, September 21). *Bruce Perry presents the 6 R's of healing trauma.* Accessed at www.adoptionlearningpartners.org/account/webinar.cfm?id=1017108 on February 12, 2022.

Perry, B. D. (2022). *Neurosequential model core slides: "Best hits" package.* Accessed at www.bdperry.com/_files/ugd/5cebf2_dd3a3ce4aef34d6794519f2418c9f043.pdf on March 18, 2023.

Perry, B. D., & Szalavitz, M. (2017). *The boy who was raised as a dog: And other stories from a child psychiatrist's notebook: What traumatized children can teach us about loss, love, and healing.* New York: Basic Books.

Perry, B. D., & Winfrey, O. (2021). *What happened to you? Conversations on trauma, resilience, and healing.* New York: Flatiron Books.

Peters, U. (2020). What is the function of confirmation bias? *Erkenntnis, 87,* 1351–1376. Accessed at https://link.springer.com/article/10.1007/s10670-020-00252-1#citeas on February 16, 2024.

Peterson, C., Florence, C., & Klevens, J. (2018). The economic burden of child maltreatment in the United States, 2015. *Child Abuse and Neglect, 86,* 178–183.

Petscher, Y., Cabell, S. Q., Catts, H. W., Compton, D. L., Foorman, B. R., Hart, S. A., et al. (2020). How the science of reading informs 21st-century education. *Reading Research Quarterly, 55*(S1), S267–S282. https://doi.org/10.1002/rrq.352

Philadelphia ACE Project. (n.d.). *Philadelphia ACE survey.* Accessed at www.philadelphiaaces.org/philadelphia-ace-survey on June 19, 2024.

Piazza, S. V., Rao, S., & Protacio, M. S. (2015). *Converging recommendations for culturally responsive literacy practices: Students with learning disabilities, English language learners, and socioculturally diverse learners.* Accessed at https://files.eric.ed.gov/fulltext/EJ1104910.pdf on March 15, 2024.

Pink, D. H. (2009). *Drive: The surprising truth about what motivates us.* New York: Riverhead Books.

Pink, D. H. (2018). *When: The scientific secrets of perfect timing.* New York: Riverhead Books.

Plemmons, G., Hall, M., Doupnik, S., Gay, J., Brown, C., Browning, W., et al. (2018). Hospitalization for suicide ideation or attempt: 2008–2015. *Pediatrics, 141*(6), Article e20172426.

Posner, M. I., & Barbey, A. K. (2020). General intelligence in the age of neuroimaging. *Trends in Neuroscience and Education, 18,* Article 100126. https://doi.org/10.1016/j.tine.2020.100126

Poth, R. D. (2023). *5 activities that promote reflection in the classroom.* Accessed at www.edutopia.org/article/reflection-learning-tool on March 18, 2024.

Preston, E. (2022, August 10). *Low pay, stress and burnout: U.S. schools face severe teacher shortage.* Accessed at www.cbsnews.com/news/teacher-shortage-schools-low-pay-burnout-incentives/?ftag=CNM-00–10aab7e&linkId=176740678 on January 30, 2024.

Price-Dennis, D., Muhammad, G. E., Womack, E., McArthur, S. A., & Haddix, M. (2017). The multiple identities and literacies of Black girlhood: A conversation about creating spaces for Black girl voices. *Journal of Language and Literacy Education, 13*(2), 1–18.

Priest, N., Rudenstine, A., Weisstein, E., & Gerwin, C. (2012). *Making mastery work: A close-up view of competency education*. Quincy, MA: Nellie Mae Education Foundation.

Prieur, J. (2022, March 11). *13 ways to create a positive learning environment in your classroom* [Blog post]. Accessed at www.prodigygame.com/main-en/blog/positive-learning-environment on March 11, 2022.

Prothero, A. (2023, April 20). *Student behavior isn't getting any better, survey shows*. Accessed at www.edweek.org/leadership/student-behavior-isnt-getting-any-better-survey-shows/2023/04 on January 30, 2024.

Rachel's Challenge. (n.d.). *Know the numbers*. Accessed at https://rachelschallenge.org/get-info/school-violence-stats on June 2, 2024.

Raleigh, V. (2018, August). *What is happening to life expectancy in England?* Accessed at www.kingsfund.org.uk/publications/whats-happening-life-expectancy-england on January 15, 2023.

Ratey, J. J., & Hagerman, E. (2008). *Spark: The revolutionary new science of exercise and the brain*. New York: Little & Brown.

Reinert Center for Transformative Teaching and Learning. (n.d.). *Resource guide: Strength-based education*. Accessed at www.slu.edu/cttl/resources/resource-guides/strengths-based-education.pdf on June 12, 2024.

Riggs, N. R., Black, D. S., & Ritt-Olson, A. (2015). Associations between dispositional mindfulness and executive function in early adolescence. *Journal of Child and Family Studies*, *24*(9), 2745–2751.

Rim, C. (2022, September 21). Emotional intelligence: Combatting the college mental health crisis. *Forbes*. Accessed at https://www.forbes.com/sites/christopherrim/2022/09/21/emotional-intelligence-combatting-the-college-mental-health-crisis/?sh=36ee01271b6c on June 6, 2024.

Ritvo, V. J. H., Turk-Browne, N. B., & Norman, K. A. (2019). Nonmonotonic plasticity: How memory retrieval drives learning. *Trends in Cognitive Sciences*, *23*(9), 726–742.

Robinson, K. (2001). *Out of our minds: Learning to be creative*. West Sussex, United Kingdom: Capstone.

Robinson, K. (2013, May 3). *Why we need to reform education now* [Blog post]. Accessed at https://huffingtonpost.com/sir-ken-robinson/reform-american-education-now_b_3203949.html on March 16, 2023.

Rock, A. (2023, December 18). *School counselor shortages by state and its impact on students*. Accessed at www.campussafetymagazine.com/mental-health/school-counselor-shortages-by-state-impact-on-students on January 30, 2024.

Roediger, H. L., III, & Butler, A. C. (2011). The critical role of retrieval practice in long-term retention. *Trends in Cognitive Sciences*, *15*(1), 20–27.

Roediger, H. L., III, & Karpicke, J. D. (2006). The power of testing memory: Basic research and implications for educational practice. *Perspectives on Psychological Science*, *1*(3), 181–210.

Rohrer, D., & Pashler, H. (2010). Recent research on human learning challenges conventional instructional strategies. *Educational Researcher*, *39*(5), 406–412.

Rosanbalm, K. D., & Murray, D. W. (2017). *Caregiver co-regulation across development: A practice brief.* Washington, DC: Office of Planning, Research, and Evaluation, Administration for Children and Families, US. Department of Health and Human Services. Accessed at https://fpg.unc.edu/sites/fpg.unc.edu/files/resources/reports-and-policy-briefs/Co-RegulationFromBirthThroughYoungAdulthood.pdf on February 15, 2024.

Rose, T. (2016). *The end of average: How we succeed in a world that values sameness.* San Francisco: HarperOne.

Rothwell, J. (2020, September 8). *Assessing the economic gains of eradicating illiteracy nationally and regionally in the United States.* Washington, DC: Gallup. Accessed at www.barbarabush.org/wp-content/uploads/2020/09/BBFoundation_GainsFromEradicatingIlliteracy_9_8.pdf on January 30, 2024.

Rotter, J. B. (1966). Generalized expectancies for internal versus external control of reinforcement. *Psychological Monographs, 80*(1), 1–28. https://doi.org/10.1037/h0092976

Ruyle, M., Child, L., & Dome, N. (2022). *The school wellness wheel: A framework addressing trauma, culture, and mastery to raise student achievement.* Bloomington, IN: Marzano Resources.

Ruyle, M., O'Neill, T. W., Iberlin, J. M., Evans, M. D., & Midles, R. (2019). *Leading the evolution: How to make personalized competency-based education a reality.* Bloomington, IN: Marzano Resources.

Ryan, R. M., & Deci, E. L. (2000). Self-determination theory and the facilitation of intrinsic motivation, social development, and well-being. *American Psychologist, 55*(1), 68–78.

Ryan, R. M., & Deci, E. L. (2017). *Self-determination theory: Basic psychological needs in motivation, development, and wellness.* New York: Guilford Press. https://doi.org/10.1521/978.14625/28806

Safir, S., & Dugan, J. (2021). *Street data: A next-generation model for equity, pedagogy, and school transformation.* Thousand Oaks, CA: Corwin.

Sanders, J., Munford, R., & Liebenberg, L. (2016). The role of teachers in building resilience of at risk youth. *International Journal of Educational Research, 80,* 111–123. https://doi.org/10.1016/j.ijer.2016.10.002

Schonert-Reichl, K. A., & Lawlor, M. S. (2010). The effects of a mindfulness-based education program on pre- and early adolescents' well-being and social and emotional competence. *Mindfulness, 1*(3), 137–151.

Schreiner, L. A. (2013). Strengths-based advising. In J. K. Drake, P. Jordan, & M. A. Miller (Eds.), *Academic advising approaches: Strategies that teach students to make the most of college* (pp. 105–120). San Francisco: Jossey-Bass.

Schunk, D. H., & Pajares, F. (2002). The development of academic self-efficacy. In A. Wigfield & J. S. Eccles (Eds.), *Development of achievement motivation* (pp. 15–31). San Diego, CA: Academic Press.

Scott, D., & Marzano, R. J. (2014). *Awaken the learner: Finding the source of effective education.* Bloomington, IN: Marzano Resources.

Seidenberg, M. S., & Borkenhagen, M. C. (2020, January). Reading science and educational practice: Some tenets for teachers. *The Reading League,* 7–12.

Seligman, M. E. P., & Csikszentmihalyi, M. (2014). Positive psychology: An introduction. In M. Csikszentmihalyi (Ed.), *Flow and the foundations of positive psychology: The collected works of Mihaly Csikszentmihalyi* (pp. 279–298). New York: Springer.

Seligman, M. E. P., Ernst, R. M., Gillham, J., Reivich, K., & Linkins, M. (2009). Positive education: Positive psychology and classroom interventions. *Oxford Review of Education*, *35*(3), 293–311.

Seven Generations Education Institute (n.d.). *Seven Grandfather teachings.* Accessed at https://www.7generations.org/seven-grandfather-teachings/ on June 2, 2024.

Shankleman, M., Hammond, L., & Jones, F. W. (2021). Adolescent social media use and well-being: A systematic review and thematic meta-synthesis. *Adolescent Research Review*, *6*, 471–492.

Shim, R. S. (2021). Dismantling structural racism in psychiatry: A path to mental health equity. *The American Journal of Psychiatry*, *178*(7), 592–598. https://doi.org/10.1176/appi.ajp.2021.21060558

Shonkoff, J. P. (2012). Leveraging the biology of adversity to address the roots of disparities in health and development. *PNAS*, *109*(2S), 17302–17307.

Shonkoff, J. P. (2016). Capitalizing on advances in science to reduce the health consequences of early childhood adversity. *JAMA Pediatrics*, *170*(10), 1003–1007.

Siddall, T. (2016, August 30). *The power of student agency in assessment and learning.* Accessed at http://nextgenlearning.org/blog/power-student-agency-assessment-and-learning on January 30, 2024.

Siegel, D. J. (2007). *The mindful brain: Reflection and attunement in the cultivation of well-being.* New York: Norton.

Siegel, D. J. (2010). *The mindful therapist: A clinician's guide to mindsight and neural integration.* New York: Norton.

Siegel, D. J. (2020). *The developing mind: How relationships and the brain interact to shape who we are* (3rd ed.). New York: Guilford Press.

Sieving, R. E., McRee, A., McMorris, B. J., Shlafer, R. J., Gower, A. L., Kapa, H. M, et al. (2017). Youth-adult connectedness: A key protective factor for adolescent health. *American Journal of Preventive Medicine*, *52*(3), S275–S278.

Simmons, R. G., & Blyth, D. A. (1987). *Moving into adolescence: The impact of pubertal change and school context.* Berlin: De Gruyter.

Simms, J. A. (2016). *The Critical Concepts (final version: English language arts, mathematics, and science).* Accessed at www.marzanoresources.com/the-critical-concepts.html on January 30, 2024.

Singer, K., & Ludlow-Broback, S. (2022, June 15). *To improve student mental health, we need more than crisis response* [Blog post]. Accessed at www.nami.org/Blogs/NAMI-Blog/June-2022/To-Improve-Student-Mental-Health-We-Need-More-Than-Crisis-Response on January 30, 2024.

Sisk, V. F., Burgoyne, A. P., Sun, J., Butler, J. L., & Macnamara, B. N. (2018). To what extent and under which circumstances are growth mind-sets important to academic achievement? Two meta-analyses. *Psychological Science*, *29*(4), 549–571.

Slopen, N., Shonkoff, J. P., Albert, M. A., Yoshikawa, H., Jacobs, A., Stoltz, R., et al. (2016). Racial disparities in child adversity in the U.S.: Interactions with family immigration history and income. *American Journal of Preventive Medicine, 50*(1), 47–56.

Smith, S. B., Simmons, D. C., & Kame'enui, E. J. (1998). Phonological awareness: Instructional and curricular basics and implications. In D. C. Simmons & E. J. Kame'enui (Eds.), *What reading research tells us about children with diverse learning needs: Bases and basics* (pp. 129–140). Mahwah, NJ: Lawrence Erlbaum Associates.

Snowling, M. J., & Hulme, C. (2005). *The science of reading: A handbook.* Malden, MA: Blackwell.

Snyder, C. R. (1995). Conceptualizing, measuring, and nurturing hope. *Journal of Counseling and Development, 73*(3), 355–360. https://doi.org/10.1002/j.1556-6676.1995.tb01764.x

Snyder, C. R. (2009). *Hope theory: Rainbows in the mind* [Abstract]. Accessed at www.tandfonline.com/doi/abs/10.1207/S15327965PLI1304_01 on February 15, 2024.

Snyder, C. R., Cheavens, J., & Michael, S. T. (1999). Hoping. In C. R. Snyder (Ed.), *Coping: The psychology of what works* (pp. 205–231). New York: Oxford University Press.

Snyder, C. R., Hoza, B., Pelham, W. E., Rapoff, M., Ware, L., Danovsky, M., et al. (1997). The development and validation of the Children's Hope Scale. *Journal of Pediatric Psychology, 22*(3), 399–421.

Snyder, C. R., Shorey, H. S., Cheavens, J., Pulvers, K. M., Adams, V. H., III., & Wiklund, C. (2002). Hope and academic success in college. *Journal of Educational Psychology, 94*(4), 820–826.

Snyder, T. D., de Brey, C., & Dillow, S. A. (2019). *Digest of education statistics 2017 (NCES 2018-070).* Washington, DC: Center for Education Statistics, Institute of Education Sciences, U.S. Department of Education. Accessed at https://nces.ed.gov/pubs2018/2018070.pdf on September 28, 2023.

Song, K. (2021). Well-being of teachers: The role of efficacy of teachers and academic optimism. *Frontiers in Psychology, 12*, Article 831972. Accessed at www.ncbi.nlm.nih.gov/pmc/articles/PMC8825852 on March 19, 2024.

Southwick, S. M., Bonanno, G. A., Masten, A. S., Panter-Brick, C., & Yehuda, R. (2014). Resilience definitions, theory, and challenges: Interdisciplinary perspectives. *European Journal of Psychotraumatology, 5*(1), Article 25338. https://doi.org/10.3402/ejpt.v5.25338

Spiteri, D. (2017). *Multiculturalism, higher education and intercultural communication: Developing strengths-based narratives for teaching and learning.* London: Palgrave Macmillan.

Srikanth, S., Petrie, T. A., Greenleaf, C., & Martin, S. (2012, August 3). *Physical fitness and academic performance: A longitudinal investigation* [Conference presentation]. American Psychological Association Annual Convention, Orlando, Florida, United States.

St. Clair-Thompson, H. L., & Gathercole, S. E. (2006). Executive functions and achievements in school: Shifting, updating, inhibition, and working memory. *The Quarterly Journal of Experimental Psychology, 59*(4), 745–759.

State Collaborative on Reforming Education. (2020). *The science of reading.* Accessed at https://tnscore.org/wp-content/uploads/2020/01/Science-of-Reading-2020.pdf on May 13, 2024.

Steele, C. M. (2010). *Whistling Vivaldi: How stereotypes affect us and what we can do.* New York: Norton.

Substance Abuse and Mental Health Services Administration. (2014, July). *SAMHSA's concept of trauma and guidance for a trauma-informed approach.* Rockville, MD: Author. Accessed at https://ncsacw.samhsa.gov/userfiles/files/SAMHSA_Trauma.pdf on January 13, 2023.

Sue, D. W., Capodilupo, C. M., Torino, G. C., Bucceri, J. M., Holder, A., Nadal, K. L., et al. (2007). Racial microaggressions in everyday life: Implications for clinical practice. *American Psychologist, 62,* 271–286.

Sugarman, S. (2021, November 1). *Three actions for building a culture of collective efficacy* [Blog post]. Accessed at www.ascd.org/blogs/three-actions-for-building-a-culture-of-collective-ef-cacy?mc_key=00Qi000001ceuWdEAI on January 30, 2024.

Sun, J., Zhang, R., & Forsyth, P. B. (2023). The effects of teacher trust on student learning and the malleability of teacher trust to school leadership: A 35-year meta-analysis. *Educational Administration Quarterly, 59*(4). https://doi.org/10.1177/0013161X231183662

Sun, J., Zhang, R., Murphy, J., & Zhang, S. (2024). The effects of academic press on student learning and its malleability to school leadership: A meta-analysis of 30 years of research. *Educational Administration Quarterly, 60*(2), 226–268.

Supekar, K., Chang, H., Mistry, P. K., Iuculano, T., & Menon, V. (2021). Neurocognitive modeling of latent memory processes reveals reorganization of hippocampal-cortical circuits underlying learning and efficient strategies. *Communications Biology, 4,* Article 405.

Symonds, W. C., Schwartz, R., & Ferguson, R. F. (2011). *Pathways to prosperity: Meeting the challenge of preparing young Americans for the 21st century.* Cambridge, MA: Harvard University Graduate School of Education.

Szalavitz, M., & Perry, B. D. (2010). *Born for love: Why empathy is essential—And endangered.* New York: William Morrow.

Tanner, K. D. (2013). Structure matters: Twenty-one teaching strategies to promote student engagement and cultivate classroom equity. *CBE Life Sciences Education, 12*(3), 322–331.

Taylor, K., & Rohrer, D. (2010). The effects of interleaved practice. *Applied Cognitive Psychology, 24*(6), 837–848.

Tedeschi, R. G. (2020, July–August). Growth after trauma. *Harvard Business Review.* Accessed at https://hbr.org/2020/07/growth-after-trauma on February 9, 2021.

Tedeschi, R. G., Shakespeare-Finch, J., Taku, K., & Calhoun, L. G. (2018). *Posttraumatic growth: Theory, research, and applications.* New York: Routledge.

Teicher, M. H., & Samson, J. A. (2016). Annual research review: Enduring neurobiological effects of childhood abuse and neglect. *Journal of Child Psychology and Psychiatry, 57*(3), 241–266.

Teicher, M. H., Samson, J. A., Anderson, C. M., & Ohashi, K. (2016). The effects of childhood maltreatment on brain structure, function and connectivity. *Nature Reviews Neuroscience, 17*, 652–666.

Thompson, D. (2021, September 14). Colleges have a guy problem. *The Atlantic*. Accessed at www.theatlantic.com/ideas/archive/2021/09/young-men-college-decline-gender-gap-higher-education/620066 on January 30, 2024.

Thompson, M., & Wiliam, D. (2007, April 9–13). *Tight but loose: A conceptual framework for scaling up school reforms* [Conference presentation]. American Educational Research Association annual meeting, Chicago, IL, United States.

Thulin, E. J., Lipson, S. K., Heinze, J. E., & Zhou, S. (2023). Suicidal ideation in American Indian and Alaskan Native college-attending students. *American Journal of Preventive Medicine*, *65*(2), 307–312. https://doi.org/10.1016/j.amepre.2023.02.031

Timmermans, A. C., & Rubie-Davies, C. M. (2018). Do teachers differ in the level of expectations or in the extent to which they differentiate in expectations? Relations between teacher-level expectations, teacher background and beliefs, and subsequent student performance. *Educational Research and Evaluation*, *24*(3–5), 241–263.

Tindle, R., & Moustafa, A. A. (2021). Psychological flexibility. In A. A. Moustafa (Ed.) *Mental Health Effects of COVID-19* (pp. 89–101). Cambridge, MA: Academic Press.

Todd, R. (2022). *How teachers can empower students who are experiencing trauma*. Accessed at www.edutopia.org/article/how-teachers-can-empower-students-who-are-experiencing-trauma on March 16, 2024.

Treacy, M., & Leavy, A. (2023). Student voice and its role in creating cognitive dissonance: The neglected narrative in teacher professional development. *Professional Development in Education*, *49*(3), 458–477. https://doi.org/10.1080/19415257.2021.1876147

TREP Project. (n.d.). *Consistency and predictability*. Accessed at www.trepeducator.org/consistency-and-predictability on March 17, 2024.

Trickey, S. (2022, November 24). *Predictability* [Blog post]. Accessed at www.teachwithmrst.com/post/predictability on February 14, 2024.

Tsai, N., Jaeggi, S. M., Eccles, J. S., Atherton, O. E., & Robbins, R. W. (2020). Predicting late adolescent anxiety from early adolescent environmental stress exposure: Cognitive control as mediator. *Frontiers in Psychology, 11*, Article 1838.

Turnaround for Children. (2020). *Strategies to build relationships with students*. Accessed at https://turnaroundusa.org/wp-content/uploads/2020/06/BuildingRelationships-WestEd.pdf on March 15, 2024.

Tyler, N., Heffernan, R., & Fortune, C.-A. (2020). Reorienting locus of control in individuals who have offended through strengths-based interventions: Personal agency and the good lives model. *Frontiers in Psychology, 11*, Article 553240. https://doi.org/10.3389/fpsyg.2020.553240

Tyner, A. (2021, August). *How to sell SEL: Parents and the politics of social-emotional learning*. Washington, DC: Thomas B. Fordham Institute. Accessed at https://files.eric.ed.gov/fulltext/ED616280.pdf on January 31, 2024.

Tyng, C. M., Amin, H. U., Saad, M. N. M., & Malik, A. S. (2017). The influences of emotion on learning and memory. *Frontiers in Psychology, 8*, Article 1454.

Um, E. R., Plass, J. L., Hayward, E. O., & Homer, B. D. (2012). Emotional design in multimedia learning. *Journal of Educational Psychology, 104*(2), 485–498. https://doi.org/10.1037/a0026609

Ungar, M., Russell, P., & Connelly, G. (2014). School-based interventions to enhance the resilience of students. *Journal of Educational and Developmental Psychology, 4*(1). https://doi.org/10.5539/jedp.v4n1p66

University of East Anglia. (2023). *People with lower literacy have greater mental health difficulties, research shows.* Accessed at https://neurosciencenews.com/mental-health-poor-literacy-22384 on March 14, 2024.

University of Kansas. (n.d.). *Positive reinforcement.* Accessed at https://specialconnections.ku.edu/behavior_plans/classroom_and_group_support/teacher_tools/positive_reinforcement on March 16, 2024.

U.S. Department of Education Office of Career, Technical, and Adult Education. (n.d.). *Making skills everyone's business: A call to transform adult learning in the United States.* Washington, DC: Author. Accessed at www2.ed.gov/about/offices/list/ovae/pi/AdultEd/making-skills-summary.pdf on January 24, 2024.

van Breda, A. D. (2018). A critical review of resilience theory and its relevance for social work. *Social Work, 54*(1), 1–18.

van der Kolk, B. A. (2005). Developmental trauma disorder: Toward a rational diagnosis for children with complex trauma histories. *Psychiatric Annals, 35*(5), 401–408.

van der Kolk, B. A. (2015). *The body keeps the score: Brain, mind, and body in the healing of trauma.* New York: Viking.

Vance, T. A. (2019, February 8). *Addressing mental health in the Black community.* Accessed at www.columbiapsychiatry.org/news/addressing-mental-health-black-community on January 31, 2024.

Vatterott, C. (2018). *Rethinking homework: Best practices that support diverse needs* (2nd ed.). Alexandria, VA: ASCD.

Verschelden, C. (2017). *Bandwidth recovery: Helping students reclaim cognitive resources lost to poverty, racism, and social marginalization.* Sterling, VA: Stylus.

Victorian Department of Education and Training. (2017). *New pedagogies for deep learning—Victorian cluster report, 2014–2017.* Accessed at https://arc.educationapps.vic.gov.au/learning/resource/9069a455-c7d9-4680-8219-a6a2783ef613?fuse=1 on February 6, 2024.

Vigano, C. (2022). *Is crackdown on social media for teenagers too late?* Accessed at https://tachopaks.co.uk/is-crackdown-on-social-media-for-teenagers-too-late.htmlifa on May 4, 2022.

Vlasova, H. (2020, November 21). *Eye-opening college dropout rates and statistics—2022.* Accessed at https://admissionsly.com/college-dropout-rates on January 23, 2024.

Vuilleumier, P. (2005). How brains beware: Neural mechanisms of emotional attention. *Trends in Cognitive Sciences, 9*(12), 585–594. https://doi.org/10.1016/j.tics.2005.10.011

Vygotsky, L. S. (1978). *Mind in society: The development of higher psychological processes.* Cambridge, MA: Harvard University Press.

Waters, L. E., Loton, D., & Jach, H. K. (2019). Does strength-based parenting predict academic achievement? The mediating effects of perseverance and engagement. *Journal of Happiness Studies, 20*(4), 1121–1140. https://doi.org/10.1007/s10902-018-9983-1

Waters, T., Marzano, R. J., & McNulty, B. (2003). *Balanced leadership: What 30 years of research tells us about the effect of leadership on student achievement.* Denver, CO: McREL. Accessed at www.mcrel.org/wp-content/uploads/2016/06/Balanced-Leadership%C2%AE-What-30-Years-of-Research-Tells-Us-about-the-Effect-of-Leadership-on-Student-Achievement.pdf on January 31, 2024.

Weinstein, N., & Algeri, M. (2018). *The empowered student: A guide to self-regulated learning.* Wakefield, MA: CAST.

Weinstein, N., & Tsai, N. (2023, November). What's behind the rise in problem behavior? It could be cognitive. *Educational Leadership, 81*(3).

Weissberg, R. P. (2015). Education to promote all students' social, emotional, and academic competence. In M. J. Feur, A. I. Berman, & R. C. Atkinson (Eds.), *Past as prologue: The National Academy of Education at 50. Members reflect* (pp. 185–191). Washington, DC: National Academy of Education.

Welsh, J. A., Nix, R. L., Blair, C., Bierman, K. L., & Nelson, K. E. (2010). The development of cognitive skills and gains in academic school readiness for children from low-income families. *Journal of Educational Psychology, 102*(1), 43–53.

What to Become. (2022, August 3). *Everything you need to know about the college dropout rate* [Blog post]. Accessed at https://whattobecome.com/blog/college-dropout-rate on January 31, 2024.

Whitford, D. K., Katsiyannis, A., & Counts, J. (2016). Discriminatory discipline: Trends and issues. *NASSP Bulletin, 100*(2), 117–135.

Wigfield, A., Eccles, J. S., Fredricks, J. A., Simpkins, S., Roeser, R. W., & Schiefele, U. (2015). Development of achievement motivation and engagement. In M. E. Lamb & R. M. Lerner (Eds.), *Handbook of child psychology and developmental science* (7th ed., pp. 657–700). New York: Wiley.

Wilder Research. (2016). *The benefits of parenting education.* Accessed at www.wilder.org/sites/default/files/imports/LitReviewSummary_10-16.pdf on February 16, 2024.

Wiliam, D., & Thompson, M. (2017). *Integrating assessment with learning: What will it take to make it work?* London: Routledge.

Williams, K. (2022). *Ruthless equity: Disrupt the status quo and ensure learning for ALL students.* Omaha, NE: Wish in One Hand Press.

Williams, L. (2018/2019, Winter). Ti wa7 szwatenem. What we know: Indigenous knowledge and learning. *BC Studies*, 200, 31–44.

Willims, P. (2017). Student agency for powerful learning. *Knowledge Quest, 45*(4), 8–15.

Willink, J., & Babin, L. (2015). *Extreme ownership: How U.S. Navy SEALs lead and win.* New York: St. Martin's Press.

Winchester, S. S., & Finney, M. I. (2021). *Healing at work: A guide to using career conflicts to overcome your past and build the future you deserve.* Dublin, OH: Telemachus Press.

Windchief, S., & Cummins, J. (2022). Considering Indigenous research methodologies: Bicultural accountability and the protection of community held knowledge. *Qualitative Inquiry, 28,* 151–163. https://doi.org/10.1177/10778004211021803

Winkelmes, M. (2013). Transparency in teaching: Faculty share data and improve students' learning. *Liberal Education, 99*(2).

Winkelmes, M. (2016, December 13). *Small teaching changes, big learning benefits* [Blog post]. Accessed at https://acue.org/blog/small-teaching-changes-big-learning-benefits on January 31, 2024.

Winkelmes, M., Bernacki, M., Butler, J., Zochowski, M., Golanics, J., & Weavil, K. H. (2016). A teaching intervention that increases underserved college students' success. *Peer Review, 18*(1–2), 31–36.

Winkelmes, M. A., Boye, A., & Tapp, S. (2019). *Transparent design in higher education teaching and leadership: A guide to implementing the transparency framework institution-wide to improve learning and retention.* Sterling, VA: Stylus Publishing.

Wise, S. (2022). *Design for belonging: How to build inclusion and collaboration in your communities.* New York: Ten Speed Press.

World Health Organization. (2020, May 17). *Health in All Policies (HiAP) training slides: Companion material to support HiAP training activities* [Slide presentation]. Accessed at www.who.int/publications/m/item/health-in-all-policies-(hiap)-training-slides-companion-material-to-support-hiap-training-activities on July 3, 2023.

World Health Organization & Calouste Gulbenkian Foundation. (2014). *Social determinants of mental health.* Geneva, Switzerland: Author. Accessed at https://gulbenkian.pt/wp-content/uploads/2016/03/SocialDeterminantsMentalHealth.pdf on January 31, 2024.

World Population Review. (n.d.). *College graduation rates by state 2024.* Accessed at https://worldpopulationreview.com/state-rankings/college-graduation-rates-by-state on June 19, 2024.

Wyoming State Board of Education. (n.d.). *Wyoming Profile of a Graduate.* Accessed at https://edu.wyoming.gov/board/wyoming-profile-of-a-graduate on January 31, 2024.

XQ Institute. (2018). *Show what you know: A landscape analysis of competency-based education.* Oakland, CA: Author. Accessed at www.gettingsmart.com/wp-content/uploads/2018/10/Show-What-You-Know.pdf on January 23, 2024.

Yeager, D. S., Bryan, C. J., Gross, J. J., Murray, J. S., Cobb, D. K., et al. (2022). A synergistic mindsets intervention protects adolescents from stress. *Nature, 607*(7919), 512–520.

Yeager, D. S., Hanselman, P., Walton, G. M., Murray, J. S., Crosnoe, R., Muller, C., et al. (2019). A national experiment reveals where a growth mindset improves achievement. *Nature, 573*(7774), 364–369.

Yeager, D. S., Romero, C., Paunesku, D., Hulleman, C. S., Schneider, B., Hinojosa, C., et al. (2016). Using design thinking to improve psychological interventions: The case of the growth mindset during the transition to high school. *Journal of Educational Psychology, 108*(3), 374–391.

Yehuda, R., Daskalakis, N. P., Bierer, L. M., Bader, H. N., Klengel, T., Holsboer, F., et al. (2016). Holocaust exposure induced intergenerational effects on FKBP5 methylation. *Biological Psychiatry, 80*(5), 372–380.

Yehuda, R., Spiegel, D., Southwick, S., Davis, L. L., Neylan, T. C., & Krystal, J. H. (2016). What I have changed my mind about and why. *European Journal of Psychotraumatology, 7*, Article 33768.

Yellow Horse Brave Heart, M. (1998). The return to the sacred path: Healing the historical trauma and historical unresolved grief response among the Lakota through a psychoeducational group intervention. *Smith College Studies in Social Work, 68*(3), 287–305.

Yellow Horse Brave Heart, M. (2000). Wakiksuyapi: Carrying the historical trauma of the Lakota. *Tulane Studies in Social Welfare, 21*(22), 245–266.

Yellow Horse Brave Heart, M. (2003). The historical trauma response among natives and its relationship with substance abuse: A Lakota illustration. *Journal of Psychoactive Drugs, 35*(1), 7–13.

Yellow Horse Brave Heart, M., & Deschenie, T. (2006). Resource guide: Historical trauma and post-colonial stress in American Indian populations. *Tribal College Journal of American Indian Higher Education, 17*(3), 24–27.

Yellow Horse Brave Heart, M., Elkins, J., Tafoya, G., Bird, D., & Salvador, M. (2012). Wicasa Was'aka: Restoring the traditional strength of American Indian boys and men. *American Journal of Public Health, 102*(S2), S177–S183.

Yemini, M., Engel, L., & Simon, A. B. (2023). Place-based education: A systematic review of literature. *Educational Review*, 1–21.

Yopp, H. K. (1992). Developing phonemic awareness in young children. *Reading Teacher, 45*(9), 696–703.

Zak, P. J. (2019). *How our brains decide when to trust*. Accessed at https://hbr.org/2019/07/how-our-brains-decide-when-to-trust on January 31, 2024.

Zenger, J., & Folkman, J. (2019). *The 3 elements of trust*. Accessed at https://hbr.org/2019/02/the-3-elements-of-trust on January 31, 2024.

Zima, B. (2021). *Mindsets and skill sets for learning: A framework for building student agency*. Bloomington, IN: Marzano Resources.

INDEX

C

D

E

F

G

H

I

K

L

M

N

O

P

R

S

The School Wellness Wheel
Mike Ruyle, Libby Child, and Nancy Dome
Your school can evolve to address trauma, promote well-being, and elevate learning. *The School Wellness Wheel* will show you how. Backed by educational, psychological, and medical research, the resource introduces a comprehensive framework for supporting students' cognitive, social, and emotional needs.
BKL064

Cultivating Mindfulness in the Classroom
Jeanie M. Iberlin with Mike Ruyle
Discover practical tools that align to the five key categories of mindfulness benefits—stress reduction, attention, emotional control, positive self-concept, and positive interactions—and explore a step-by-step process for establishing a formal school or classroom mindfulness program.
BKL035

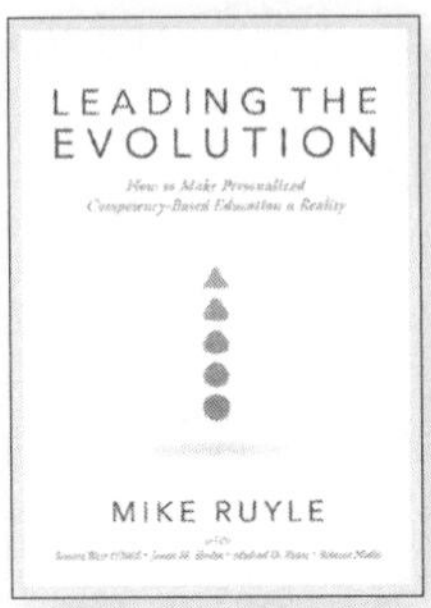

Leading the Evolution
Mike Ruyle with Tamera Weir O'Neill, Jeanie M. Iberlin, Michael D. Evans, and Rebecca Midles
Take action to evolve the existing model of schooling into one that is more innovative, relevant, and effective. *Leading the Evolution* introduces a three-pronged approach to driving substantive change—called the evolutionary triad—that connects transformational leadership, student engagement, and teacher optimism around personalized competency-based education.
BKL042

A Handbook for Personalized Competency-Based Education
Robert J. Marzano, Jennifer S. Norford, Michelle Finn, and Douglas Finn III
Ensure all students master content by designing and implementing a personalized competency-based education (PCBE) system. Explore examples of how to use proficiency scales, standard operating procedures, behavior rubrics, personal tracking matrices, and other tools to aid in instruction and assessment.
BKL037

Building Bonds With Learners
Patricia Erbe
Learn to harness the power of relationships and foster a sense of belonging in this research- and experience-based model. K–12 teachers will gain a practical teacher-student relationship methodology for purposefully forming vital connections and lessening academic and behavioral challenges and equity gaps.
BKG170

MARZANO Resources

Visit MarzanoResources.com or call 888.849.0851 to order.